NETWORKS WITHOUT A CAUSE

NETWORKS WITHOUT A CAUSE
A CRITIQUE OF SOCIAL MEDIA

GEERT LOVINK

polity

The right of Geert Lovink to be identified as Author of this Work has been asserted in
accordance with the UK Copyright, Designs and Patents Act 1988.

First published in 2011 by Polity Press

Polity Press
65 Bridge Street
Cambridge CB2 1UR, UK

Polity Press
350 Main Street
Malden, MA 02148, USA

ISBN-13: 978-0-7456-4967-2
ISBN-13: 978-0-7456-4968-9(pb)

A catalogue record for this book is available from the British Library.

Typeset in 10.5 on 12 pt Sabon
by Toppan Best-set Premedia Limited
Printed and bound in Great Britain by Clays Ltd, St Ives plc

The publisher has used its best endeavours to ensure that the URLs for external websites
referred to in this book are correct and active at the time of going to press. However, the
publisher has no responsibility for the websites and can make no guarantee that a site will
remain live or that the content is or will remain appropriate.

Every effort has been made to trace all copyright holders, but if any have been inadvertently
overlooked the publisher will be pleased to include any necessary credits in any subsequent
reprint or edition.

For further information on Polity, visit our website: www.politybooks.com

CONTENTS

ACKNOWLEDGMENTS

More than four years have elapsed between my "Berlin" study *Zero Comments* and the making of this latest book. It has become an Amsterdam production, part IV in my series of studies into critical internet culture. Whereas *Dark Fiber,* written in Sydney in 2001, brought together material ranging from cyber culture to dot.com-mania, *My First Recession*, wrapped up in Brisbane in 2003, looked at the transition period of the dot.com crash and to the early blogging years. *Networks Without a Cause* is similar to the previous studies in that it contains a mix of theory, reflections on dominant motifs, concept development, critical essays, and case studies. Needless to say, this monograph describes the late Web 2.0 era, dominated not just by Google, Twitter, YouTube, and Wikipedia, but also, more recently, WikiLeaks and Facebook and Twitter revolutions in North Africa and the Middle East. For me, the period can be best described as the era of the Institute of Network Cultures, which I founded in 2004, with its research initiatives, conferences, and publications on Wikipedia (Critical Point of View), online video (Video Vortex), critique of the creative industries (MyCreativity), urban screens, search (Society of the Query), and a large, onsite experiment concerning organized networks (Winter Camp).

This period of writing has been marked by the departure of Emilie Randoe, the founder of the School of Interactive Media where our Institute of Network Cultures is based, due to the centralization and related institutional politics at the Amsterdam University of Applied Sciences (HvA). On the University of Amsterdam side, where I teach, we saw the growing popularity of the new media masters program within Media Studies. Part of this was the collaborative student blog Masters of Media, which I set up in September 2006. Because of the great interest in my essay "Blogging, the Nihilist Impulse," I continued to develop this topic. A collaboration with Jodi Dean did not result in a common publication. Jodi wrote *Blog Theory* (2010), also published by Polity Press, and in this book the largest chapter is devoted to this topic.

I tested different chapters in February 2009 at a mini-seminar at the Critical Theory Emphasis program at the University of California, Irvine. I want to thank Elizabeth Losh for facilitating this. I also benefited from the collaboration with the Eurozine network that not only published a number of my essays, but also invited me to give a lecture at their September 2008 conference in Paris on the role of language in the internet.

Sabine Niederer and Margreet Riphagen's support at the Institute of Network Cultures has been invaluable in creating an atmosphere that made it possible for me to write, surrounded as I was by production activities, visitors, applications, and deadlines. My friendship and collaboration with Ned Rossiter can be felt throughout the book. I am very grateful for his ongoing support, suggestions, and editorial work, in particular concerning the introduction. Morgan Currie, whom I was lucky to work with on the Economies of the Commons II and the Unbound Book conferences, contributed greatly to the structure of the argument. Thanks, Morgan, for all the changes you made in the structure of the material and the copy-editing. Linda Wallace also stepped in during the last phase of editing, devoting a lot of her time to bringing the text into its final shape. John Thompson commissioned the book at Polity Press after we met in San Francisco in May 2007. He had the patience to wait until it was time to wrap it up. Thanks go to him, Sarah Lambert, and anonymous (!) readers of the first draft. My commentators are mentioned in the individual chapters. This book is dedicated to my dearest, Linda, and our son Kazimir, for their amazing support.

Amsterdam, April 2011

INTRODUCTION: CAPTURING WEB 2.0 BEFORE ITS DISAPPEARANCE

> The introduction is over, the chapter begins.
>
> Johan Sjerpstra

Once the internet changed the world; now the world is changing the internet. Its mainstreaming is well and truly over, and the forgettable Web 2.0 saga has run its course. The participatory crowds suddenly find themselves in a situation full of tension and conflict – an unwelcome state of affairs for the pragmatist class who oversaw the internet's formation from the beginning. Criticism of Google and Facebook's privacy violations is on the rise. Conflicts over Net neutrality and WikiLeaks demonstrate that the friction-free days of "multi-stakeholder" governance – a loose coalition of corporations, NGOs, and engineers who kept state officials and old-school telecoms at bay, most notably through the World Summit on the Information Society (WSIS) meetings – are now over. A bubble has burst again, but this time in the form of the collapsing libertarian consensus model. Internet regulators who favored business and barred state intervention are moving into defense mode. Now that society has overruled their freewheeling ethic, the notion of the internet as an exceptional, unregulated sphere evaporates. The moment of decision bears upon us: which side are you on?

As a distributed (many-to-many) communication infrastructure, the internet has long been celebrated for its potential to overcome the asymmetries of top-down broadcast media – and even representative democracy itself. The horsepower of the many would dissolve the rusty institutions bit by bit. At first the internet appeared to solve many of the long-standing shortcomings of the old "public sphere," and early research on forms of public discourse emerging online were

1

strongly framed in this seemingly dead tradition. Platforms such as blogs, discussion forums, and participatory news sites fostering "citizen journalism" were considered a new frontier of free speech, where anybody with an internet connection could participate in political communication. So much for critical imagination. It is one thing to make such claims, but the internet was not rolled out in a vacuum. Some critics have since debunked the notion that public discourse within online forums and blogs increases "democratic participation." Participation in what? In online petitions, maybe. But decision-making? Many "users of blogs" do not conform to larger ideals but display a culture of "detached engagement." Jodi Dean argues that a new form of "communicative capitalism" has emerged, where discourse proliferates but is completely devoid of genuine political potency.[1] Finally, rather than foster new public engagements, online discussion tends to take place within "echo chambers" where groups of like-minded individuals, consciously or not, avoid debate with their cultural or political adversaries.

Society has now caught up with the internet and disrupted the techno dreams of cyberspace as a parallel virtual reality. Visiting the 2011 South by Southwest (SXSW) technology event in Austin, Texas, the *Guardian's* Oliver Burkeman is simply overwhelmed, sighing that "the internet is over. This, for outsiders, is the fundamental obstacle to understanding where technology culture is heading: increasingly, it's about everything."[2] That is, the internet as a project with a distinct set of protocols separate from our daily lives, with their existing conflicts and ambivalent circumstances, has lost its sense and purpose. With children online well before the age of four there is no longer any urge to explain how computer networks operate. How can a medium that is so accepted and embraced cause such friction? New media have definitively passed beyond an introductory phase, but they continue to clash with existing social and political structures, as corporations and traditional knowledge institutions face the disruptive implications of networking. While the implementation of computer networks over the past decade drastically altered daily business routines and workflows, procedures at decision-making levels still cling to old organizational trees. Take the centralized service Twitter: a good PR tool for politicians, but one that did not halt the growing crisis of political legitimacy or make politicians any more directly responsive. Is the medium just passing through adolescence – will it mature in the end? Or will web culture, like most of its male operators and decision-makers, remain in a stage of eternal childhood?

2

This study situates an internet culture caught between self-referentiality and institutional arrangements. It is no longer sufficient to complain about network society's dysfunctionalities in terms of usability, access, privacy, or copyright infringements. Instead, we need to investigate that slippery nexus between the internet's reinforcement of existing power structures, and parallel – and increasingly interpenetrating – worlds where control is diffused. Ideological criticism coupled with moral outrage over abuses, from political censorship to child pornography, falls short as it too easily gets caught up in the 24-hour news spectacle. All too often Web 2.0 debates end in careful considerations about what journalism should but fails to do, as witnessed at the height of the blog wave. Deconstructing the hype and downplaying over-optimistic reporting have also proven insufficient. Web 2.0 cultures are remarkably resilient against the op-ed style of public opinion. They created secluded online environments where literally tens of millions of users work, hang out, chat, and play, irrespective of what parents, teachers, columnists, or celebrities have to say about social networking. Be it the *Wall Street Journal*, *The Australian*, *Der Spiegel*, or the *Guardian*, we read what major news outlets make of the internet phenomenon – not what is actually discussed in forums, exchanged on peer-to-peer networks, or how people use search engines.

More often than not, network cultures don't fit in. For decades consultancy gurus called for "change," but when the "perfect storm" of WikiLeaks arrived, techno-optimists displayed significant unease. We witness "deep penetration" of network technologies in society – but the outcome is not what the MBA club expected. Why? We cannot understand this complex process simply by reading the signs of the time. We need a sixth sense beyond the zeitgeist for untimely configurations appearing out of nowhere, scaling up like a G6 private jet. Netspaces are noncommittal, and users unrepentantly move on as if their addiction never happened. Let us not extrapolate the digital natives' *Weltbild* from all the contradictions of their fractured self-perception. We should stop repeating the upbeat intentions of a never-ending stream of start-ups zooming by on TechCrunch and instead dig into the real conflicts that emerge from the network condition. Should we wait in vain for the agonizing, flawless story about our intoxicating lives on Facebook? If it is not going to be a novel, what else do we look for?

A Brief History of Web 2.0

Sociality is the capacity of being several things at once.

G. H. Mead

Let us once and for all contend with Web 2.0 before this episode comes to a close. Popularized in 2004 by publisher Tim O'Reilly, the term "Web 2.0" regrouped the half-dead start-up scene on the US West Coast in the aftermath of the dot.com crash. The story goes something like this: in 1998 the cool cyberworld of geeks, artists, designers, and small entrepreneurs were bulldozed overnight by "the suits": managers and accountants going after Big Money provided by banks, pension funds, and venture capital. At the height of dot. com mania all attention became focused on e-commerce, touting it as the New Economy. Users were first and foremost potential customers, and they needed convincing to buy online goods and services. The AOL-Time Warner merger in January 2000 was the symbolic height of the dot.com era. With the sudden influx of business types, early cyberculture and other creative enclaves suffered a fatal blow and lost their avant-garde positions for good. When the New Economy bubble burst into a cloud of scandals and bankruptcies in March 2000, the hyped-up dot.com entrepreneurs sprinted equally fast from the scene, and stocks never fully recovered.

We should judge Web 2.0 for what it is: a renaissance in Silicon Valley which nearly vanished due to the 2000–01 financial crisis, the political reorientation of G. W. Bush's election, the 9/11 attacks and successive US invasions in Afghanistan and Iraq. If West Coast internet start-ups were to regain (global) market supremacy in 2003, after the worst of the Enron-WorldCom drama was over, their focus had to shift from e-commerce and quick and greedy IPOs (flotation on the stock market), toward a more "participatory culture" (Jenkins) in which users (also called prosumers), and not venture capitalists or bankers, had the final say. The "free and open" business model moved into place as ideal start-ups were bought by larger players such as Yahoo and Newscorp. The unimpeachable attitude of the past had to be repackaged, and Silicon Valley found its renewed inspiration in two projects: the vital energy of the search start-up Google and the rapidly emerging blog scene, gathered around self-publishing platforms such as blogger.com, Blogspot, and LiveJournal. This situation became evident when I visited Sunnyvale in early 2003, passing the deserted Silicon Graphics office, and where the only full parking lot seen was Google's.[3]

4

Both Google's search algorithm, which is explored further in chapter 9, "Society of the Query," and Dave Winer's RSS invention (the underlying blog technology) date back to 1997–8 but managed to avoid the dot.com rage to resurface as the duo-core of the Web 2.0 wave. Whereas blogging embodied the non-profit, empowering aspect of personal responses grouped around a link, Google developed parasitical techniques to exploit other people's content, also known as "organizing the world's information." So-called "user-generated content" aggregates profiles that can be sold to advertisers as direct marketing data, and Google soon discovered it could profit from all the free information floating around the open internet, from amateur videos to news sites. Google's late public offering in August 2004, six years after its founding, should be seen as the symbolic launch of Web 2.0: a comprehensive set of web applications driven by the rapid growth of users with access to broadband.

Web 2.0 has three distinguishing features: it is easy to use, it facilitates sociality, and it provides users with free publishing and production platforms that allow them to upload content in any form, be it pictures, videos, or text. Search 'n share: the users themselves recommend more than the professionals. The subsequent focus on profiting from free user-generated content can therefore be seen as a direct response to the dot.com crash. The killer apps weren't based on direct financial transactions (e-commerce) but on personalized ads that sold indirect information and data-mining of user profiles, with demographic details that are then sold to third parties. Companies no longer profit at the level of production, but instead through the control of distribution channels, and users do not immediately realize how their free labor and online socializing is being monetized by Apple, Amazon, eBay, and Google, the biggest winners in this game. Now, as the IT sector takes on the media industry, the cult of free and open is nothing more than dubious revenge on the e-commerce madness that almost ruined the internet.

Another consequence of Web 2.0 is that news media are, at best, secondary sources. This is an ironic reversal of Habermas's description of the internet as an informal public sphere submitting to the higher authority of established outlets such as publishing houses, newspapers, and cultural magazines.[4] In the end, the Habermas paradigm is nothing but a moral judgment on how the world should function, since for most young people "old media" lost their legitimacy a long time ago. But both positions seem perfectly valid – networks are both powerful and dissolve power. The internet can be "secondary" and dominant at the same time: whirlpool dialectics.

5

This is exactly why "leading" intellectuals remain unaware of current transformations. The outgoing generations read newspapers and sit in front of their TV, watching their favorite talk shows and wondering what the fuss is about; is there really anything spectacular about all this invisible status updating? Only a handful of those in power have the courage to openly express their real resentment toward all the useless twittering and chatting.

Meanwhile, welcome to the social. These days the social is a feature. It is no longer a problem (as in the nineteenth and twentieth centuries when the Social Problem predominated) or a sector in society provided for deviant, sick, and elderly people. Until recently, employing an amoral definition of the social was unthinkable. Either the social was an ideal that you subscribed to through lifelong dedication, a religion that provided a secure identity for millions, or a vision of horror: the invading Others who were after your belongings and property. Now the beast has been tamed. In the long post-war era from 1945 to 1989 the social became neutralized, and for the twenty-first century it returns as a special effect of technological procedures, written into protocols and distinct from the community. The social lost its mysterious potential energy to burst suddenly onto the street and take power. We might be moved by Catholic and Gramscian images of the common people gathering in squares to celebrate their unity, but this sentiment is short-lived and cannot replace the feeling of discontent that society, as Margaret Thatcher rightly stated, no longer exists. Blame neo-liberalism, individualism, consumerism, globalization, and new media. They all have destroyed the homogeneous feeling of community that so many ran away from in the post-World War II period. Social media as a buzzword of the outgoing Web 2.0 era is just a product of business management strategies and should be judged accordingly. The citizen-as-user has not yet left the social media *epocha* behind, encapsulated as he is in Flickr, Wikipedia, MySpace, Twitter, Facebook or YouTube. Platforms come and go (remember Bebo, Orkut, Friendster?) but the trend is clear: the networks without cause are time eaters, and we're only being sucked deeper into the social cave without knowing what to look for.

What is Critical Web 2.0 Studies Today?

Not much is available in terms of thorough and critical Web 2.0 research, but that should not surprise us. PhD research cannot keep up with the pace of change and condemns itself to capturing vanishing networks and cultural patterns. Ever since the early 1990s, user cultures have emerged from nowhere, and researchers cannot antici- pate or synthesize the speed with which these large structures come and go. User cultures long surpassed the imagination of IT journal- ists, and society is way ahead of its theorists (including this author). The response is either to panic or to leave the topic of new media altogether. The object of study is in a permanent state of flux and will disappear shortly – the death of everything cannot be denied. The realization that theory in the form of detailed case studies is condemned to history writing can induce a state of depression and drag us further into a pharmacological state of mind, as Bernard Stiegler calls it.[5] Along with the demise of French theory, there is a clear lack of guidance. Op-ed writers and stand-up comedians deal with new media as gadgets, but smartphones are not handbags. We want informed debates full of wit and irony, but instead we discuss current affairs as defined by the news media. A possible way out is the development of critical concepts that migrate from one generation of applications to the next, without falling back on speculative theory that merely celebrates the liberating potentialities of buzzwords while waiting to be translated into market value.

Let us discuss the state of Web 2.0 criticism (and leave aside justi- fied privacy concerns that are widely covered elsewhere by writers such as danah boyd). Andrew Keen's *The Cult of the Amateur* from 2007 is considered one of the first critiques of the Web 2.0 belief system. "What happens," Keen asks, "when ignorance meets egoism meets bad taste meets mob rule? The monkey takes over." When everyone broadcasts, no one is listening. In this state of "digital Dar- winism," only the loudest and most opinionated voices survive. Web 2.0 "decimate(s) the ranks of our cultural gatekeepers."[6] Whereas Keen comes off as a grumpy and jealous representative of the old media class, this is not the case with Nicholas Carr, whose book *The Big Switch* (2008) analyzes the rise of cloud computing. For Carr (who we visit again in chapter 1, "Psychopathology of Information Overload"), this centralized infrastructure signals the end of the autonomous PC as a node within a distributed network. The last chapter of Carr's book, entitled "iGod," indicates a "neurological turn" in Web 2.0 critique. Starting from the observation that Google's intention has always been to metamorphose its operation into an Artificial Intelligence "an artificial brain that is smarter than your brain" (as Google founder Sergey Brin told *Newsweek*), Carr focuses his attention on future human cognition: "The medium is not only the message. The medium is the mind. It shapes what we see and how

7

we see it." With the internet's stress on speed, we become the Web's neurons: "The more links we click, pages we view, and transactions we make, the more intelligence the Web makes, the more economic value it gains, and the more profit it throws off."[7]

In his famous 2008 *The Atlantic* essay, "Is Google Making Us Stupid? What the Internet is Doing to Our Brains," Carr sharpens this point by arguing that constantly switching between windows and sites and frantically using search engines will ultimately dumb us down. Is it the individual's responsibility to monitor her internet use to prevent a long-term impact on her cognition? In its extensive article on the ensuing debate, Wikipedia refers to Sven Birkerts's 1994 study *The Gutenberg Elegies: The Fate of Reading in the Electronic Age*, and the later work of developmental psychologist Maryanne Wolf, who points out the loss of "deep reading" capacity. Internet-savvy users, she claims, seem to lose the capacity to read, and to enjoy thick novels and comprehensive monographs. Carr and others cleverly exploit the Anglo-American obsession with anything related to the mind, brain, and consciousness. Mainstream science reporting meanwhile cannot get enough. A thorough economic (let alone Marxist) analysis of Google and the free and open complex is seriously uncool. The cultural critics must sing along with the Daniel Dennetts of this world (loosely gathered on edge.org) in order to communicate their concerns.

In his book-length essay *Payback,* Edge member and editor of *Frankfurter Allgemeine Zeitung* Frank Schirrmacher also addresses the internet's impact on the brain.[8] Whereas Carr's take on the collapse of the white male's multitasking capacities had the *couleur locale* of a US IT-business expert moonlighting as an East Coast intellectual, Schirrmacher moves the debate to the continental European context, where an aging middle class recoils in defensive anxiety over Islamic fundamentalism and Asian hypermodernity. Like Carr, Schirrmacher seeks evidence of a deteriorating human brain that cannot keep pace with iPhones, Twitter, and Facebook in addition to the already existing information flows of television, radio, and print. On permanent alert, we submit to the logic of constant availability and speed. Schirrmacher speaks of "I exhaustion." Most German bloggers responded negatively to *Payback*. Apart from factual mistakes, they took issue with Schirrmacher's implicit anti-digital cultural pessimism (something he denies) and the conflict of interest between his roles as newspaper publisher and as critic of the zeitgeist. Whatever the cultural media agenda, Schirrmacher's alarm will remain with us for quite some time. What place should we give digital devices and applications in our everyday life? Will the internet overwhelm our senses and dictate our worldview? Or will we have the will and vision to master the tools?

In *You Are Not a Gadget* (2010), Jaron Lanier asks: "What happens when we stop shaping the technology and technology starts shaping us?"[9] Lanier is a special case. He is not a journalist or academic but a mega-nerd, a computer scientist belonging to the pre-Web "hippie" cyberculture. Politically, Lanier is hard to pin down and perhaps best labeled as countercultural and anti-corporate (we always must be careful applying the anti-capitalist label to the American West Coast). What makes Lanier's story special is his status as a Silicon Valley insider, and we should read his long-awaited book just as Kremlin watchers once deciphered central news media. In his very own way, Lanier is the contemporary version of the Soviet dissident. Much like Andrew Keen, Lanier's defence of the individual points to the dumb-down effect of the "wisdom of the crowd" as unique voices are suppressed in favor of mob rule, manifested on sites such as Wikipedia. Lanier asks why the past two decades have not generated new music styles and subcultures, and he blames the strong emphasis on retro in contemporary, remix-dominated music culture. Free culture not only decimates the income of performing artists but also discourages musicians from experimenting with new sounds. The democratization of digital tools did not herald any "super-Gershwins"; instead, Lanier sees "pattern exhaustion," a phenomenon in which a culture runs dry of variations on traditional designs and becomes less creative in general. "We are not passing through a momentary lull before a storm. We have instead entered a persistent somnolence and I have come to believe that we will only escape it when we kill the hive."[10] Whether or not we agree with Lanier, we should at least take up his critique and formulate exactly which forms of experimentation and invention are working successfully in the online realm in electronic music or hacker culture.

Thierry Chervel of the German cultural aggregator Perlentaucher writes: "According to Schirrmacher the internet grinds the brain and he wants to regain control. But that is no longer possible. The revolution eats its children, fathers, and those who detest it."[11] Is this going to be the destiny of the new wave of Net critics such as Siva Vaidhyanathan, Sherry Turkle, and even Evgeny Morozov?[12] Internet and society debate should be neither "medicalized" nor moralized, but should instead address the politics and aesthetics of network architecture.

Instead of repeating what Carr, Schirrmacher, and others proclaim, I argue that Web 2.0 critique needs to take other avenues. Rather than mapping mental impacts and pondering the Net's influence on our lives, or discussing over and over the fate of the news and publishing industry, let us next study several less obvious emerging cultural logics – real-time, linking vs liking, and the rise of national webs – that extend beyond particular platforms and corporations. This is the Net criticism approach that I'll employ over subsequent chapters of this book. I intend to unearth aspects of everyday internet use that often remain unnoticed. I point to the slightly invisible transition from internet use as a tool to the creation of collaborative widespread "user cultures" that start to develop their own distinguished characteristics, which then infuse life inside the technology. It is in this relatively new ecology that concepts find a breeding ground for immediate trial and error. Concepts can be seen as abstract ideas, but in the context of lively Net cultures they emerge from within and do not fall out of the sky. In my approach, I both pinpoint the adoption of concepts and propose new concepts that are designed to play a productive role. I perceive the internet context as still fluid; otherwise why bother and not move on to more urgent and interesting topics? The battle for the internet is not over yet. As long as something is at stake new enclosures will produce new generations of outlaws – and critical positions that further their projects.

Slogans and quotes for the networked many:
No idea? No problem (advertisement) – Feeling Smart Again – Yes We Comment – When you are bored you are boring – Yearning for the Common Good – Fall of the Digital Hegemon – The despair of mass dandyism – Register Here to Become a Partizan – Filling In the American Void – The Growing Internal Distance – Experience the Beauty of Indirect Intensity™ – a quiet extacy – I serve as a blank screen – The observer is alone. That's the solitude of the free person – Belief as a rational choice – ... superior software for the perplexed multitudes ... – "France was the center of the world and nowadays it is suffering from the lack of great historic events. This is why it revels in radical ideological postures. It is the lyrical, neurotic expectation of some great deed of its own which however is not coming, and never will come" (Milan Kundera) – Giving people back their most reliable asset, theory (promotional billboard) – We are not desperate for investments – "He is a running dog of Google. Lower than animals" – We are enjoying independence (Chatroulette) – Multitasking is for the Poor – Fatum of Tech (mini series) – Noble Lies for Social Media – I like to think about myself – Linking the unintended revolts – "Overprogrammed, furious,

10

lonely" (Zadie Smith) – Favorite colour: opaque – With no power comes no responsibility.

The Colonization of Real-time

Forget the browser; real-time is the new crack. Dave Winer promotes it on *Scripting News,* and Nicholas Carr writes about it in his blog series *The Real Time Chronicles.*[13] We see the fluid, ever-changing trend popping up in metaphors such as Google Wave and Twitter, the most visible symptom of this transitory tendency, but you can also find it in chatrooms, internet telephony such as Skype, live monitoring of internet traffic (Deep Pocket Inspection), and dynamic pricing such as trade in stocks, and in video streaming. In December 2009, Google introduced a real-time search interface that automatically updates search results without requiring a browser refresh.

Real-time signifies a fundamental shift from the static archive toward "flow" and the "river." Who responds to yesterday's references? Time speeds up and we abandon history. In a 24/7 economy, we transmit tweets while the visible part of the archive diminishes to the last few hours.[14] Silicon Valley gears up for the colonization of real-time and moves away from the static web "page" that persists as a reference to the newspaper. Why store a flow? Users no longer desire to keep information offline on their own devices, and the "cloud," along with hardware developments (think MacAir and its various technical restrictions), facilitates this liberating movement. We outsource our archives, trusting institutions to manage them for us. If Google keeps our files, at some point we can toss out the clumsy, all-purpose PC. Away with the big, ugly, grey office furniture. The Web has transformed into an ephemeral environment that we carry around in our pockets. Some have already said goodbye to the very idea of "search" because it is a time-consuming activity, often with unsatisfactory outcomes. This could be the point when the Google empire starts to crumble, which is why they are keen to be at the forefront of a situation that the French philosopher of speed, Paul Virilio, predicted a long time ago.

Nowadays live television is too slow, so news shows turn to Twitter for up-to-the-second information. The televisual apparatus itself may be fast enough, its signals travelling at light speed, but these days we need multiple and omnipresent viewpoints. The real space of the TV studio must dissolve. CNN, once a mighty global initiative, turns out to be hopelessly slow and narrow in scope while mobilizing its

11

multiple live channels. Even real-time is relative. Much like finance, the media industry is forced to maximize surplus value by exploiting milliseconds. The industry can only return profits by utilizing the colonization of these streams on a planetary scale and in a distributed fashion.

May 2009 saw the introduction of the online, real-time collaborative editing platform Google Wave. It merged email, instant messages, wikis, and social networks, integrating, for instance, feeds of Facebook, Twitter, and email into one real live event on the screen. It was a meta-online tool for real-time communication that provided contextual spelling and grammar checking with automated translation among 40 languages. Seen from your "dashboard," you experienced Wave as if sitting on the banks of a river watching the current flow by. A year later Google decommissioned Wave, citing lack of interest and reports about dismal usability. The service was so bad that "humans weren't able to comprehend it."[15] Should we bother to synthesize multi-channel live streams? For what purpose again? Have you already installed – and mastered – your personal intelligence dashboard that assists you in solving the information overload question?[16]

Utopian promises suggest we will no longer wait around while the PC computes our questions. The internet comes closer to the messiness and complexities of the existing social world. Yet, in terms of design, one step forward also means two steps back. Just look at Twitter on a smartphone; it resembles 1981 ASCII email and SMS messages on a 2001 cell phone. To what extent is this a conscious visual effect? Raw, typo-prone HTML-style may not be a technical imperfection but rather a reference to the incompleteness of the Eternal Now in which we are caught. There is simply no time to enjoy slow media. Back in Tuscany mode, it is nice to lean back and listen to the offline silence, but that is an exception reserved for quality moments.

Microblogging is the pacemaker of the real-time internet, but we can also look at it from the reverse perspective of social media urging users to cough up as much as possible. Twitter first asked: "What are you doing?," "What's on your mind?," "What's happening here?" If the machine is not reading your thoughts, you are kindly requested to insert and share them. Get with the program. Give us your best self-shot. Expose your impulses. This inclination produces frantically updated blogs, frequently refreshed news sites, and petabytes of milli-opinions. The driving technology behind these applications is the constant cascade of RSS feeds, making it possible to get instant updates of what's happening elsewhere on the Web. The proliferation of mobile phones plays a significant background role in "mobilizing" your computer, social network, video and photo camera, audio devices, and eventually also your TV. With the miniaturization of hardware, combined with wireless connectivity, technology becomes an invisible part of everyday life. Web 2.0 applications respond to this trend by attempting to extract value from our every situation. The Machine constantly desires to know what's going on, which choices we make, where we go, who we talk to. All the while we are data-mined without any concern that our semi-private and mostly public selves are making the owners of social media joyfully wealthy. This is the price of the free, and we seem more than willing to pay it.

The cyber-prophets were wrong: there is no evidence that the world is becoming more virtual. Rather the virtual is becoming more real; it wants to penetrate and map out our real lives and social relationships. Self-management and techno-sculpturing become crucial: how do you shape the self in real-time flows? No longer encouraged to act out a role, we are forced to be "ourselves" (in a form that is no less theatrical or artificial). We constantly login, create profiles, and post status updates to present our Self on the global marketplace of employment, friendship, and love. We are allowed multiple passions but only one certified ID on Facebook, because the system response cannot deal with ambivalence. Trust is the oil of global capitalism and the security state, required by both sides in every transaction and at every checkpoint to allow the passage of both our bodies and information. The idea that the virtual liberates you from your old self has collapsed. There is no alternative identity.

The Web 2.0 Self is therefore post-cosmetic. The ideal is neither the Other nor the better human. *Mehrmensch*, not *Übermensch*. The perfectly polished personality lacks empathy and is straight-out suspect. It is the flaws (affairs, drug taking, bad dresses, weight gain, bad skin) that make the celebrity so irresistible. Becoming, now, implies revealing who you are, as social media invite users to "administer" their all-too-human dimensions, beyond the hiding or exposing of controversial aspects. Our profiles remain cold and incomplete if we do not expose at least some aspect of our private lives. Otherwise we are robots, anonymous members of a vanishing twentieth-century mass culture. In *Cold Intimacies*, Eva Illouz articulates a problem of online identity that we will return to in chapter 2 on these issues, "Facebook, Anonymity, and the Crisis of the Multiple Self": "It is virtually impossible to distinguish the rationalization and

13

commodification of selfhood from the capacity of the self to shape and help itself and to engage in deliberation and communication with others."[17]

And so every minute of life is converted into "work," or at least being available, a condition of perpetual online presence that corresponds with what Tiziana Terranova terms "the social production of value."[18] But at the same time that we appropriate and incorporate technology into our lives, we also create spaces in which to pull back and pause a moment for ourselves. How do we measure the balance? It is impossible to speed up and slow down simultaneously, but this is exactly how people lead their lives. We opt for either speedy or slow tasks according to our character, skill-set and taste – and then we outsource the rest.

> Quotes of no one and everyone:
> Worries Over Unexpected Growth of Ego Inflation (headline) – Look at my Distributed Grandiosity – Critique of Hyper-caffeinated Marxism – "Ever found out what is not important?" – Recommended Cascade Effects – unfriending one's lover – Join the Abolition of Self-Realization – Important Emails – Becoming Princess – Design your Struggle with Us (Pro. $150 a year) – Natural-Born Dissident – "Being able to create something that makes you feel smarter without having to do a lot of work has been difficult. Only a few ideas have ever gained traction with white people, the most notable of which being documentary films and public radio – However, in the past decade a new item has been added to this very short list: TED Talks" (Stuff White People Like) – "Ignore what you don't understand" (XML) – There ain't no such thing as a neutral lunch – "Downvoting is good for you" (scientific skepticism website)

From Link to Like

Contemplate the following: "This link is not an endorsement."[19] But wait a minute; it is. That's why lawyers are fighting court cases over the link issue. "You may not establish and/or operate links to this website without the prior written consent ..." says Ryanair. "Such consent may be withdrawn at any time at Ryanair's own discretion."[20] Linking makes one complicit. Geeks and cyber-optimists are in denial about this when they make passionate explanations of value-free linkage. Wikipedia defines the hyperlink as "a reference in a document to an external piece of information," but absent in this definition is agency. If you do not agree with a statement, then you ignore it. You make a non-link. If a video is uncool, you do not recommend it. You skip boring pictures and do not listen to bad music. Why would this basic law not apply on the Web? Besides, linking invites your website's visitors to jump ship and explains why most "calculating" internauts are wary of too many links on their pages.[21] Jumping around is a basic mode of behavior in postmodern societies. If used at all, links should support your argument or business. Links are "ties" that symbolize "reputation" (which then can be measured and mapped) and are the very basis of Google's search algorithm. Google is built on positive affirmation.

Until recently there were no subconscious links but only tedious HTML work. That changed with social bookmarking buttons, described by Anne Helmond as "pre-configured links that take us back to the 'mother' platform when clicked. The thumbs-up 'like' button, activated with a click, so popular on Facebook, is far less intentional than linking, as the connection they create is less a relationship but more of an affective association, requiring less effort."[22] Unless you subscribe to Habermas's interest-free public sphere of civil debate, or you're a right-wing populist shock-blogger whose hobby is to provoke and openly attack, why link to competitors, to trash, to false information, to your political or social enemies?

These are the traps that the link rhetoric finds itself in. The "freedom to link" willingly negates the linked-to party. So what if we have "anti-linkage software" that automatically launches a DDoS attack on servers linking without permission to your document (including search engines)? Is there a freedom to unlink? Links create traffic, which in turn generates revenues. If millions would take down links to their pages from the Google search engine, this could possibly be the end of the service – the vital pillar of an empire. The problem is, so far they haven't. External links are accepted, tolerated, and mostly ignored or unknown. Techno-materialists say links feed machines created for cybernetic consumption. Blog spam, with its long lists of links, perfectly exemplifies how the economy of mass manufactured linkages works. Links are the basic unit used by the global information economy to investigate, map out, and reproduce its own existence. Google's empire is based on the link work that others put into their websites and documents. The very beginning of Page and Brin's analysis of web links in 1996 is rooted in the idea of linking as a positive endorsement of the Other. In David Vise's book on Google we read that "counting the number of links pointing to a Web site was a way of ranking that site's popularity." According to Page: "A large number of citations in scientific literature means your work is important because other people thought it was worth mentioning."[23] If one disagrees and doesn't want to add to a work's existing popularity, the best way to reverse this process is not to mention or link to it at all. But, as we shall see later on, this logic puts the category of criticism itself into jeopardy.

Take the case of US Judge Richard Posner who proposed to ban linking to newspaper articles or any copyrighted material without the copyright holder's consent. Richard Posner writes:

> Expanding copyright law to bar online access to copyrighted materials without the copyright holder's consent, or to bar linking to or paraphrasing copyrighted materials without the copyright holder's consent, might be necessary to keep free riding on content financed by online newspapers from so impairing the incentive to create costly newsgathering operations that news services like Reuters and the Associated Press would become the only professional, nongovernmental sources of news and opinion.[24]

TechCrunch responded: "I am sorry Judge Posner, but I don't need to ask your permission to link to your blog post or to a newspaper article online. That is just the way the Web works. If newspapers don't like it, they don't need to be on the Web." Blogs and other sites take content from newspapers, Posner asserts, but they share none of the costs of news gathering. TechCrunch:

> Of course, that blanket assertion is simply not true. A growing number of blogs, including TechCrunch, do their own newsgathering and send writers to cover events at their own cost. But even if we limit the discussion to cut-and-paste sites, the free rider argument still doesn't hold much water. You can't be a free rider if you are giving something back of value. As such, a link is valuable. (...) Where does Judge Posner think all of these newspaper sites get their readers? It is mostly through links, not direct traffic. Removing the links would obliterate the majority of the online readership for many newspapers.[25]

The recent decline of the link should be discussed as a gradual, subtle, almost invisible process. First, search engines lowered their status. We no longer click from page to page, using links to get somewhere, but take the direct route of the query. Radicalizing this, we can say that search engines have a parasitic attitude toward links. Engines are the largest benefactors of links while links erode their power at the same time. This mechanism is aptly described by Anne Helmond in her study *Blogging for Engines*: "There is a second linking process in the background, with the search engines. Bloggers are still linking to other bloggers but also put a lot of time and effort into formatting their content so that it can be easily consumed by search engines."[26] This is a clear example of the failing, distributed nature of links. Links do not comply with Clay Shirky's power laws or suffer from the tyranny of nodes as described by Ulises Mejias, but are produced, from the very start, to push the blog higher up in search rankings. Producing links becomes not only a means but an end in itself.

This process becomes further eroded inside the walled gardens of social networking sites where recommendation (liking) takes over from linking. Introduced in April 2010, the Facebook "like" button is the newest standard in blog promotion. The idea is that a blog post is "shared" on Facebook. The like button enables users to make connections to pages and share content with their friends with one click and to show logged-in users which friends have already "liked" the page. At stake is the politics of traffic. Inside social media, the link is reduced to a recommendation of content visited with the explicit aim to return to the platform – to say something about it, or share it with others, for instance. The move from link to like as the dominant web currency symbolizes the shift in the attention economy from search-driven navigation to the self-referential or gated dwelling in social media.[27]

Netizens and the Rise of Extreme Opinions

Inside Web 2.0 we look in vain for well-behaved members. The internet is a breeding ground for extreme opinions and border-testing users. If this virtual space is an oasis of freedom, as its reputation claims, then let's see what we can get away with. This attitude avoids true dialogue, which in any case would take us back to the communication utopia of Habermas. We never find out if the one-liners of mostly anonymous posters are true. Sustained interaction happens elsewhere, in more hidden, quasi-private forums. The public internet has turned into a battle zone, which explains the success of walled gardens such as Facebook and Twitter that seal off the aggressive Other (or at least give this impression, since the rise of Facebook stalkers, bullies, and even killers heralds the entry of the violent Other into the sanitized security of social media sites). Web 2.0 therefore provides users with tools to filter content and other users.

While Web 1.0 had secluded areas, the feeling of the public internet as a toxic environment had not yet arrived. The idea of the "netizen" is a mid-1990s response to the first wave of ordinary users who took over the Net. The ideal netizen moderates, cools down heated debates, and responds in a friendly, non-repressive manner. There was always a sense of the netizen being something like the "good cop" on a methadone program. The netizen embodies the idea of governance from below, does not represent the Law, and acts like a personal advisor, a guide in a new universe. The netizen operates in the spirit of good conduct and corporate citizenship. Similar to the neo-liberal citizen, users were encouraged to take social responsibility for themselves – the Net was explicitly designed to keep state legislators out. Until the early 1990s, in the late academic stage of the Net, all users were presumed to know the rules (also called netiquette) and to behave accordingly. Of course, this was not always the case (in the early Usenet days there were no "netizens": everyone was a pervert). But when misbehavior was noted, the individual could be convinced to stop spamming or bullying, for instance. This was no longer possible after 1995, when the internet opened to the general public. With the rapid growth of the World Wide Web and its easy-to-use browsers, the code of conduct developed by IT engineers and scientists could no longer be passed from one user to the next.

At the time, the Net was regarded as a global medium that could not be easily controlled by national legislation. Perhaps there was some truth in this. Cyberspace was out of control, but in a nice and innocent way. That authorities installed a task force in a room next to the office of the Bavarian Prime Minister in order to police the Bavarian part of the internet is an endearing and somewhat desperate image. At the time we had a good laugh about this predictably German measure. But 9/11 and the dot.com crash cut the laughter short. Over a decade later, there are reams of legislation, entire police departments dedicated to cybercrime, and a whole arsenal of software tools to oversee the National Web, as it is now called. Retrospectively, we easily dismiss the rational netizen approach as a libertarian Gestalt, a figure of the neo-liberal age of deregulation. However, the netizen was invented to address issues that have grown exponentially. These days they are framed as a part of education programs in schools and as general awareness campaigns. Identity theft is a serious business. Parents and teachers need to know how to identify and respond to cyberbullying amongst children. Much like the mid-1990s, we still face the problem of massification. A data visualization of its hyper growth would be the image that summarizes

18

Web 2.0. The sheer number of users across the globe and the intensity with which people engage with the internet is still overwhelming to insiders, and many no longer believe that the internet community can sort out these issues itself.

In times of global recession, rising nationalism, ethnic tension, and collective obsession with the Islam Question, comment cultures inside Web 2.0 become a major concern for media regulators and the police. Blogs, forums, and social networking sites invite users to leave short messages, and young people have particularly impulsive reactions to (news) events, often posting death threats to politicians and celebrities without realizing what they have just done. Professional comment monitoring is now serious work. Just to give some Dutch examples, Marokko.nl oversees 50,000 postings on a daily basis, and the right-wing *Telegraaf* news site gets 15,000 comments on its selected news items daily. Populist blogs like Geen Stijl encourage users to post extreme judgments, a tactic proven to draw attention to the site. Whereas some sites have internal policies to delete racist remarks, death threats, and libelous content, others encourage their users in this direction, all in the name of free speech.

Current software invites users to leave short statements but often excludes the possibility for others to respond. Web 2.0 was not designed to facilitate debate with its thousands of contributions. If the Web goes real-time, there is less space for reflection and more technology facilitating impulsive blather (an issue we'll return to in chapter 3, "Treatise on Comment Culture"). What the back-office software does is merely measure "responsiveness": in other words, there have been that many users, that much judgment, and that little debate. This development only invites authorities to interfere further in the few existing online mass conversations that do take place. Will (interface) design bring a solution to this hyper-growth in all directions? Wikipedia is a good example of a project that has managed to retain critical mass without exploding into fragments. However, on Wikipedia, too, bots play an increasing role in the automated policing of this large website. Bots merely work in the background, doing their silent job for their master. How can users regain control and navigate complex threads? Should they train their own bots and install dashboards to regain an overview à la Google Wave, or simply walk away and come back when the matter is resolved?

Sloganize with Us:
Introvert shopping – Low-noise Networking – Unite in Self-Government – Decommission Society – Friends are Toxic – No More Mindless

Suspense – Be the first to unlike this – Memorial for the Terror of Recommendation – Working for the Archive – Perception minus MyReality – I left Facebook. I am not nobody – "PHP is about as exciting as your toothbrush. You use it every day, it does the job, it is a simple tool, so what? Who would want to read about toothbrushes?" (Rasmus Lerdorf, creator of PHP) – Error establishing a connection to Funkopolis – Each generation will have to build its own media (after Marinetti) – Mobile Social Real-time Civil War – Don't believe the database – Uncertain Organizations – My Time is More Valuable than Yours – Target: reduce scholastic transmissions by 10% in 2020 – service security – Learning from mistakes is overrated – like.com has been acquired by Google – "Ideas don't make you rich. The correct execution of ideas does." (Felix Dennis)

The Rise of National Webs

Whereas "digital rights management" is in crisis due to copy cultures such as peer-to-peer networks, control within the nation-state is certainly on the rise. With a Net user base of 2 billion, focus has shifted from "global governance" to the national and local levels where the action is. People care about what happens in their immediate surroundings, a truism predicted in the 1990s; it just took a while to find a way to develop the technical implementation. With 42.6 percent of internet users located in Asia, the transatlantic era is over. In August 2008 it was announced that, for the first time, the Chinese user population surpassed that of the US. Now only 25 percent of the Web's content is in English.

The technical background of national webs is the development of tools to oversee and isolate the national IP range (the IP addresses allocated to a country). These geo-sensitive technologies can be used in two directions. First, they block users outside the country from viewing public television channels online (such as Norway, UK, Australia) where taxpayers or viewer license fees have funded content production, thus reproducing an ideology of cultural nationalism. Websites of public libraries hosting copyrighted cultural heritage are also blocked for similar reasons. Second, citizens residing within the nation's geo-technical borders can also be prevented from visiting foreign sites (mainland Chinese residents are not able to use YouTube, Facebook, or Twitter, for instance). In a recent development China exported its national firewall technology (built with the help of countless Western IT firms) to Sri Lanka, which used it to block "offensive websites" of exiled Tamil Tiger groups. Whereas in the past China

20

was considered a backward-looking exception, it is now rapidly the norm, even for OECD countries that claim to support internet freedom.

Culturally, language is the main vehicle for creating these "national webs." Very important to this process was the development of a system called Unicode, a protocol that attributes a unique piece of code to all the symbols of every language in the world. Unicode allows people to read and type symbols in many major languages. Software, however, still lags behind in these localizing efforts. There are still cases where older web browsers and operating systems are not able to display some Hindi and also Japanese characters. At some stage Blogger.com participated in the creation of specialized software, so that people could blog in Hindi. As time went on, blogging culture started to develop its own national characteristics, as I examine in the blogs chapter of this book. Google, opening up offices throughout the African continent, is still concerned with the localization of the Google search engine for respective African languages. These days it is possible to include Mandarin characters in your URL, and we may soon start to see code programmed in languages other than English.

Politically, however, the rise of national webs is an ambivalent development. Whereas communicating in one's own language rather than Latin script keyboards and domain names sounds liberating and is necessary for bringing the remaining 80 percent of the world's population online, the new digital enclosures also present a direct threat to the free and open exchange the internet once facilitated. Nationally defined spaces allow security agents to closely monitor telecommunications within state borders. As I discuss in chapter 10 on "Organizing Networks," authoritarian regimes such as Iran make increasingly tactical use of the Web in order to crack down on the opposition – reminding us that the internet does not work so easily as a revolutionary tool. Against all predictions, the Great Chinese Firewall, built with Western expertise from Cisco,[28] is remarkably successful at both preventing hostile content and monitoring internal populations on an unprecedented scale. This achievement proves that power these days is not absolute but dynamic and focused on control-ling the overall population. Cyber-dissidents, with their own proxy servers for circumventing the Wall, remain in a marginal position if they cannot transport their memes into larger social contexts. If there are protests and uprisings (and there are many) they seem to emerge out of nowhere, reach an incredible intensity and then disappear again, sending out a "planetary shock wave through the networks."[29] As the saying goes: regardless of your size or intent, it is all about governmentality. So how do you manage complexity? The only way to challenge this administrative approach is to organize: social change is no longer techno-warfare between filters and anti-filters, but a question of organized networks that set a marathon of events in motion.

Waiting for Network Theory

These thoughts and the following chapters are part of a "Net criticism" project that seeks to develop sustainable concepts. Separately, chapter 4, "Disquisition on Internet Criticism," builds on previous thoughts contained in *My First Recession*, from 2003, and is dedicated to the state of the arts of this genre-in-the-making. Past examples of concepts include sovereign media, organized networks, and distributed aesthetics, with tactical media being the most well known. The presupposition here is that by using concepts as individual building blocks, assembled through endless dialogues and debates, such collaborative efforts will ultimately culminate in a comprehensive materialist (read: hardware- and software-focused) and affect-related theory. This has not happened so far on a large scale, but maybe we should slow down, relax, and be patient.

When scientific network theory arrived, researchers eagerly adopted it across disciplines because its generalizations seemed to offer what the "social physics" analysts of the network society had long been waiting for. Because of its all-too-human perspective and lack of techno-interest, the sociological focus of "social network analysis" of interpersonal dynamics proved ill-suited to the contradictions of the network society. The result is fading enthusiasm for general network theories that offer only a one-size-fits-all approach, which is also the case for Actor Network Theory (ANT). If we study the use of networks by large institutions or bots as examples of autonomous software behavior, ANT might be useful. But what if we look at web aesthetics or social media politics? Online subjectivities? Big silence. With "internet studies" (organized by AoIR, the Association of internet Researchers) focusing on social science methods, the absence of a larger humanities project in this field is becoming obvious. As I argue in chapter 5, "Media Studies: Diagnostics of a Failed Merger," it is time to look for elements that can make up a network theory outside of the identity-obsessed cultural studies and ethnographic or quantitative social sciences approaches. What we need are appealing critical concepts that will survive as robust memes and transform into socio-technical protocols.

If we look at internet-specific theory, the object of study has congealed from virtual communities (Rheingold), space of flows (Castells), smart mobs (Rheingold), weak ties and tipping points (Gladwell), crowdsourcing, participatory culture (Jenkins), and wisdom of the crowds (Surowiecki), into general labels such as Web 2.0 (O'Reilly) and social media. Often these theories effectively describe how networks emerge and grow, and what shapes and sizes they take, but remain silent about how they are being embedded into society and what conflicts this evokes.

Why, after a good two decades, does no (general) "internet theory" exist? Are we all to blame? We need a contemporary network theory that reflects rapid changes and takes the critical and cultural dimensions of technical media seriously. Network theory still emphasizes the science-focused "unified network theory," to paraphrase the language of Albert-László Barabási. But we cannot merely study potentiality and growth patterns as pseudo-natural phenomena. There is hope: we can revolt against the mathematical shapes of networks. Humanities should do more than describe the times we're living in. We can match untimely aphorisms with future scenario planning, speculative thinking with data journalism, and computer programming with visual studies. The overall aim is to ignite speculative futurism and celebrate singular modes of expression rather than institutional power plays. Many want to know how networks can guarantee "trust" while remaining open, flat, and democratic. How can rapidly emerging concentrations of power be counterbalanced? If networks are so distributed and decentralized in nature, then why don't they oppose the economies of scale that produce the Googles and Facebooks? The answer may lie in the organized networks concept, introduced in *Zero Comments*, that now yields case studies described in the last chapter of this book. In any case, rough consensus has vanished.[30] Are you ready for the conflict age?

23

— 1 —

PSYCHOPATHOLOGY OF
INFORMATION OVERLOAD

To live is so startling that it leaves little time for anything else.

Emily Dickinson

Tentacular, protuberant, excrescent, hypertelic: this is the inertial destiny of a saturated world. The denial of its own end in hyperfinality; is this not also the mechanism of cancer? The revenge of growth in excrescence. The revenge and summons of speed in inertia.

Jean Baudrillard

Information overload has been with us for some time. Marshall McLuhan and Herbert Simon discussed it in the 1960s. The causes of attention breakdown shifted from the proliferation of channels and titles to storage capacity, but the symptoms remained the same: not coping any more and leaving incoming data flows to pile up until the system breaks down. It is only in the 2000s that billions became confronted with data explosion – having to browse and search 24/7, often on the go, on tiny mobile screens. Reading and answering hundreds of emails a day can no longer be dealt with under the paradox of choice or the "less is more" rubric. There is no "tyranny of the small decision" here. It's simply work.[1]

Information overload is a fashionable media topic that presents itself as a tech-related sentiment amongst the stagnant middle classes. It should in fact be discussed in the context of burgeoning workloads, longer working hours, and less pay. While communication and media may be an opportunity – and a necessity – for the global poor, it causes headaches for the more affluent segments of society. Because discontent is not expressed in political terms, we translate the problem into medical discourse. The user turned patient needs to compensate sensory overload with offline quality time. Or the inability of a user to participate in the knowledge society is described as a generational issue. Whereas fresh synapses and empty brains can suck up gigabytes of various information streams, the grey suits in power sooner or later crack up. To make things worse, because of their limited multitasking skills males are more likely to suffer from info overload than women. The wannabe digital natives neglect their diet and are hit by a data attack. They freak out when their BlackBerry is stolen, laptop breaks down, email box overflows, or friend requests remain unanswered.

In his 1901 *Psychopathology of Everyday Life*, Freud writes about forgetting names, misspellings, and other lapses of the brain. Feeling upset, we wonder about the origin of such errors and mistakes. Our senses are playing tricks on us. Like last century's discontent, in the information age we blame ourselves without knowing why we're at fault. Is it education, socio-economic structures, or human limitations that we have yet to be reconciled with? The difference is the sudden attention shift away from human memory capacity toward architectures of information systems. A century after Freud, the anxiety shifts from forgetting to finding. We no longer blame ourselves for forgetting names of friends or family but instead are upset if we fail to find the right file folder or enter incomplete query terms.

Users embrace the world and start making lists. We are honored to be invited by the Machine to submit our opinions and preferences. How do you categorize yourself? There must at least be some "good-value" content out there as a reward, after we feed the databases. Once we stumble upon "good value" we start forwarding, blogging, twittering, and linking to our latest discoveries. As long as there's content there's hope. We give in to the pressure to categorize data and join swarms of "collective intelligence." Donate your wisdom to the crowds. Websites display the most read, viewed, and sent content, and give advice on what like-minded users thought and bought. What is fascinating is not so much the flux of opinions, as Jean Baudrillard once described democracy in the media age, but the ability to indulge in similarity with others. We are invited to create reading lists, rank music, and evaluate the products we consumed. User bees working for queen Google. It is so tempting to become part of the online "pollination" world, as French economist Yann Moulier Boutang coined it, with billions of users acting like bees that fly from one website to the other, adding value for the owners.

Soft Narcosis of the Networked Condition

In April 2010, I went to Bologna to visit the Italian media theorist Franco "Bifo" Berardi. He was a member of the 1977 post-Operaist movement (often associated with Antonio Negri, Paolo Virno, and others), founder of the pirate radio station Radio Alice, involved in the tactical media Tele-street movement, and editor of the web discussion forum Recombinant. Berardi, who teaches at an art academy in Milan and recently turned 60, has a remarkably sharp eye for the contemporary "precarious" conditions of overworking, short-term contracts, anti-depressants, BlackBerries, and credit card debt. Finally, Berardi's work is available in English. In *The Soul at Work*, from 2009, he describes the transition in the last 30 to 40 years from alienation to autonomy, from repression to hyper-expressivity, from the hopes and desires of schizo activism to the diffused, if not to say depressed, subjectivity of the pharmacological Web 2.0 citizen.[2]

In a 2009 anthology of recent essays, entitled *Precarious Rhapsody*, Franco Berardi remarks: "While cyberspace is conceptually infinite, cybertime is not infinite at all. I call cybertime the ability of the conscious organism to actually process (cyber-spatial) information."[3] In the Net economy, he writes, flexibility has evolved into a fractalization of work. The worker is paid for his or her occasional, temporary services. We are all too aware of this fragmentation of activity time. As Berardi states:

> Today psychopathology reveals itself ever more clearly as a social epidemic and, more precisely, a socio-communicational one. If you want to survive you have to be competitive, and if you want to be competitive you must be connected, receive and process continuously an immense and growing amount of data. This provokes a constant attentive stress, a reduction of the time available for affectivity.[4]

In an attempt to sync their bodies, workers take drugs such as Prozac, Viagra, cocaine, or amphetamines. If we bring this analysis to the internet we see these two movements – the expansion of storage and the compression of time – making online work so stressful. It is the "origin of contemporary chaos." A chaos that occurs when the world goes too fast for your brain.

According to Berardi, we have to focus on the "digital natives" if we really want to understand info overload. Whether older generations suffer from info saturation should not determine our analysis. Berardi:

> Do not ask yourself if you can or cannot cope. It is not about adaptation or choice. The Greek god of hunting and rustic music, Pan, is a symbol

26

of plenty and abundance and has never been stigmatized as a problem. Humankind was always impressed by the billions of stars shining in the clear night sky – and never was in a panic about its plentitude.[5]

For Berardi, we must imagine how humans grow up in the info sphere. The nonconformist Berardi questions the current emphasis in contemporary arts and other fancy circles of "becoming," a central concept in the work of his teachers Gilles Deleuze and Félix Guattari, with whom he collaborated and about whom he wrote a book. Desire was always good, but now that's not always the case. We are no longer "becoming" digital. We're in the midst of the network para-digm – and it is pretty busy in here.

Berardi recommended Mark Fisher's 2009 *Capitalist Realism* to me, which describes what happens when postmodernism is natural-ized. Fisher defines this unstated worldview as "reflexive impotence." "They know things are bad, but more than that, they can't do any-thing about. But that 'knowledge,' that 'reflexivity,' is not a passive observation of an existing state of affairs. It is a self-fulfilling proph-ecy." An obstacle to implementing any response to such content overload is that one can retreat into a position of indifference. Young people experience a world where nothing can be done. They sense that society is falling apart and nothing will change. Fisher correlates the impotence to widespread pathologization, foreclosing the possi-bility of politicization. "Many of the teenage students I encountered," Fisher writes, "seemed to be in a state of depressive hedonia, consti-tuted by an inability to do anything else except pursue pleasure." Young people respond to the freedom that post-disciplinary systems offer "not by pursuing projects but by falling into hedonic lassitude: the soft narcosis, the comfort food oblivion of Playstation, all-night TV and marijuana."[6] Having a psychoanalytic background, Franco Berardi connects the condition described by Mark Fisher to the shift away from the affection of the mother and the voice of the father to the machinic realm of television and the computer as the prime source of language acquisition.

Indolence becomes a virtue after one no longer misses the news headlines. This is the strategy of the Network Sovereign. No more calls for restraint or attempts to filter the rubbish in the hope of finding vital info gems. Instead we surf 'n' search for perfect serendip-ity with our eyes wide shut. We are fully connected yet don't care. The flashy visual seductions of PR firms and software engineers run aground on this paramount attitude. Data flows no longer penetrate our mental armature; deflector shields do their job.

Berardi claims that we do not live in an "attention economy," which is a concept based on the idea of choice and preferred by the liberal and conservative outgoing generations. As if there was any choice to participate in Facebook, Twitter, and to have your mobile phone on 24/7. For those post-baby boom Gen-Xers, growing up under capitalist realism, this simply is not the case. Berardi: "The problem is not in the technology. We have to come to terms with it. The killing element is the combination of info stress and competition. We have to win, and to be the first. The real pathogenic effect is the neo-liberal pressure that makes the network condition so unlivable – not the abundance of information in itself."

The (Self-)Mastery of Information

Should we make the claim for info-sovereignty? Tokyo Net wizard David d'Heilly described this demand once as the road to "personal information autonomy," the ability to design your own data cloud. Much like other addictions and conditions, you must become strong enough to switch off your iPhone. This needs training, self-restraint, and education, much like other aspects of life. What is required is a serious reconsideration of "media literacy," not just in terms of info ethics, gadget mastery, or "media wisdom" (which is the name of the Dutch policy on media literacy now that the entire population is online), but in terms of determining one's destiny. An important aspect of literacy is the ability to walk away from the screen. You will master the tools not only once you know how to use them, but also once you know when to put them aside. This training must take into consideration how much email, Twitter, and SMS is vital, what work can be done later, what defines entertainment, and what is pure distraction.

The problem with this strategy of refusal and withdrawal is not a lack of Truth but a lack of popularity. This post-enlightened position is not exactly in fashion. We cannot live the Nietzschean lifestyle and expect wide endorsement. The world thrives on being normal and boring, not exceptional. Difference remains within the choices of the pull-down menu. When discussed in public, self-restraint of one's information intake often borders on the pedagogic and the moralistic – translated into policies, it can easily end up in the soft persecution of firewalling others. A "solution" for the middle classes and ethically indifferent is to outsource info-management to a personal assistant in China. Gamers buy their avatar updates from gold farms; having

28

someone delete your spam for you each morning would be a similar trend.

It will not be sufficient to prescribe info-saturation diets. An anatomy of accelerating information exchange needs to deconstruct this breakdown like a film and play it back in slow motion to extract the vital microseconds in which panic manifests itself. If we want to develop info sovereignty it is of strategic importance to reclaim time. In addition to Fair Trade we could see an emerging Fair Time movement. First we need to oppose the "real-time internet" strategies of Google and Twitter and stretch the work sequence. Think of Hakim Bey's temporary autonomous zones (TAZ). In the past, emphasis was placed on creating spaces (such as parties and squats), while the TAZ of the contemporary age will emphasize the first element, its temporary nature, and celebrate Chronos, the art of the *longue durée*.

After slow food, slow communication? This time it will not be a reformist lifestyle movement obsessed with its own positive image. It may not be sufficient to repair what Clay Shirky calls "filter failure." Time goes to the core of capitalist exploitation. To sabotage "time management" is not an innocent gesture. But Franco Berardi has his doubts about this classic, proletarian-workerist strategy of disruption. Virilio's argument for reintroducing time, the interval, and moments for reflection, doesn't have a political edge. It lacks engagement with existing work conditions under neo-liberalism – the internalization of competition, the voluntary aspect of working long hours, and the role of drugs and medicines to combat structural illnesses such as panic and depression. Like Mark Fisher, Berardi calls for an anatomy of the malaise caused by "semio capitalism" before we dream, again, of mutinous subjects and the liberation of collective imagination.

Back in the Netherlands I got on the train to Delft and met up with Wim Nijenhuis, the architecture theorist and Virilio expert. Did Nijenhuis believe that we could uphold or resist the tendency toward real-time and expand time again in order to restore space for reflection? He answered that, according to Virilio, absolute speed tends to create what he calls "polar inertia." The more we are exposed to communication at the speed of light, the more we will reach a relative state of inertia – interpreted, that makes it impossible to move in relation to the systems of communication and tracking. In the era of light speed everybody will be traceable. The trend toward communication in real-time, the real movements and real events of our lives that are immediately reduplicated in the representational sphere of the media, will cut us off from the material time needed for action, chronology, and history, including concrete objects of experience, confining us in what German philosopher Peter Sloterdijk calls "spheric time."

Instead of the world, the individual's focus will be on the matter of his or her body. At the same time we will experience a feeling of failure in the face of a demanding worklife that has been speeded up by real-time communication. Nijenhuis told me that we should emphasize the very real bodily responses to info overload, such as panic, stress, burnout, and trauma, as a part of what he calls "the strategy of negative anticipation" that is performed not by individual consciousness but by the living body itself. Anyone who gives up the chronological time of action and concrete objects of experience will gradually become a "fragile personality," experiencing depersonalization, falling apart, difficulties with a vulnerable ego, and weak self-esteem.

This involution or regression is the dominant experience in neoliberal society, producing the feeling that everyone is already a failure. This is where we should look as we ask ourselves "what is to be done" when faced with information overload. Referring to Peter Sloterdijk's 2009 *Du mußt dein Leben ändern* (*Thou Shalt Change Your Life,* not yet translated into English), Nijenhuis favors the ascesis as Sloterdijk redefined it, correcting Foucault's aesthetics of existence. For Sloterdijk, ascesis means much more than restriction or resignation. He sees it as being the art of retreat and the overcompensation of initial deficiencies such as physical handicaps and psychological feelings of failure through exercise and training, aimed at a new post-Kantian anthropology: the exercising human who claims distance from information overload. But ascesis also reveals reminiscences of another post-Kantian thinker: Arthur Schopenhauer. Nijenhuis: "What can we learn from Schopenhauer's indifference towards progressive time and his philosophy of relief?"

We should neither portray ourselves as victims of speed politics or the availability economy, nor simply slow down and have a break. What's at stake is to turn what seems to be a private failure into a public affair and become aware of what it means to depend on real-time media. "My Phone is Off for You."[7] There may be a multiplicity of voices but there is also zero time to reflect on the constant stream of incoming news sources. Howard Rheingold describes our situation as "mindful infotention" and encourages us to make more use of user interfaces that create overview. In an attempt to formulate an alternative, the Slow Media Manifesto states that "slow media are not about fast consumption but about choosing the ingredients mindfully and preparing them in a concentrated manner."[8] Another aspect the manifesto discusses is monotasking, emphasizing the importance of quality conversation. Ned Rossiter put it well in an email correspondence: "slow media is important inasmuch as it says 'no way' to the mono-temporality of real-time."

Wasn't it Alan Ginsburg who said that it was all about making life bearable? A concrete step could be to sign off social networking sites such as Facebook and Twitter in an attempt to take back the availability economy. Together with tens of thousands I joined the May 31, 2010, Quit Facebook day of action, deleting my profile and related data – not the first and also not the last initiative of this kind. It wasn't the time consumed by managing my nearly 2000 "friends," or the privacy concerns; my main motivation to join the exodus was to question the growing role of centralized internet services offered to us at no cost in exchange for collecting our data, profiles, music tastes, social behaviors, and opinions. It is not simply that we have something to hide. Let's hope we all do. What we need to defend is the very principle of decentralized, distributed networks. This principle is under attack by corporations such as Google and Facebook, as well as by national authorities who feel a need to control our communication and the data infrastructure at large.

There is a growing awareness that we need to take the architecture of social networking into our own hands. This trend started a while ago with Ning, but it is still a centralized commercial venture initiated by Netscape's Marc Andreessen. We see the free software and open-source communities coming on board with initiatives like Diaspora, Crabgrass, and GNU Social. There are political reasons to support such initiatives. I don't want to overestimate the CIA's role, but it is well known that activists must be very cautious using Facebook. For a while it was OK to spread the message for this or that campaign, but Facebook is becoming too dangerous as an internal channel to coordinate civil disobedience. It's not enough to simply caution youngsters when uploading compromising party pictures onto social networking sites. We should all be more careful and envision the most effective forms of political expression today. Let's strengthen the self-determination of the nodes against the data cloud's central authority and keep the Web decentralized.

The Canon Question

Connected with the populist turn to the right after 9/11, 2001, public interest in collectively creating lists of the top 100 best novels, historical buildings, and fashion designers exploded. If the West is under attack, we'd better know what there is to defend. The necessity of a "canon" came as a response to the notion that the average level of knowledge about the nation's history, literature, and arts had declined. Cultural institutions started identifying their masterpieces. Even more upsetting than a lack of historical insight or declining professional standards was the absence of shared knowledge among people who live in a certain country or work in a common discipline, the presumed absence of "community." What we know by heart defines a country. Heritage is a part of active memory and cannot be outsourced to a search engine. In this way the nation-state is a living body of shared, communal knowledge. The collective selection of the nation's "eternal works of beauty" becomes a therapeutic moment in a time of rising ethnic tension, recession, and job losses. The idea is that the more we know where "we" come from, the better "we" can deal with the risks and failures of neo-liberal policies.

The rise of cultural studies within the arts and humanities, according to Ronan McDonald in *The Death of the Critic*, led to suspicion of the "canon" amongst liberal-progressive intellectuals. "The neo-Marxist orientation of cultural studies regards the 'best' as a politically dubious category, with selections made in its name often nurturing hidden and hierarchical agendas."[9] As Pierre Bourdieu proved, taste is a class-based category and an important battlefield, and despite all efforts to erode high culture with pop, the cultural elites of Western society remain focused on a small number of mainly white, male artists. Pop culture, mass media, and democratized higher education have so far not resulted in the disappearance of cultural enclaves celebrating self-referential artistic autonomy. This is despite the fact that in growth-driven liberal Western societies the dichotomy between vulgar pop trash and serious elite art turned out to be a false one. Even in times of budget cuts the choice is not between high and low culture. Sponsorship, donations, high fees for concerts, and indirect subsidies all distort the opposition of state vs market in terms of the financing of culture. In the neo-liberal austere view, "free culture" backed by venture capitalists should be considered a communist project.

The issue here is not to propose an inclusive canon but to seek new criteria for determining relationships in information-rich environments, which supersede the role of the traditional cultural critic. The promotion of classics selected by either experts or fans mirrors the existing explosion of online content. Instead of calling for a better understanding of the "quantitative turn" in our culture, as done for instance by Lev Manovich's "cultural analytics" research, the canonists stick to the idea of a "Leitkultur" to show us the way. According to Wikipedia, the term "Leitkultur" is a "politically controversial concept, first introduced in 1998 by the German-Arab sociologist Bassam Tibi. It can be translated as 'guiding culture' or 'leading culture'." The canon approach walks away from a contemporary understanding of mass culture as manifested in what Chris Anderson coined the "Long Tail," which expresses the need for "leading content" in a time of cultural diffusion. The self-appointed cultural opinion leaders from "old media" such as print, radio, and television express their own inability to deal with complex, layered processes of hybridization and dislocation and computed, computable difference. "It no longer makes sense to speak of a single public sphere – rather, there are now multiple publics, distributed in various ways, sometimes geographically, sometimes within the same national or urban space; and an individual might participate in more than one public."[10] Critics today need extraordinary "cultural competence" in terms of language skills, cross-disciplinarity, technical training, and global awareness. The nostalgic call for a canon limits our ability to develop personal styles and reduces the role of the growing class of creative workers to soldiers in a national program.

In an interview on the New York digirati website edge.org, the editor-in-chief of the German newspaper *Frankfurter Allgemeine Zeitung* (FAZ), Frank Schirrmacher, relates the question of content selection to the loss of concentration.[11] A computer that starts to think for us overwhelms people. "Thinking itself leaves the brain and uses a platform outside of the human body. And that, of course, is the internet and it's the cloud." Or is there a hidden message here – Germans as anxious, inward-looking Luddites? Schirrmacher:

> The question of what survives, which idea survives, and which idea drowns, which idea starves to death, is something which, in our whole system of thought, is very, very known, and is quite an issue. What is and what is not important? What is important to know? Can we still decide what is important? It starts with this absolutely normal, everyday news. But now you encounter, at least in Europe, a lot of people who think, what in my life is important, what isn't important, what is the information of my life. And some of them say, well, it's in Facebook. And others say, well, it's on my blog. And, apparently, for many people it's very hard to say it's somewhere in my life, in my lived life.

Schirrmacher's concern is that we know a lot about others, and nothing about ourselves. This is what the debate about overload and selection, in the end, comes down to: the loss of the Self. The autonomous Western individual is delegating skills and knowledge to what Clay Shirky terms the "Algorithmic Authority," and instead of gaining power, this act of outsourcing only further weakens the subject.

What remains is the Art of Self-Curation, much like Michel Foucault's "technology of the self," aimed at creating ever-changing temporary collections inside our netbooks and iPhones – Adilkno's data dandyism as a mass practice.[12] By nature we filter, forget, hear, and see selectively, but that doesn't mean that we must agree that all the filtering should be done on our behalf. The danger of filters is their invisibility. What we need is a growing awareness of the existence and architecture of the filters that surround us. Our cultural bias is something to be aware of, not to run from. "The problem is filter failure, not information overload" is the title of one of Clay Shirky's lectures that you can watch online.[13] I would rephrase this as the lack of awareness of the filter architecture that produces the feeling of information overload. We need to distrust Google's intention to "organize the world's information" and see it instead as a worldwide move toward data manipulation, driven by a curious dynamic of state control and corporate interest. Before we start to condemn the powers to be, we need to ask ourselves some key questions. How do we overcome this paradoxical era of hyped-up individualization that results precisely in the algorithmic outsourcing of the self? How do we determine significance outside of the celebrity paradigm and instead use intelligence to identify what's at stake?

The Carr Effect

In *The Shallows, What the Internet is Doing to Our Brains*, from 2010, Nicholas Carr has surprisingly turned into a doomsday preacher. In contrast to his previous IT industry insider critiques of major players in the internet game, Carr has transformed himself into a public intellectual who voices general concerns about long-term impacts on society. It is interesting to see how Carr changed from a *Harvard Business Review* editor into a North American philosopher of technology in the lineage of Lewis Mumford and Langdon Winner.

By any standard *The Shallows*, which was shortlisted for the 2011 Pullizer Prize, is a measured, well-researched piece of writing. It can be useful to remind the busy, well-educated middle classes that technology is reshaping their brains. Those who followed Carr's Rough Type blog will have been surprised to see Carr's razor-sharp Google critique morphed into popular science writing. In *The Shallows* Carr's famous "Is Google Making Us Stupid?" essay has been elevated into a comprehensive analysis, accomplished by discussing neuroscientific journal articles. Nicholas Carr's potential split personality suggests various directions internet criticism can take. On his blog Carr's postings are witty, cynical, and right on target, and miles ahead of Jeff Jarvis's defensive mode of writing as a Google evangelist, or Clay Shirky's default appraisal of Anything 2.0. In his Gutenberg incarnation Nicholas Carr repositions himself as a pop science writer of the John Brockman school.

We can summarize and popularize the relevant neuroscience literature but shouldn't be surprised when other neuroscientists come up with opposite research outcomes. Carr writes: "We can assume that the neural circuits devoted to scanning, skimming and multitasking are expanding and strengthening, while those used for reading and thinking deeply, with sustained concentration, are weakening or eroding."[14] No, we cannot assume this. The discussion about our altered neurons is a dead-end street forestalling change. At best this meme installs regimes of guilt and fear-driven restrictions of use.

Carr: "What the Net diminishes is the ability to know a subject for ourselves, to construct within our own minds the rich and idiosyncratic set of connections that give rise to a singular intelligence."[15] But users are not "suckers for irrelevancy." If used in the wrong context such a description can so easily be read as the "arrogance of the better people." We all struggle to make sense of these new tools. Wasting time on useless procedures is a universal gift to mankind. We're born to wait (until we die). What a shame, all those hours spoiled on "thinking deeply" about the wrong topic! There is still a considerable group that will have to subject itself to therapeutic measures to kick the habit. Curiously enough, Carr does not explicitly talk about internet addiction. There might be a class element here. Information workers as a social group are reluctant to diagnose themselves as (potential) patients, because heavy computer use is still seen as an empowering activity resulting in more skills and increased social mobility. What if you do not recognize yourself in Richard Foreman's image of us as "pancake people – spread wide and thin as we connect with the vast network of information accessed by the mere touch of a button"?[16]

I would instead propose a liberating, sovereign point of view on mastering the internet. *The Shallows* gives a number of clues in this direction. In a similar way to Frank Schirrmacher's *Payback*, Carr opens with a first-person confession of a busy, middle-aged male unable to cope with the multitasking demands of real-time communication. During the writing of *The Shallows,* Carr switched off Facebook, RSS, and Twitter and cut back on email. Toward the end of the book he admits that he eased his diet regime and returned to his initially heavy internet use. In line with Sloterdijk's philosophy of "lifelong training" we should not just train the mind to become less distracted. What we need are tools that no longer primarily focus on real-time and instead favor circumstances where counter-intuitive thought can occur. The perpetual state of distraction can be overcome by "uncooling" and "undesigning" the cult of multitasking and updating. The going offline movement will not be so anti-tech but anti-real-time. Technology will have to become our servant again. How do we design in favor of attentive thought?

What *The Shallows* did not anticipate was the "Carr effect." Massive reporting about the downside of multitasking, the distraction of email and Twitter, information overload, and the effect of search engines on learning is itself having an impact on average new media usage. Imagine neglecting work email late at night from home, switching off smartphones during dinner, or even further restricting children's "screen time." The messenger is not a neutral outsider who merely observes. The popularity of the book and the eagerness of reviewers to report and respond to Carr's thesis is an indication that Carr has hit the zeitgeist. After the Web's introductory phase for the academic few that lasted till 1993, the dot.com hype that busted in 2000, its rebirth as Web 2.0 around 2003, and its evolution into a mass medium in 2011, we are entering the fourth stage of internet culture, characterized by conflict in the public realm and (self-) mastery on the individual level. In this next phase the internet will find its place in everyday life, embedded in the fridge, taking over television, integrating with cell phones, facilitating as a recipe assistant in the kitchen, and so on. What may sound like even more intense usage could in fact demand less of our attention. As soon as we understand its workings and limitations, users can move on and leave behind years of tension from idiosyncratic software, failed broadband connections, viruses, and endless upgrades.

The therapeutic process of (self-)mastery proposed by Sloterdijk might not only be necessary for those prone to specific gadget or platform addictions, but should be part of school education. Internet culture is rapidly entering the "vacuum cleaner" stage. All technologies, regardless of how "disruptive" they are, are eventually pushed into the background where they have even more power on the level of the collective unconscious. Mid-twentieth-century white goods

36

revolutionized daily living. The appliances made domestic work more efficient and after a while became self-evident. We still use them but no longer talk about them, let alone discuss the protocols of microwave switchboards (maybe we should!). There are no heated debates amongst civil society delegation members who participate in global toaster governance forums. One day the "internet debate" will end up in a similar way.

FACEBOOK, ANONYMITY, AND THE CRISIS OF THE MULTIPLE SELF

Man is least himself when he talks in his own person. Give him a mask, and he will tell you the truth.
Epigraph of Oscar Wilde, chosen by Julian Assange

In Jeff Kinney's 2007 *Diary of a Wimpy Kid* we find the following entry:

In school today they had a general assembly and showed the movie *It's Awesome to Be Me*, which they show us every year. This movie is all about how you should be happy with who you are and not change anything about yourself. To be honest with you, I think that's really a dumb message to be telling kids, especially the ones at my school.[1]

Many conceive of the internet as a lively exchange of arguments and files. We talk through Skype, send pictures, check the weather, and download software. Only with the rise of the blogosphere in 2003–04 did the internet become inundated with self-promotion. A culture of "self-disclosure" established itself. Social networking sites, coming shortly after, unleashed a collective obsession with "identity management." The massive uptake of Facebook in particular has spurred an identity crisis of yet unknown dimensions, circling around the question of who we are and how we should present ourselves online. In the age of social media we're not looking to externalize other possible selves but the True Self, deep inside. But this is not soul searching – what started off as an address book to find lost friends and schoolmates has turned into a massive self-branding exercise: "it's awesome to be me." But who exactly am I?[2]

In an interview with the Dutch daily *NRC-Handelsblad*, portrait photographer Rineke Dijkstra observed that, between 2005 and

2010, Europeans, in particular adolescents, "have developed two faces: a private one in which to see how they really feel, and a public face for use in the outside world, which they perfect on YouTube and Facebook. The public face seems to gain importance, as if it is an instinct to put it on, an evolutionary development in order to survive."[3] The confusion over who we are and how much we should reveal about our private lives and opinions is on the rise, just as the growing pressure "to be yourself" increasingly conflicts with social conformism. If it is true that the distinction between the real and the virtual is diminishing, and that offline and online are blending, does that also mean we can no longer pretend we are someone else on the internet? And if privacy is under threat, how do we distinguish between private and public? What is "the Self" anyway in a society where millions aim to be unique yet are steered by identical desires? Perhaps the concept of "mass anonymity" presents a possible way out.

Celebrating Multiple Identities

It all started so harmlessly in the last years of the Cold War. The first internet generation, well protected by the walls of academia, chose a random user name and the outcome was a wild hippie culture played out on Usenet and bulletin board systems. Early cyberculture was driven by a shared desire to become someone else. In *Life on the Screen*, from 1995, Sherry Turkle describes how taking on a different persona online had possible therapeutic effects. At the time, computer networks were used as vehicles to escape "official reality," design alternative futures, enhance bodies, and extend minds. Burning Man, smart drinks, George Gilder, Ray Kurzweil, and Mondo 2000 were the cultural landmarks representing the values of the internet's first inhabitants. Back in the roaring nineties the opponent was no longer the Soviet Union but the slow-moving Corporation, with its bureaucratic Organization Man (William Whyte) from the suburbs waiting for top-down orders from management. In contrast the internet stood for distributed empowerment: a flexible, ever-changing openness toward the world, wary of the control-obsessed Orwellian institution. For almost a decade the internet's remake of the flower-power Self dominated the outside world's perception, as transmitted through the "old" print and broadcast media. Techno-libertarian utopia was a strong meme. It would give generations to come the idea of the internet as a tool for personal freedom, a concept that would sooner rather than later collide with the bureaucratic security regime of the Web 2.0 age.

White male geek culture, found on sites like Slashdot, still blends obsessive gaming and code hacking with ironic post-ideological media consumption. Use of aliases in online gaming communities is still widespread. In these subcultures we find techno-medieval role-playing is as important as cryptographic software protecting its members from state intrusion. The "whatever" attitude here is one of supreme distance, cool and calm. The multiple Self is not seen as an act of liberation but is simply played out as a technological given. What binds these subcultures together is their distance from both the old " 'high culture" and from politically correct projects devoted to class, gender, race, migration, ecology, and imperial wars. Within these techno-cultures, the Self is seen as a fundamental lie (I am not me), an antagonism that one should have chucked out a long time ago. If you live a thousand lives, you can easily switch to another identity. There is no true Self, only an endless series of interchange-able masks. A remainder of this pioneer belief system is the often-heard statement in tech circles that there is no such thing as privacy – but that is not the concern. Instead, left without a core, the person-ality can engage in never-ending play.

The hedonistic dot.com excesses at the turn of the millennium were over by the 2001 financial crisis and 9/11 attacks. The war on terror aborted the desire for a serious parallel "second-self" culture and instead gave rise to a global surveillance and control industry. To this assault on freedom, Web 2.0 tactically responded with coherent, singular identities in sync with the data owned by police, security, and financial institutions. Thanks to this ideology of "trust" that offers "walled gardens" and online malls safe for e-commerce, cheap, centralized cloud computing makes it possible to have "the stuff you care about all in one place"[4] – a place of filtered material retreat, where ordinary users can meet their friends and be protected from the wild, anarchic Web, with its viruses, spam, and online fraud. Instead of resisting corporate power and calling for government regu-lation, techno-libertarians built up self-confidence: we're on the right side of history. Your private data will not be used against you. There will be no Last Judgement Day or second January 30, 1933, when Hitler came to power. Either we have lived under the sign of Big Brother for decades without realizing that the handover occurred ages ago, or the regime change to Behemoth that we all fear will never happen.

Within Facebook there are no hippie dropouts, just a pathological dimension of commitment to the Real Self going hand in hand with the comfort of being only amongst friends in a safe, controlled environment. And no punks or criminalized migrant street culture either. Differences of choice are celebrated so long as they are confined to one identity. Facebook CEO Mark Zuckerberg puts it like this: "having two identities for yourself is an example of a lack of integrity."[5] Says venture capitalist Peter Thiel: "Facebook rival MySpace is about being someone fake on the internet; everyone could be a movie star." Thiel considers it "very healthy that the real people have won out over the fake people."[6]

As a result there is little freedom any more to present yourself in multiple ways online. Social networking sites, anticipating this movement toward security (that is, toward one identity) coupled with our personal desire for comfort, offer their users a limited, user-friendly range of choice for submitting private and professional data to the world. In her film review of *The Social Network* (David Fincher, 2010), Zadie Smith despises Facebook's normalcy as defined by its autistic computer-nerd founders. "Maybe the whole internet simply becomes like Facebook: falsely jolly, fake-friendly, self-promoting, slickly disingenuous." The Web 2.0 generation deserves better: "Facebook is the wild west of the internet tamed to fit the suburban fantasies of a suburban soul." Smith asks if we shouldn't struggle against this pacification. "We were going to live online. It was going to be extraordinary. Yet what kind of living is this? Step back from your Facebook Wall for a moment: Doesn't it, suddenly, look a little ridiculous? *Your* life in *this* format?"[7]

Should we seek an out from this limited scenario? Should we all just go playfully anonymous again? Before looking into a few possible exit strategies, we need to grasp the rise of the modern self and why it has so blithely endorsed the limited Web 2.0 social environment.

From Self-Disclosure to Self-Promotion

The public pressure to refrain from anonymity cannot be countered without a better understanding of the "self-management" wave manifesting in online portfolios, dating sites, and Facebook.[8] In the Web 2.0 age the drive to self-realization is deeply embedded in society. According to Israeli sociologist Eva Illouz, the modern self is an autonomous entity incapable of valorizing itself, enmeshed as it is in social and political structures. Social media should be seen as only the latest incarnation of these institutions. In her 2007 book, *Cold Intimacies*, Illouz illustrates how capitalism has been turned into an "emotional culture," complicating the commonly held view that

41

commodification, wage labor, and profit-driven activities create "cold" and calculated relationships. She describes the rise of "emotional capitalism" within a public sphere saturated with the exposure of private life (and vice versa, the "hot distance"). Through the service industry, affect becomes an essential aspect of economic behavior – and a fashionable object of contemporary theory. According to Illouz, "it is virtually impossible to distinguish the rationalization and commodification of selfhood from the capacity of the self to shape and help itself and to engage in deliberation and communication with others."[9] There is a narrative in the making, says Illouz, which aspires to self-realization, and that plays itself out within institutional and semi-public settings such as the self-help sector and online platforms. "The prevalence and persistence of this narrative, which we may call as shorthand a narrative of recognition, is related to the interests of social groups operating within the market, in civil society, and within the institutional boundaries of the state."

Illouz emphasizes that it becomes harder to distinguish between our professional and private self. In the competitive networking context of work, we are trained to present ourselves as the best, fastest, and smartest. At the same time we are aware that this is only an artificial, made-up image of ourselves and that our "real" self is different, which is what celebrities have been grappling with for decades. This distinction is critical if we're looking for intimate relationships or partners for our life online. On dating sites, for instance, people look for authentic experiences, even as, according to Illouz, the technology they use all but destroys the desperately sought intimacy.

In a Skype interview I did with Illouz in June 2010, she stressed the long-term decoupling of private life from the private sphere. She said: "We should not blame technology for the loss of private life. The pornofication of culture and the political-economic push for increased transparency of private life have been on the rise for decades, and the internet has only institutionalized these trends." According to Illouz, networking through websites like Facebook displays two forms of social capital:

> showing that one is loved and showing who we are connected to. Showing off one's position in the hierarchy is not only modern obviously. We could read the current anxiety about social networking as a replay of the late 19th century motive of the liberal-bourgeois subject being overwhelmed by the masses on the streets of the industrial world.

42

Modernity was, and still is, as much about creating as about polluting the boundaries between high and low, public and private. Calling for more regulation and control is often associated with cultural fears about the breakdown of boundaries. This response is normal. We should remember that it is the patrolling of the boundaries itself that keeps a culture alive.

Religion of the Positive

There might be three ways to counter the self-promotion machine. One way is to disrupt its self-evidence. Talking about the dark side of positive thinking is a first step to recover from the mass delusion of smile or die, and more effective than simply joking about the absence of a "dislike" button in Facebook, or about the one-dimensional representation of relationships where "friending" is the only option. In her 2009 book, *Bright-Sided: How the Relentless Promotion of Positive Thinking Has Undermined America*, Barbara Ehrenreich shows how relentless promotion requires "deliberate self-deception, including a constant effort to repress or block out unpleasant possibilities and 'negative' thoughts."[10] In the context of social networking sites we cannot say that the optimistic bias undermines "preparedness" and "invites disaster" (as US sociologist Karen Cerulo does), but what it does do is flatten everyday experience by ruling out more complex feelings. Ambiguities are not allowed. Reckless optimism rules out the very possibility of questioning the rules. We need to study these new limitations in terms of what French philosopher Bernard Stiegler called "a pharmacological critique of libidinal economy."[11] Reduced choices steer and eventually desensitize users, who, on a positive note, will then desert these platforms in search of better alternatives. It wouldn't be a problem for the rest of the world if cheerful Americans bother only each other with their optimistic folklore. The problem is that these design principles are applied to software that billions use across the globe. The culmination here is to reject this, sign off, and delete your user profile.

The self as a creative and knowledgeable agent is trapped for the simple reason that there is no one, true Self that we absolutely must unveil. As Polish-English philosopher Zygmunt Bauman said, beyond the binaries of self and other, the fractionalized self is also highly fictionalized, self-defeating, and illusionary.[12] Even on Facebook, amongst "friends," we play theater, acting as if we play ourselves. This is not an act of "self-mastery" but rather a technical translation of data to drown out mundane life. The sheer number of paradoxical experiences is evidence that there is no one being, so we should ask why we still need to perform a synthesis. A variety of platforms and functionalities allow different facets of the self to thrive as long as they remain within social norms and do not openly contradict each other. Social networking is not about affirming something as truth but more about making truth through endless clicking. As a way out, it is fine to admit "I am not who I am." It's a step in the right direction – modern people as the people who try to (re-)invent themselves.

Triumph of the Airheads

Another way out is to dismantle the consumer desire that drives the self-promotion machine to begin with. In this argument, the marketing of the self is not so much a narcissistic venture aiming to satisfy one's inner needs but is primarily powered by the fast consumption of objects external to us, the unstoppable drive to collect more and more stuff – from friends and lovers to brand products, services, and other quasi-exclusive short-lived experiences. Signing up has become irresistible, in part because of the ruthless way the Facebook algorithm contacts potential new users, for instance via imported email address books, inviting them to become your friend. This is the naive model of eternal growth promoted by sites like Facebook, or by Twitter that never stops measuring you by your amount of tweets. To live a tweetless life is constructed as not living.

There are three Australian publications from 2005 to 2007 that summarize this particular discontent in hyper-consumerist societies that are driven by debt, overwork, and related illnesses. Even though none of the three authors explicitly examines Web 2.0, the mechanisms they describe could very well explain its cult of self-disclosure with its built-in algorithms to collect more and more "friends." First, social media can be seen as both producer and symptom of what Clive Hamilton in 2005 coined "affluenza," the plenty that makes you sick. In *Affluenza: When Too Much is Never Enough*, Hamilton defined it as: 1. "the bloated, sluggish and unfulfilled feeling that results from keeping up with the Joneses. 2. An epidemic of stress, overwork, waste and indebtedness. 3. An unsustainable addiction to economic growth."[13] We see social media further accelerating the McLifestyle, while at the same time presenting itself as a channel to relieve the tension piling up in our comfort prisons.

In *Blubberland, the Dangers of Happiness* (2007), architecture writer Elizabeth Farrelly presents variations on the "affluenza" theme. According to the blurb, her critique of the Western lifestyle "joins the dots between consumerism, sprawl, obesity, depression, McMansionism, sustainability and desire." If we search for a general cultural framework for social media, this is one of the possible directions. "Blubber is unused energy, neither good nor bad in itself but aquiver with potential, anything spare or surplus, the spare time in the day."[14] There is also the physical blubber of the super-mall, the four-wheel drive, Pentecostal mega churches, home theaters, and the MP3 player. We want it all, now – lubricant devices such as the smartphone, packed with apps, guiding us through shapeless urban spaces, lingering in the pain of who we are supposed to be. "Big is beautiful" results in diabetes, depression, and despair. Farrelly writes: "the (virtual) shell, like the cave, is as much trap as shield. The thicker the mask, the more it encloses us, inhibiting the very interaction we need to heal the trauma."[15] Her critique of the built environment can easily be adopted for living-apart-together media.

The Triumph of the Airheads and the Retreat from Commonsense, by journalist Shelley Gare (2006), foreshadows the "new media as pop culture" critiques of Keen, Carr, and Lanier. In these Teflon-times, "airheads" adore luxury brands; they do not read much beyond the glossies and self-help literature, "which makes them so receptive to jargon, slang and management speak."[16] They are devoid of self-doubt and are self-obsessed up to the point of ignoring the public infrastructures crumbling all around them. Imagine if you could have all that tax money for yourself? "The children of the real-time revolution" are only driven by how the next five minutes turn out. They cannot see the difference between something and nothing, and have been taught that it is their right to voice their opinion on everything. According to Gare, "theory is paramount in the airhead universe," and "theory too often gets it wrong, but airheads have the memory of goldfish so it's not as if anyone cares or has to worry in hindsight."[17] Gare argues against the postmodern relativism that reduced education standards. She warns of the long-term ramifications when style is elevated over substance or PR messages over expert knowledge. What Shelley Gare describes so well is the state of mind of the hovering subject, constantly browsing, checking, and updating without sense, purpose, or commitment.

Moralistic zeitgeist critiques such as these by Hamilton, Farrelly, and Gare can easily be dismissed as the grumpy remarks of outgoing "down-to-earth" baby boomers, staring in the mirror of the

45

mainstream media they cannot stop quoting. However, in the context of "Net criticism," they are important for providing an extra-academic cultural framework to help understand not just the architecture, but also the success of social media. Being bad is always much sexier than being good, but, as Gare notices, for a society that has lost the plot, it is not so much about being bad as "being foolish, thoughtless and irresponsible." Social media have only further amplified the non-speak that is spread by reality TV shows such as *Big Brother*. We should read these authors' raves of resentment against such empty cultural offerings against the grain, to offer an amoral analysis as a way out of the consumerist trap.

Reintroducing Anonymity

The third way to dismantle the performance of the self and self-disclosure is to revisit anonymity in today's context. The question is how to re-imagine anonymity not as an attainable categorical state, but as a way to recoup an energy of metamorphosis, the desire to become someone else. Yet, in the political sphere, we are told we don't have a right to perfect anonymity at all any more. In his 14 theses on the "Foundations of a Common Internet Policy for the Future," German Police and Justice Minister de Maiziere wrote: "The free citizen shows his face, tells his name and has an address"[18] – a perfect summary of the self-disclosure culture we find on Facebook. In a lively debate, the German Carta website asked its readers if there was such a thing as the right to anonymity. Journalists make headlines by revealing certain identities, while in other cases they have to protect their anonymous sources. There are codes of conduct to regulate these cases, but what about the rights of citizens who use the internet?

What would become of the democratized self if voting decisions were made public? Wouldn't that be the moment when the self splits apart to create a double? American e-democracy activist Steven Clift is concerned with "the fundamental poisoning of local democracy and communities by online newspapers with anonymous commenting."[19] For Clift, the use of real names in local exchanges is crucial. Yet it is not clear how we would handle those who question our (politically correct) consensus-based culture. In a system that aims to prevent the outbreak of nonconformism, open personalities and fluid identities will only beget problems with the law. Most users are not comfortable with a parallel existence anyway: they want to remain themselves and hide inside the silent majority, participating in informal dialogues inside the Walled Garden. I do not exist as another version of myself, and Facebook knows perfectly well how to exploit this, which explains its success with over half a billion users by early 2011. Yet, in certain combustible political contexts, the activist use of Facebook can experience a Thermidorian Reaction,[20] as I will discuss later in chapter 10, "Organizing Networks in Culture and Politics."

Nonetheless, a decade after September 11, 2001, there are still strongholds that cultivate variations of anonymity, from blogs, Wikipedia, P2P, Tor, and Chatroulette, to the image board 4chan. Short, bitchy remarks are in fashion and increasingly anonymous. These online cultures can be interpreted as expressions of "pseudonimity" that build up a respectable reputation of the Other Self under a stable user name, used for instance by the Wikipedia editor. This "state of the self" has less and less room to maneuver. We can sign up for Second Life and draw up the avatar of our fantasies, design a virtual world of our liking, but such parallel identities cannot be taken into other contexts. Chatroulette eventually changed its rules. Gossiping may be healthy but can be lethal in environments where everyone tracks each other. Whereas the old – but still mainstream – internet ideology claimed to be safe ground for freedom of speech, the post 9/11 reality is proving otherwise. Sophisticated tracing technologies employed by police investigators and security agencies, which identify users' internet protocol addresses, have effectively destroyed online anonymity. Yet, despite this fact, the vast majority of the internet population still considers the internet a free-for-all playground where you can say anything you like.

Anonymous is Not Your Friend

> We are Anonymous. We are Legion. We do not forgive. We do not forget. Expect us.
>
> Anonymous

This sets up a dangerous scenario. Collective self-confidence can lead to serious miscalculations, as happened when the group which calls itself Anonymous organized *Operation Payback*. This was a solidarity campaign in support of WikiLeaks, which aimed to bring down Mastercard, PayPal and Visa websites. Following the US diplomatic cables leak in December 2010, Anonymous supporters commenced

Distributed Denial of Service (DDoS) attacks on websites of companies that had withdrawn WikiLeaks' banking facilities. A security site reported: "for the first time, people with minimal technical skills were acting like professional hackers and engaging in mass destruction of technology infrastructure."[21] Often young and inexperienced users downloaded software onto their computer (called botnets) and their identity (IP address) was easily detected by the authorities. A message originating on 4chan warned anyone who was on Anonymous Operations IRC channels, or who downloaded and used the LOIC DDoS attack software, that law enforcement potentially logged their IP addresses.

The people behind Operation Payback were easily traceable. "If you send out a press release on behalf of Anonymous and leave the identifying metadata in the PDF file, there's not much you can do to hide from the police. Someone named Alex Tapanaris made that facepalm-worthy mistake."[22] Such stories exemplify the rift between old-school security hackers (groups like 2600 and CCC), who are skeptical of DDoS attacks, and the nihilist 4chan pop culture that explicitly refrains from hacker nomenclature. What we see is a reprise of the late 1990s debate between coders and activists over "hacktivist" strategies, this time on a much larger scale. In the end WikiLeaks itself is also not anonymous.[23] Operation Payback reveals how difficult it is to educate mass online culture about basic security issues. The Anonymous group may be a sexy, mysterious movement, but why isn't it concerned with the anonymity of its members and supporters? We may also reverse this question toward hackers: wouldn't it be wiser to admit that there is no absolute anonymity any more (as if there ever was)? There are risks if you engage in acts of civil disobedience. Belarussian-US Net critic Evgeny Morozov called the DDoS attacks "a legitimate expression of dissent,"[24] which might be the case, even though virtual sit-ins may not have the same legal status as strikes or demonstrations. The question emerges whether protesting anonymously is indeed a basic citizen right. If voting remains anonymous – one of the arguments against dodgy electronic voting machines – what actions invite us to stand up and express our opinion in public? Or has this become too dangerous, as we see in today's authoritarian regimes?

By questioning the self-evidence of Facebook and its befriending algorithm, we already make a first step toward refusing corporate-controlled social media platforms: "I prefer not to." The next step could be to actively shape new manifestations of collective anonymous action: "I need to become anonymous in order to be present."[25]

Anonymity as an exercise in play may be a necessary delusion that saves us from the idea of the true self, advocated by Facebook as our one and only option. We are told to believe there is no true face behind the mask, or rather, told to ask what the mask is hiding, instead of what its wearer is performing. What we need to make clear is that the internet provides the potential for self-performance and creative play.

It is no longer sufficient to fight for some constitutional right to vote anonymously. Trolls, zombies, and other fake personas unite in movements such as Anonymous. Whether organizing protests for WikiLeaks or against Scientology, the starting point is the idea that "visibility and transparency are no longer signs of democratic openness but rather of administrative availability." How are public visibility and strategic camouflage related in an online context? Will we "oscillate between the hyperpresence of a mask and visual redundancy?"[26] What can we do to become invisible, imperceptible? As Matthew Fuller explains, "this implies the generation of an inverse structural coupling between what exists as unseen and what is yet blind to it, a mutual unfolding of nonsensibility in which each edges away." He calls this the "aesthetics of insensible things."[27] Opposed to this strategy of blurring into the background is the burka as an artistic device for intervention in public space. The burka proves to be the ultimate provocation to Western transparency as *Kulturideal* and norm of a universal lifestyle.[28]

In 1929, Virginia Woolf, in *A Room of One's Own*, wrote: "I would venture to guess that Anon, who wrote so many poems without signing them, was often a woman." In the context of social media, the question is how to integrate offline acts into the equation without turning the real world into the next wave. Can the existing platforms only be used in the shadow of events to come? Networks prepare the groundwork through their "weak links"; it's what they are good at. Their role in real-time communication, once events unfold, remains overrated. If everything had worked out, networks would have already kicked off the erosion of existing power structures. What will happen if we overcome the fear of surveillance and control? Will anonymous action, like voting in public elections, no longer be necessary because that information will be publicly available by other means? Or should we remain cautious and see the *carnaval balle masque* as the temporary state of exception?

— 3 —

TREATISE ON COMMENT CULTURE

In memory of German media theorist Cornelia Vismann (1961–2010)

In fact, interpretation is a means in itself to become master of something.

Friedrich Nietzsche

Wo kommt Information her? Es gibt nur eine Quelle und das ist der lebende Mensch. Eine Nachricht die ich erhalte verwandele ich zu Information indem ich sie interpretiere. Die Interpretation ist die Arbeit die aufgewandt werden muß, um eine Nachricht, eine Signal- oder Bitkette, in Information zu verwandeln.

[Where does information come from? There is only one source and that is the living human. I turn a message that I receive into information by interpreting it. Interpretation is the effort that needs to be expended to change a message, a chain of signals or pleas into information.]

Joseph Weizenbaum

There is little life in the Long Tail. Is anyone still reading blogs? Individual blogs rarely receive comments, a condition described in *Blogging, the Nihilist Impulse*.[1] Either blog owners have shut down the opportunity to leave comments, put their blog on moderation mode, or have simply forgotten to approve the cued responses. Comments can hardly be distinguished from spam. Additionally, blogs get low traffic. There may be nine followers and a dozen or so friends, with 43 views of the video on YouTube. This is the harsh reality laid down in the Power Law. Long Tail and "most visited sites" are not opposites, as Clay Shirky writes in his 2003 posting *Power Laws, Weblogs and Inequality*: "A new social system starts, and seems delightfully free of the elitism and cliquishness of the existing systems.

Then, as the new system grows, problems of scale set in. Not everyone can participate in every conversation. Not everyone gets to be heard. Some core group seems more connected than the rest of us."[2]

While my last book, *Zero Comment* from 2007, focused on average blogs, the first part of this treatise investigates the other end of the Power Law diagram and presents a theory of comment cultures that have reached a critical mass. Responses attract curious visitors and provoke more replies. This basic rule of how crowds gather, described by mass psychologists, is also operational on the internet, as if the masses want to celebrate their own presence by demonstrating their sheer quantity. As we read in Elias Canetti's magnum opus, *Crowds and Power*, attracted by rumors, the swelling and density of the crowd seems unstoppable. The mob becomes invincible. On the Web we see similar concentrations of users. Instead of being distributed throughout the network, debating culture clusters around a few sites, often in response to particular authors, issues, and longer-running threads. The more news and the faster the turnover of postings, the more users are inclined to leave comments. We see this pattern everywhere, from forums, blogs, and Twitter to newspaper sites.

Talking Back to the Web

The freedom to respond has long been a quintessential internet feature, equal to file sharing and online publishing itself. Network cultures are overwhelmingly "discursive" and have fostered an unprecedented scale of comments, different from any other in history. Participation has moved from something that had to be fought for to something entirely normal, expected, and, indeed, encouraged by commercial platforms. As one of the most common (because simple) forms of communication, the practice of commenting is not only central to blogging and forums but defines the experiences of social networking and twittering too (also known as micro-blogging), which are entirely focused on responses. These innumerable, mundane forms of public discourse increasingly constitute the everyday interactions of the online billions.

Whereas traditional media "push" content in a top-down fashion, the internet has a vitalist image of an ever-changing yet equal social space. Newspaper "Letters to the Editor" were treated with suspicion because of their potentially "manufactured discontent." They had little impact because of editorial "repressive tolerance" with the few column inches reserved for reader opinions. Online content is different in that it is surrounded by a lively social sphere grouped around the posting, not just through comments but also through linking in blog postings, tweeting, and the like, combined with the share and recommend buttons within social media. At least, that's the ideology. For some, it is enough to value these technical possibilities. The reality often looks different. Rarely do we see respondents talking to each other. Lively debates are the exception and often depend on labor-intensive lobbying behind the scenes of the moderator(s). Comment cultures are not self-emergent systems but orchestrated arrangements. This is not always obvious, even for insiders. Most of us, pleasantly blinded by techno-optimism, believe that the sheer availability of open-reply functionalities will result in animated discussions and lead to a deeper, higher, and richer understanding of the topic. But writers, editors, and moderators play a vital role in establishing a culture of frequent commenting.

Time and again, twentieth-century thought has proven that texts and readers are one and the same, with text constituted through interpretive conventions. This was still an imaginative process that occurred in the heads of readers. Audience interaction is now a given, not only with the text or artwork but even with the author directly through Twitter, blogs, call-ins, or live engagements during conferences, festivals, and talk shows.[3] We need to keep in mind that in this age of self-representation, commenting often *lacks* a direct confrontation with the text or artwork. The present act of replying does not seek a one-to-one dialogue with the creator. Internet comment culture needs to be distinguished from online dialogues and discussions. Another reading of today's thriving "comment culture" could be that it s(t)imulates traffic. First and foremost, comments are a software feature (that can be switched on or off) ultimately related to revenue streams of the service providers who invite us to speak out at – but not so much speak to – others. Users are well aware of this underlying economic principle, and their often cynical contributions reflect the knowledge that their comments are features contributing to the overall reputation of the site, and in particular to the popularity of that specific topic or thread.

Internet comment culture is the opposite of what Adorno described as the "jargon of authenticity." Instead of being "societized chosenness, noble and homey,"[4] users attempt to go as low as possible, often in the name of briefness. We often hear that online comments represent the unmediated voice of the people. There are no "concerns" voiced here. That would be too polite a description. We have to attribute the rise of online "re:actions" to an increased willingness to publicly articulate "resentments." In a mix of slang, ad-like slogans, and half-finished judgments, users mash up phrases and sayings they have heard or read somewhere. Small talk is not the right term. What's performed is a desperate attempt to be heard, to achieve any impact, and leave behind a mark. Users no longer contribute merely to "correct" the author, or to contribute to the "general intellect" – they want to have an effect.

So you want to join the comment posters? After you read an article, see a photo, or status update, and feel the need to respond, you have to register (if you are not inside the Facebook wall), get through the identity hoop (real name, type email address twice, URL of website), and then just type your two cents and press submit. Click refresh and there it is: your very own micro-opinion. Perhaps you may return to the article in a little while to see if anything has happened, and, if so, whether the author, moderators, or well-known contributors have taken up your point (if there was one). You wait for others but their much needed contribution doesn't come, or, as Bob Stein formulated in his Inverse Law of Commenting on the Open Web, unfortunately, "the more you'd like to read someone's comments on a text, the less likely they are to participate in an open forum."[5]

Even though early internet cultures such as Usenet, lists, and forums dealt with trolls, anonymity, and violent threats, the scale and visibility of today's mass comments are of an entirely different order. It is easy to judge the screaming and yelling as the fall of civilization. Instead, it is proposed here to analyze today's comment cultures as perpetual machines. What's striking are their erratic jumps. It is unlikely that you will read all comments – 54? 156? 262? – but what remains is the fascination and horror of the naked numbers.

Welcome to the age of mass hermeneutics – but how do we make sense of such amounts? Will we develop new ways to interpret these contributions or are they merely signs of life of individual users, special effects of the interactive systems that aren't worth noticing? Even if we do not jump on the info overload bandwagon, and, with Clay Shirky, interpret this data fest as "filter failure," should we simply ignore it all and move on? Just to mention two examples: on a given day, the geeky tech Slashdot homepage had 15 stories and an average of 135 comments per story; on the same day, the Dutch populist schockblog Geen Stijl had an average of 223 comments per story with a high of 835.[6] But there is no way of knowing how many comments are posted by the same people supplying different user names. Emails obtained by the Anonymous group from the US cyber-security firm HBGary Federal confirm that companies use "Persona

Management Software" to multiply the efforts of each "user" they employ to support or attack a certain cause, creating the impression of major support for what their client (either a corporation or government) is trying to do. The software creates all the online features a real person would possess: a name, email account, web page, and social media identity.[7] And perhaps you have already heard about the YouTube Comment Poster Bot?[8]

We either ignore or engage in content, but what are the politics of comments? How much of the attention economy is devoted to commentary? Knowledge is tested through dialogue and response, and presumably reaches a higher degree of rationality through this process of cleansing and examination. Cybernetics for all: this is the age of feedback and input as default procedures in almost every institutional activity. Resentment and bad temper are taken into account in such procedural thinking. This is even more the case on news sites where commentary is obligatory. How do we escape the cynical reading of comments as a necessary yet wasted human compulsion?

An Archaeology of Commentary

Let's contrast online comment culture with the tradition of hermeneutics and philology, with the aim of unearthing its architecture. Is there continuity in the interpretive tradition? A comparison with Torah comments in the Jewish tradition is obvious, but do we want such a one-on-one method? The role of comments in hermeneutics, the philosophical practice that "lays out" different text interpretations in literature, is very much limited to paper editions of canonical texts. But this should not stop us from borrowing insights and categories, or even reading philology itself as a metaphor. We execute some find-and-replace commands and come up with interesting but predictable findings. For instance, if we talk about the growing role of respondents, the reference to the role of the choir in Greek drama is all too easily made.

Media history doesn't show a linear progress toward open texts. What we see are waves of intensities grouped around the platform of the day. This is particularly the case with commentary. The German anthology that takes us right back to Mesopotamian and Egyptian times is that of J. Assmann and B. Gladigow's *Text und Kommentar* from 1995, produced by the "ancient history wing" of German media theory that works on the archaeology of literary communication. In the introduction, Assmann writes about the earliest manifestation of text, delivered by a messenger, as a "message that is taken up again."[9] He reports on a 1987 conference entirely devoted to the earliest forms of canonization: once a text is fixed, and nothing is added or changed, can a piece of writing become a "founding text" to define certain practices or procedures (such as law)? Only after the closure of the text do we see the rise of commentary, and then the text becomes open for interpretation. Assmann is using a broad cross-cultural definition of text. The Latin word *textus* (meaning: weaving the signs) occurs in opposition to *commentarius*. What defines early text is not its material storage but the transmission of commitment. Cultural texts, which are different from the restricted-access holy texts, are common property of the people, and exegesis can take place. Comments occur when these texts are passed on from one generation to the next in the context of teaching, learning, and reading. In this process the pupil interprets the text as part of the experience of learning. Understanding, however – as Assmann stresses – happens through oral explanation, also called hodegetics.[10]

How are comments on texts stored over time and reproduced from one generation to the next? In the late Gutenberg era this was mainly done through critical editions. With the production of annotated, completed works in the nineteenth century there was a move from comments toward genesis and criticism. This development is reflected in the professional separation of the editor of classic texts from the literary history commentator. According to Bodo Plachta, writing in the 2009 "commentary" issue of the journal *Zeitschrift für Ideengeschichte*, the move to include commentary occurred around 1970 (with new Kleist and Heine editions). It is also Plachta who points to the relevance of comments outside of academia, the space without limits in digital media, and how easy it is to make changes.

In their essay *Comments, Code and Codification*, Markus Krajewski and Cornelia Vismann stress the temporary, lively aspect of comments. Needless to say, comments are also text – as deconstruction is itself a form of commentary.[11] What distinguishes comments from text is their unfinished nature. There is no end to a comment. Whereas texts can be interpreted as hermetic or authoritative, commentary is seen as oral, informal, fast, and fluid. Comments circulate around the static, inflexible source text. Ever since manuscripts came with margins, room for comments has been designed in order to bring the silent original to life. To better understand internet commentary, we could also further explore its oral background. In a heated debate we often no longer precisely hear what others say. This might also be the case when we skim texts and browse through comments. The amount of information that we do not "hear" when we use search engines is even higher.

Krajewski and Vismann summarize the history of Roman law, its once lively culture of commentary, and tell how in 533 BC it was all "codified" into the Codex. From then on, no additional comments were allowed. The book became a closed object according to the law. This split between frozen text and outlawed chatter has since then haunted Western discourse production: once separated and codified, text cannot be transferred back into a casual conversation. What is stalled within the legal system has been taken up by the computer industry as a way to reintroduce comments as a productive element in software production. Much like lawmaking in the sixth century, it is the compiler who codifies source code. The text literally consists of source and code. Comments are not placed outside but can be read in conjunction with executable code. It is only through the compiler that the two become separated.

Krajewski and Vismann then make a surprising jump and discuss the Request for Comments (RFC) procedure of the Internet Engineering Task Force (IETF). According to the official history of the internet, this feedback loop of comments produces network code (or protocol, as Alex Galloway refers to it) that in turn provokes a next round of comments that culminate into new code. The authors conclude that also in these cases the codifying power, however invisible, still exists. If, in technical terms, the compiler codifies source code, then what mechanisms could be envisioned that metamorphose blog commentary into a next text? There are no codification procedures for the ordinary users – yet. This is where, for Krajewski and Vismann, the Kittlerian analogy, with its emphasis on the supremacy of the operating system, has to stop.

Whereas the interwovenness of code and comment is obvious to programmers, this is not at all the case if we move to the graphic interface. There is a brutal rupture between Donald Knuth's "literate programming" principle that describes the advantages of the programmer directly "talking" to the computer, and highly closed environments such as Facebook where next to nothing can be programmed (but where users are constantly commenting on each other). Seen from the current chaotic situation, codifiers who pick and choose the best comments and then take these to the next level of the discourse – as Krajewski and Vismann describe in reference to the jurist Tribonian (500–547 BC), who used this method to revise the legal code of the Roman Empire – are creatures of some distant future. Maybe it could be a role taken into consideration while designing Web 3.0?

In their editorial to the *Zeitschrift* commentary issue, Vismann and Krajewsi noted that up to the time of Hegel, commenting on classic texts belonged to the philosophical repertoire.[12] Annotating was not merely a skill; it was part of one's art of living. Writing comments declined as a scholarly activity in the nineteenth and twentieth centuries and, until the uptake of the internet, was only practiced by legal scholars, theologians, and editors of collected works. However, as they point out, commentary has not lost its capacity to create significant texts. Here is where we drop our anchor, to further study the role of comments in contemporary internet culture.

Beyond Taming the Commentators

Let's not fall into the trap of thinking that only ancient societies will give us insight into how a once pure and unmediated humankind witnessed the birth of commentary. What we can do is utilize certain elements from historians' tales, such as the role of cultural memory, and apply that to our age of democratized media use. In contrast to printed commentary, today's comment culture is a product of the techno-secular age. Its aim is an amoral form of participation, designed with the intention of checking what citizens are up to and to what subjects they respond. Its textual flows are designed and built by new authorities, the engineers, not by teachers or priests. They have created systems that are no longer solely concentrated on interpretation of the text itself. We do not care so much what the text precisely "says" but what the wider ecology is. Instead of a close reading, we practice intuitive scanning. If we submit a comment it is often an ironic meta-remark, an observation on what the possible implications of the referred posting could be or what the author-as-celebrity could mean. Content is no longer judged in a vacuum but automatically read within the political, cultural, and media context in which it operates. It is the media system of texts, moving images, and lived media experiences that is being stored and reproduced through re-use and re-mixing.

What we need to overcome is the high–low distinction and read the internet onslaught of comments against the grain, as a blueprint for a society in which commentary is becoming a built-in feature of all communication devices and services. Let's reread the German master of twentieth-century hermeneutics and the updated Hans-Georg Gadamer 2.0 could look like this. If the ontology of understanding and the hermeneutics of interpretation are interwoven, as

Paul Ricoeur argues, and we want to make a serious effort in "understanding media," we can no longer push aside online exegesis as mere noise. Some even see in such a project a future for the endangered humanities.[13] Writing about Brecht's poetry, Walter Benjamin emphasized the role of commentary in the making of classic texts. Today, online comments are an integral part of the network effect, and to ignore or dismiss this element is to understand only half of the story.

"No history of ideas without media history," the editors of the *Zeitschrift* wrote. We should implement such insight into future scenarios: on what design concepts could a rich, diverse, and controversial comment culture be based? What would a contemporary text curatorship look like – one that actively embraces the quantitative turn of internet comment culture, and in fact does something with it? How can we overcome the tired complaints about trash and information overload? The question we set out to answer is what a "distributed scripture" would look like. The hypertext tradition paves the way here. Today, knowledge is hyperlinked and open for comments and collaboration. This may sound banal and utopian at the same time. The implications of the shifting relations between primary and secondary texts are vast.[14]

How can comments, even if they are posted by the millions, escape the margins and become integrated into the source? Or should we separate the two? This issue is not merely a scholarly one but is part of a growing movement to design radical media literacies. It is not enough to draw up lists of counter-classics in an attempt to resist national campaigns to canonize cultural and scientific heritage. The reactionary call for national canons, heard worldwide in so many different contexts, is a clear response to the unheard explosion of untamed commentary and the loss of authority of the artist formerly known as author.

On the other hand, it is not necessary either to repeat the numerous critiques of the Wisdom of Crowds meme here. What is so interesting – and disturbing – about internet comment cultures in the early twenty-first century is their hostile anxiety to engage with other neighboring voices. The actual existing lapse of rationality results in an avalanche of random and repetitive comments. There is a widespread unwillingness to reach consensus and to come to a conclusion in a debate. Software can try, by producing "mind maps" and counting the frequency of used words, with illustrations of them in clouds, but neither blog nor forum software has made much progress since the mid-nineties. The schematic Decision Making Software (DMS)[15] has not been widely accepted as a model to be implemented in crowded and messy debates, and rightly so. Comment rating is another way out; deleting by editors or the community is another, but the Web 2.0 "bee economics," as articulated by Yann Moulier Boutang,[16] require platforms to exploit mass participation, not to curtail it. Data sparks fly around everywhere, luring us to comment. What is information for some is interpretation for others and useless ballast for most. Please say something about me, transport me further, link to me, like me. But once the debate is raging, we do not quite know how to summarize the People's interpretation.

Designing Mass Hermeneutics

To get away from the radical banality we are confronted with while trying to understand online comment cultures, we could adapt certain material from Leo Strauss's *Persecution and the Art of Writing*. Persecution, he writes, "gives rise to a peculiar technique of writing and therewith to a peculiar type of literature, in which the truth about all crucial things is presented exclusively between the lines."[17] A similar tactic should be followed if we want to regain control over collaborative forms of online meaning production. Strauss: "That literature is addressed, not to all readers, but to trustworthy and intelligent readers only." Leaving the obvious elitism aside, this is crucial: "It has all the advantages of private communication without having its greatest disadvantage – that it reaches only the writer's acquaintances." For Strauss, the solution has to be found in the axiom "that thoughtless men are careless readers, and only thoughtful men are careful readers." What we could do is translate Strauss's axioms into code. As we know, it is not enough to go offline and then create some secret society. Signing off is a leisure gesture for those who can afford to delegate their "relationship management" to their private staff who are responsible for PR matters such as Facebook status updates, twittering, blog postings, and corporate email. (Funnily enough, smartphones are considered private and personal communication devices, as was the case with US President Barack Obama who, after his election, refused to give up his BlackBerry.[18])

In Michel Foucault's *The Order of Discourse* we read about the limitations that society puts on textual exchanges: "In every society the production of discourse is at once controlled, selected, organised and redistributed by a certain number of procedures whose role is to ward off its powers and dangers, to gain mastery over its chance events, to evade its ponderous, formidable materiality."[19] What limitations does Web 2.0 lay on textual exchange? The facilitating ideology of participatory culture, with its claims of all-inclusivity, is blurring out its own editorializing selection mechanisms (with Wikipedia as the classic case). How many entries and comments are deleted? Is it difficult to log in? Did the user have to register first somewhere else like Facebook, before they could start? How can we create an internet-specific hermeneutics as "a discipline that proposes to understand a text" – to understand what it attempts to say?

For Paul Ricoeur, "every interpretation reveals a profound intention, that of overcoming distance and cultural differences."[20] But what if we do not even understand the hermeneutics machines that are at our disposal? We may as well reverse our expectation toward software developers and demand from next-generation software and interface design that it brings together understanding and interpretation. According to Günter Figal, understanding means "to be able to come back to something."[21] We need to refer to and take data out of the archive in order to create new relations between entities. To understand means to return to a previous topic. How do we do this when "re:sponding" is reduced to a short impression? It is too easy to give the strict answer that there can only be responses if they are comprised of an earnest analysis based on time-delayed reflection. What we need is an introduction of "re:search" in real-time flows to give us easier access to the relevant archives, both inside and outside the current thread. It is not sufficient to be able to use a search engine and have the technical ability to insert a link. What is needed is a form of contextualizing, such as references to other contributors or background articles that explain more about the date and place of the original entry.

This software architecture debate should start with the premise of the freedom of the interpreter, which, as Figal emphasizes, is actually the freedom of the text itself.[22] There is a freedom of interpretation that builds on the ambiguity of meaning. This freedom thrives on the energy that is unleashed by the separation of author and recipient. This is where we have to say farewell to tensions created by those who privilege the classic text over interpretation, and it is where the "mass hermeneutics" project starts. It is no longer the majority that is silent but its supposed spiritual leaders and intellectual cadres that are incapable of speaking out when confronted with sudden changes in society. Modern sovereigns in politics, the arts and pop culture are often mute, but interpretation of their empty (while "correct") statements is rather dull and limited in scope. Instead of focusing on the anxieties of the big ego creators (the writer as default celebrity), the reader shifts to become a default respondent.

In Hans Ulrich Gumbrecht's *Powers of Philology* (2002), we find a passage that directly deals with the question of how the editorial tradition of creating and understanding collected works of canonical authors will alter in the digital age. He sees a historical link between the "return to commentary" and the rise of hypertext, culminating in a "high tech philology."[23] For Gumbrecht, it is obvious that within a short time all human texts, including all recorded commentary, will become available online. Think of Google Books, Europeana, and other digitization projects. This will mean the end of the limited space that was once available in the margins of books. The question is what the long-term effects might be of this abundance and structural emptiness of the margins, on the five basic activities of philologists as Gumbrecht describes them: the collection of fragments, the editing of texts, the production of comments, historicization, and teaching. Can we imagine doing the same with large collections of internet commentary? Bodo Plachta adds the multimedia dimension to the e-book: video files, radio interviews, and lectures.[24] If we look at comments on 2.0, it is easy to draw up the necessary next steps: we process comments through in-depth interpretation and later it all ends up in a canon. We could then predict the radical halt of commentary inside printed editions of collected works, and a move toward a new cult of large, private collections of digital (book) files that may – or may not – include (online) commentary.

The signs are everywhere: text is coming alive (again?). To show that "social text" is already a workable concept one only has to look at Commentpress, developed by Bob Stein and his fellows at the Institute for the Future of Book. It is a plug-in for both fixed documents and blogs that allows "readers to comment paragraph by paragraph in the margins of a text. Annotate, gloss, workshop, debate: with Commentpress you can do all of these things on a finer-grained level, turning a document into a conversation."[25] With Commentpress, comments are turned into "collaborative thinking and writing." Social reading and social writing are blurring – with all the possible consequences for the collective ownership of ideas. Commentpress is a pragmatic example of running code with the desire in mind to design the comment ecology – and yet another proof of the thesis that software does not result in a creed or a set of dogmas, but in a social order.

"In place of a hermeneutics we need an erotics of art," Susan Sontag concluded her essay *Against Interpretation* in 1964. She demanded that commentary make works of art more real. Criticism should produce less meaning and instead cut back content so that we can start seeing the object again. Would we also say, "like the fumes of the automobile and of the heavy industry which befoul the urban atmosphere, the effusion of interpretations of art today poisons our sensibility"?[26] No. The danger of politicians, corporations, and taste police interfering on the internet with the aim of shutting down websites is all too real. Freedom is an absolute value and should not be negotiated on a case-by-case basis. Otherwise there would be no whistleblower sites like WikiLeaks, image boards such as 4chan, or large scanned book collections of theory like aaaaarg. But we cannot be liberal either. That would shut down our minds. We have to keep asking questions. How can wild comment cultures be cultivated that resist the philistinism of interpretation, as Sontag calls it? What would it mean in our situation to recover our senses, apart from simply going offline, introducing slow media, or other sustainable measures?

The currently excessive online comment cultures raise the question of what creative singularity could be in a deeply quantitative world. What if comment culture devotes all its efforts to mass producing aphorisms – Project Dada for the twenty-first century? Do you know how slogans morph into poetry and how a comment can flip into an aphorism? The fact that there are no meta-narratives out there is no longer a post-structuralist truism but a hardwired reality. Today's interpretative grids that Sontag rebelled against are of a technological nature. The power of professional critics that she wanted to reign in has effectively been diminished. The storage revolution that we're in the midst of eliminates all content and leads to the danger of all-out data relativism. Sontag writes: "by reducing the work of art to its content and then interpreting that, one tames the work of art." In which cases would we resist the temptation to interpretation and instead add an extra dimension to an online debate, as well as publicly call for an end to the "cultures of complaint" that merely replicate ideology? We have to face comment cultures head on, not in praise of interpretation, but in order to remain alert and in touch with the signs of the times – no matter how unpleasant they sometimes might be.

— 4 —

DISQUISITION ON INTERNET CRITICISM

I don't believe you can predict human behaviour or human conditions. Planned economies have never functioned. People will automatically embark on a path of resistance. When Gutenberg invented the printing press, a flood of information followed. It was possible to print anything and most of it was a pamphlet: a call to civil war, a call to religious war, and a call to intolerance. People fought back by inventing criticism. Kant is the answer to the superiority of the printed word. Today you can observe that people who use the Internet are immune towards the glut of information, they read the first 40 words and ignore the remaining 18,000. Such reductionism has its good and bad sides. This kind of user is hardly going to sit down in the evening and read Anna Karenina. But he's also not going to drown in information. Man creates his own clarity.

Alexander Kluge[1]

This chapter raises the question of the genre of "internet criticism" and its analytical contours. Taking into account the pressure to remain light and positive, it is perceived as a sign of cultural pessimism to question mainstream internet concepts.[2] No negative reasoning please. So does critique equal civil courage? We need to keep in mind that criticism is a necessary yet boring job; developing a compelling argument consisting of related concepts can be profoundly unsexy. Critique needs to be built up, time and again, and, despite its rich history, can't simply be pulled out of a drawer. How can we develop a rhetoric that follows the footsteps of literary and theater criticism, yet is tailored to the technological specificities of the internet and the twenty-first-century global condition? Will Net criticism generate a literary style of its own, similar to the review or essay with their connections to the rise of book culture in the eighteenth century? We do not need to start from scratch. There are beginnings, from nettime to Nicholas Carr, but we will also look out for African voices, Indian Facebook critiques, and radical Brazilian concepts. Internet criticism can also take new forms besides well-known genres such as the article, review, essay, and the book. In terms of software, one could think along the lines of email threads, forum discussions, blog postings, tweets, and other comment cultures. Before we look into the foundations of the emerging genre we must pass through the desert of the real and deal with the perceived crisis mode of criticism in neighboring fields such as visual arts, film, and book culture. So let's join the never-ending search for the whereabouts of critique.

Criticism in the Age of Overload

In *The Death of the Critic* (2007), Ronan McDonald proposes to historicize criticism as a relic of the modernist age. The critic guided the audience in their quest to improve their taste. Before the cultural revolution of the late 1960s, it was the perceived task of the critic to define the canon – not with a restrictive agenda, but from the perspective of emancipatory enlightenment. In those days, critics had to endeavor to learn and to propagate the best that is known and thought in the world. Elite tastes were shared – and prescribed – to the masses as an educational policy to elevate ordinary people and make them part of Western civilization. Beauty with a cause.

Deep into the twentieth century, it was still the critic who defined taste and determined the authenticity of cultural artifacts. Looking back, the heyday of criticism occurred during the age of the newspaper, magazines, and journals – mass circulation that centralized, captured, and steered collective attention, prompting citizen readers to discuss the latest novel or last night's theater play. In criticism, sense and reason met. According to Ronan McDonald, the decline of criticism set in with the "democratization of taste" during the 1970s. In response to the rise of pop culture, criticism retreated behind the walls of academia. The study of aesthetics became "increasingly inward-looking and non-evaluative."[3] Over recent decades, the gap between academic theorization and journalistic coverage of the artist-as-celebrity increased, resulting in the "death of criticism" meme. Michael Schreyach writes that art criticism these days "can do little more than establish some context for the art under consideration, and offer a few remarks about the art's market value, popularity, it's social significance (or lack thereof)."[4] At best, critique has become *Flaschenpost*, a message in a bottle.

Together, these two related forces – pop culture and the withdrawal of literary criticism into academia – undermined the authority of the critic. The velocity of "un-authorized" critique witnessed in blogs and on Amazon, and the retreat inside universities, where experts wage a self-referential battle of discourses, are two sides of the same coin. In the context of the internet, you get statements like this from John Sutherland: "there are those who see web-reviewing as a 'power of the reader' trend – the democratization of something traditionally monopolized by literary mandarins. And there are those who see it as a degradation of literary taste."[5]

For McDonald, criticism oscillates between media and the academy. He says: "the democratization of objective critical standards may have partly derived from the anti-authoritarian, anti-hierarchical cultural currents of the 1960s and 1970s. Popular and academic trends share their dislike for evaluation as the task of the critic."[6] In the internet age we still operate under the same conditions. Both the baroque postmodern language and the short amateur responses on the comment pages shy away from the traditional critic-as-professional's normative descriptions. We don't require judgment any more, but what are critics to make of the constant onslaught of new applications, publishing tools, and social media? Critics, pushed into a defensive mode, must constantly respond to a steady flow of new products, services, and communication paradigms, making it harder to see the general trends.

While comment wars are raging on the Net, most insiders of the traditional disciplines agree that their mode of criticism is in a crisis. A 2008 anthology, *The State of Art Criticism*, edited by James Elkins and Michael Newman, full of starting points, transcripts of seminars, and assessments, expresses this uncertainty. Art criticism is "unsure of its place and function within society."[7] According to Elkins, art criticism is "massively produced, and massively ignored and is in a state of vigorous health and terminal illness."[8] There is an overproduction of ephemeral criticism, causing numerous interpretations of "meaning" and lack of codification. "Anyone with access to the internet can become a critic. There are now multiple publics, distributed in various ways," Newman writes, concluding: "the role of critical judgement is thrown into question again, as it was in the 1960s and 1970s. But have not reflective judgements always had to discover their criteria, which are never given in advance?"[9]

In the *Guardian* (online edition) February 22, 2010, Jonathan Jones wrote that it is the job of the critic to reject the relativism and pluralism of modern life. All the time, from a million sources, we are bombarded with cultural information. A new film or the music of the moment can enter our minds regardless of quality and regardless of our interest. In fact, in this age of overload, indifference is the most likely effect of so many competing images. If we do make an aesthetic choice it is likely to be a consumerist one, a passing taste to be forgotten and replaced in a moment.

In late 2009, I co-curated an event at De Balie's centre for cultural debates in Amsterdam on the crisis of criticism with the Dutch AICA chapter (the professional society of art critics). Called *Critics Floating in the Virtual Sphere: Will Art Criticism Survive?*, it discussed the relation between art criticism and the rise of the Web. In her opening speech, curator Maria Hlavajova reminded the audience that around 1989 the pronounced death of the art critic occurred simultaneously with the fall of the Berlin Wall and the invention of the World Wide Web. Presenter Regine Debatty, who blogs at *We Make Money Not Art*,[10] began by saying that she was a blogger, not an art critic. She asked why people associated blogs alone with terms such as "impressionistic," "subjective," and "populist" when both *Art Forum* and *Art Review* had gossip sections. Lately the art world has started accepting blogs, said Debatty, and remarkably it now sees blog writing as a style that certainly has a quality of its own. Debatty often is requested "can you write in the style of your blog?" On her blog, Debatty is always positive and only writes about what she likes, does not practice negative criticism and is not provocative. The blog does not ask questions. There is a lot of traffic, but few comments.

The last presenter was the North American art critic Jennifer Allen, based in Berlin since 1996; there she writes for *Zitty*, *Monopol* and *Die Süddeutsche Zeitung*. Allen sees less and less money for art critics. Art criticism has transformed into egocentric, celebrity-driven reporting, dominated by amateurs. The trend started with artforum. com, then crept into the magazine itself, with its "Seen and Heard" rubric. She said that serious art criticism in book form is harder to publish because the press no longer cover book lecture tours. Magazines have lost their audiences to online editions, even though "writing for the online world marks you for life and reduces your income to one third." Another problem she sees results from increased speed. Recently, the feature film *Brüno* was killed because of bad tweets during the opening night. After the negative judgment people no longer showed up at the box office. Then there is the lack of authority. Blogs and Twitter might be popular but they have not taken over the position that leading magazines once had; nor do they take up an alternative position. Why don't they take on Christies, *Artforum*, the biennales, and the curators? On the Net there is often no response, concluded Allen, and online reviews do not generate opinion. They do not take up renegade positions or change the elitist power structure of the contemporary art world.

The debate illustrated a few trends. Art criticism has entered the informal networked media age and there is no way back. As a consequence, personal style has taken over from the formal language of theory. People who still discuss how to co-mingle art criticism and new media lag behind. As Jennifer Allen pointed out, art criticism, be it online or in print, is failing to convince society of the relevance of the arts: "we fail to communicate the excitement and passion we have for culture." Young people know so much about running shoes and cell phones, she observed. "Why not look at art as we look at cell phones?"[11]

Can these insights be useful for Net criticism? We might ask ourselves, why flog a dead horse? What's the point of re-introducing "criticism," a genre that is said to have lost its vitality and may already have vanished? Should we move toward or away from the "fatal" position that Jean Baudrillard offered as a counterplayer of critique?[12] What would it mean to propose a new wave of criticism in a time characterized by absence of judgment? Why not embrace the object in order to kill it? Doesn't the Net criticism proposal fall into the trap of being identified with historical "critical theory," where, before we can even start, we have to cross the icy plains of abstraction and speak with Walter Benjamin, after being forced to compare notes with Adorno, Horkheimer, Habermas, and Honneth.[13] Instead of a productive source of inspiration or philosophical current to compare notes with, in fact the idea of Net criticism as a follow-up to the Frankfurt School has proved a dead-end street. The reference itself ends conversations. You can be critical without being critical – and that is perhaps the main reason why a (public) link with the Frankfurt School should best be avoided. What remains is clandestine reading, silent admiration, and an informal interpretation of their work.

Shaping Net Criticism

Discourse is not progressing linearly from one concept to the next. Why should the internet, with all its newness and untold features take up the heavy legacy of this ailing text species? Perhaps criticism is a historical stage that now supposedly comes back to life as cool attitude. Net criticism could be nothing more than one writing mode amongst many, a basic form of reflection also known as an alternative lifestyle for the rebel who likes to question hierarchies. Instead of going in this cynical direction, I, along with Ronan McDonald, view criticism not as an ideological program but as a much needed basic craft to create literary styles, and as an invitation to engage in radical thought, away from frivolous commentary and chatter about the latest tweet. How might this be expressed? In this internet age, the antidote for critique is news jargon and public relations speak, fostering quick skimming. If the future critic has any adversary to oppose, it would be the anonymous professional information editor, entire frenzied clone armies of them, receiving, repackaging, and releasing text and visual material for the global participatory users who then link, like, and forward. The Net critic operates in a parallel Kafkaesque universe by not engaging with these spin doctors, whose traditional home turf has thus far been television and print, and who now embrace cyberspace with a vengeance.

Let's get real. We should start with the observation that the internet is now a mainstream technology. While its ever-changing qualities continue to fascinate us, there is nothing spectacular about it. We've gone post-spectacle. This is the information society made real – welcome to the society of the query. We approach power with a question and wait while the cloud computes. What exactly happens is rather abstract and visually poor. This is exactly why leading intellectuals and theorists are not aware of the current transformations. It is indeed hard to keep up with the exponential rise of applications and services. Most corporations and institutions are also still in the process of fully understanding the impact that network technologies are having on their organizations, while integrating some elements and blocking off others (mostly the interactive, upstream bits). The introduction of computer networks within organizations over the past decade has changed workflows but hasn't reached the level of decision-making. We seem stuck in a period of permanent transition. We receive confusing answers to the question of whether "new media" are yet fully part of our culture. Even in countries with high usage of broadband and mobile phones, there is a hesitant "leading culture" that does not know whether new media should fully institutionalize as a separate sphere, or dissolve and be integrated into existing traditional branches like film, television, print, and radio.

Here, the internet which is now so pervasive is in itself somehow, strangely, invisible. Following this logic of invisibility, Net criticism so far occupies a marginal position in academic research, corresponding with the diminishing role of criticism and theory in society. Most research still relegates the internet to a secondary role in relation to print and broadcast media. Yet the internet is no longer simply a tool; it has become an inseparable part of economic, social, and cultural processes. By now the academic world itself fully depends on networked information technologies. This shift requires a new level of thinking in which humanities scholars have not yet played an active role. The idea is simple. Much like theater, visual arts, film, and literature, the internet as a medium deserves an informed and sophisticated form of criticism and theory, one that goes beyond journalism and reporting. Interestingly, however, its marginal status has allowed Net criticism to incubate over the past 15 years in spaces outside the academy: contemporary art festivals, online mailing lists, and media activist networks. The history of this cultural-artistic refuge era has yet to be written.

How can we get beyond the news paradigm? We cannot understand this state of the internet's invisibility by merely reading the offerings of traditional media outlets and institutions and, in essence, deconstructing the agendas of these old media messengers. We cannot understand the Web by deconstructing *The New York Times*. Again and again, it has proved insufficient to analyze simplified sound bytes and lament the deceptive side of marketing techniques. What Net criticism therefore should do if it wants to deal with hype is to demonstrate how normative ideas become transformed into their opposite, into practices of domination.

Net criticism must progress beyond *Ideologiekritik* and discourse analysis. The goal of Net criticism is to hardwire self-reflexivity into the feedback loop to change the architecture. The idea is to develop long-lasting concepts and insights that dig deep into the network architectures. Instead of focusing on a fast-changing social reality, as Manuel Castells proposes,[14] I have made it my task to develop a better understanding of the role that concepts such as *free, open, network, community, blog, share, change, friends, link,* and *like* are playing in the making of the network society. We do not need to be idealists to recognize the importance of studying how concepts that simmer for years seem to suddenly appear out of the blue, then turn into small initiatives that scale up overnight into systems used by hundreds of millions of people. There is a need to revise the way theory is used and implemented. Internet criticism as a project is a common search for media-specific concepts that can then be implemented in code, policies, rhetoric, and user cultures.

This is a trial-and-error process. Surprisingly, some of the 1990s concepts I was involved in formulating are still meaningful, such as *sovereign media*, the *data dandy*, and, most of all, *tactical media*.[15] *Net criticism* is another example from 1995, developed with Pit Schultz. More recent examples are *organized networks*, *distributed aesthetics*, and the broader concept of *network cultures*. Sometimes it is useful to invent dozens of them just to see if and how they resonate. In other times it is worthwhile to invest a lot of (collective) time and energy to turn one of them into a proper machine. Obviously this metaphor is borrowed from Deleuze and Guattari who, like few before them, have theorized this process.

Pragmatic thinking threatens to banish conceptual development into the background. "Wild thinking" remains essential, be it in the form of essays, slogans, case studies, or discussions. If the humanities want to reclaim lost territory it is essential that concepts are developed and then translated into real-world action, which includes political activity, mobility, work cultures, and social relations, as well as embedding them into code and protocols. Can a critical concept be further developed into services, software, orgnets, and teaching materials? Criticism can be a productive act that develops a set of workable concepts. It is through concept development that the project will go beyond the constantly morphing, news-reporting level of internet thinking to reach another level where understanding leads to code. Here criticism is linked to its ability to change the object of study.[16] The turn here is one that folds the critical into the networked mode itself.

Review Culture in the Internet Age

As an example of one strategy to establish a lively set of practices, "Net criticism" could analyze how reviewing practices alter when they enter the digital online realm. In other contexts such as film, literature, and theater, often criticism is the equivalent of reviewing recent works. In the context of the internet, what would a comprehensive review of a website or a new app consist of? How has it come to pass that "usability" criteria are framed through the protestant-corporate idiom of Jacob Nielsen – and still remain unchallenged? Can we popularize highly technical software reviews? What would form a good app review, beyond the description of its functionality? Over the years, we've seen a steady rise in the intellectual level of

70

game reviews, bouncing off from film and cultural studies, but this cannot be said of broader internet culture. Reviews in general are considered slow reading in comparison with the instant gratification of the search process. One could even say that a rich and diverse review culture would do away with most of our search queries. The radical democratization of reviews at sites like Amazon is obviously of concern for old-school commentators who feel overloaded with rapid data accumulation. Gail Pool's 2007 *Faint Praise, The Plight of Book Reviewing in America* discusses the steady downfall of traditional book reviewing. "Reviews help us decide what we are to read and to find out what is out there to be read. [...] We read reviews because we take pleasure in the play of ideas, or in reading about reading, or in the well-written review as a literary form. But essentially we want consumer advice and cultural guidance."[17]

According to Pool, the reviewing community has long placed faith in generalists, who are nonetheless authorities as public intellectuals, which is contrary to the Web's bookselling and review sites that have "the democratic idea that every reader has something of value to offer."[18] The distinction between a generalist approach, expert reading, and amateur impression is of importance here. Net culture needs to give more space to well-read experts that can communicate complex techno-protocological issues to a wider audience. How can we transcend the massive output of product reviews that mainly look at communication mishaps, factory mistakes, version incompatibilities, and delivery problems of the latest consumer goods? Gail Pool describes the classic navigation problem as such:

> does anyone really want to read through six hundred reviews of a single book, each with its own description and evaluation, to try to identify the good ones? I can think of few reading experiences less rewarding: the scrolling alone would be wearing, and by the time I'd read a few dozen reviews, I suspect I'd no longer either need or want to read the book.[19]

The problem is, how can we sign up for Martin Amis's *War Against Cliché*, which calls for an end to banality? Should Amazon close down the review option or should Web users filter it out? Take care not to blame only the "self-appointed critics." On the professional end, publishers are instrumentalizing reviewers as blurb machines: *please come up with short, juicy statements, solely written for promotion purposes*. It is the rise of news reporting that has pushed challenging reviews aside. According to Pool: "we need to devise better means of choosing books for review. Our current system inevitably

leads to overlooking good books, overpraising bad ones, and under-
mining the book page."[20]

Interestingly, Gail Pool mentions Virginia Woolf, who in her 1939
pamphlet, *Reviewing*, called for the genre to be abandoned altogether, describing the reviewer as a "a louse, a distracted tag on the
tail of the political kite." A dedicated website describes her intention
as longing "for the obscurity of the dark workshop in which authors
are respected and not ridiculed like some hybrid 'between the peacock
and the ape'."[21] In this hypertext age it is impossible to make such
distinctions between primary (source) and secondary (interpretation)
literature, as George Steiner outlined, suggesting that we prefer the
"mandarin madness of secondary."[22] For writers and readers alike it
becomes a question of "internet mastery" if we want to avoid being
distracted – and disturbed – by the folly of the crowd. It becomes a
matter of survival to tactically move in and then move out of the
public arena. The public nature of the 1930s that drove Virginia
Woolf insane is nothing compared to the TV and radio interviews,
book tours, email requests, and increasing 24/7 social media obliga-
tions that contemporary writers are exposed to. Today's print reviews,
no matter how short and shoddy, are an oasis of content in comparison with social media's crude and invasive short messaging. The
question thus becomes: how can readers decide for themselves, unper-
turbed by Amazon-like recommendation algorithms? It is too easy to
say, as Pool does, that we need "commentary that is impartial,
informed and critical"[23] yet not mention that we already collabora-
tively navigate, search, and filter.

Another relevant reference for our context is L. E. Sissman's 1978
essay *Reviewer's Dues*, where he drew up the following rules: "never
review the work of a friend. Never review the work of an enemy.
Never climb on bandwagons. Never review a book in a field you
don't know or care about." And last but not least: "never fail to take
chances in judgements."[24] What rules would be imperative for cyberspace? I would suggest the following. Never review an artifact that
no one else is talking about. Never review a thing that is not available
online and cannot be freely referred to. Never review a matter that
you cannot discuss in online forums or on mailing lists.

Network Culture as Concept and Agenda

For another example of Net criticism in operation, let's next look
into the "network culture" concept. Net criticism can only come into

existence if there is first a lively network culture at work. This condition is a vital a priori and highlights the subtle difference between adaptation and development: usage alone won't suffice. For Net criticism to thrive there must be a productive relation to the technology itself. Both "network cultures" and "network theory" point to wider contexts that move away from the real/virtual binary often found in popular literature and news reporting.[25] This binary was especially dominant in the nineties, and a recent example was the "real life" versus Second Life meme. Today's large and complex networks override this binary opposition. Networks integrate sociality with software, interfaces, and routers. The term "network" has a specific ambiguity, as it at once talks about the social as well as the machinic. The social structure formed by the technological infrastructure is of interest here because there is no longer any "pure internet technology" without massive swarms of users.

Netzkritik, as it is known in German, handpicks issues and case studies that can be situated in the middle of the peculiar self-referentiality of networks at one end, and mainstream arrangements within media and organizations at the other. Internet culture continues to clash with the latter, with their existing institutional arrangements and social structures. We should be fully aware of this. Network culture disrupts academia, funding bodies, cultural institutions, television, and the fine art and performing arts scenes. Everywhere, the powers that be are ready to hit back, as the WikiLeaks case has shown. This is not a progressive era. At the same time we need to understand that the "new media networks" (whoever or whatever that may be) are not trying to steal existing resources in order to take over. Power itself will have to be redefined. Networks are informal, fluid, and invisible, and it is this aspect that is causing panic and confusion. As the business gurus preach: technology is disruptive. This disruption, creative or not, does not indicate a simple victory of the new over the old, and also never seems to materialize in the form that the consultant class and think-tank futurists predict.

Network culture, therefore, is both a wider phenomenon in society and a resonating concept that can be used for research and action. As an open-ended denominator, it suggests an existing condition and, even more crucially, is a strange attractor that brings people together. In 2004, it became incorporated into the name of an overall program when I founded the Institute of Network Cultures (INC), following my appointment as research professor (*lector*) within the School of Interactive Media at the Amsterdam University of Applied Sciences. These *lectorates* were seen to be small units to kick-start much needed research within the Dutch polytechnic system (*hogescholen*). Ned Rossiter, Sabine Niederer, and Linda Wallace were involved in choosing the name. The year 2004 is also when Tiziana Terranova published her book *Network Cultures*. The name is a good example of a hybrid concept that is both a strange attractor and empty signifier. This "second-order" term, network + cultures, coming as it does *after* the technology, points to assemblages that might emerge over time once the excitement of the new has faded. Paraphrasing UK scholar Irit Rogoff, we could say that the INC as a brand name expresses a mixture of cultures that, through intense exposure to technology, have lost their "originary identity."[26] The chosen topics – from urban screens to online video to search to Wikipedia – advance beyond remediation; what fascinates are the elements that escape this logic.

The INC research extends to design, activism, art, philosophy, political theory, and urban studies, and is not confined to the internet alone. The internet can only be understood as the conjuncture of these various fields and lines of inquiry. But make no mistake, this is not a naive, multidisciplinary proposal with vastly different players in size, age, and power. There is a need for the other disciplines to contribute (with ideas and resources) to the critical study of the internet, not the other way round. "Network cultures" should be read as a strategic term for humanities-based internet studies, enlisted to diagnose political and aesthetic developments in user-driven communications. Network cultures can be understood as social-technical formations under construction. They rapidly assemble, and can just as quickly disappear, creating a sense of spontaneity, transience, even uncertainty. However self-evident it is, collaboration is the foundation of network cultures. What is new here is that working with others in distributed online networks frequently brings about tensions that have no recourse to traditional protocols of conflict resolution.

Ever since its founding, the INC has been a framework for the realization of a diverse array of projects with a strong emphasis on reseach as content – not as policy, business development, or as code. Its goal has been to create open, organizational forms that give an early institutional context to ideas from both individuals and organizations. A key focus is the establishment of (more or less) sustainable research networks around emerging topics. After a number of years, these research networks either vanish, become independent entities, or are taken up by others. This strategy can be summarized as "criticism in action" or "action research."

A long-term goal of Net criticism is to support and develop new media literacies. Today's "wo/man of letters" is a contested figure.

Are the digital natives reading less or more? Digital literacy as a concept has mainly been a topic for creative industries and cultural studies research seeking to defend popular internet use by arguing that education and professional fields should "learn" from entertainment and participatory new media such as games. The INC approach, while stressing the progressive potential of the internet, offers an alternative to this well-meaning agenda that is mostly concerned with neutralizing anxieties while promoting public investment in digitalization, the use of computers in classrooms, and the reformation of regulatory regimes and government policy frameworks. Net criticism is not about the promotion of use. The trick here is to understand and share the power of concept development as such. It is to devise ways for concept development to be implemented in both code and lived practices, from customs and culture to new forms of organization and revenues.

Another even more important aspect of network cultures is the geo-political, post-post-colonial dimension: the hyper-growth of internet users outside the West – Brazil, China, India, Southeast Asia, parts of the Middle East, and Africa. INC's research is embedded in these developments and sets the ambitious goal to increase the role of global cultural theory. The objective is to "hardwire" arts and humanities into internet culture and to turn around the current apathy among academics (who feel that they must "keep up" with technology) into a vital international movement of "critical anticipation." We urgently need to move beyond the interpretation of news and master the real-time flows that surround us. In order to get there we should remain open to input from "digital natives" and the research methods that are emerging out of the networked technologies themselves. What does it mean when we say that Net criticism must become technical? The technical has to be foregrounded through negations and falsifications, not by stating a positive truth. Critique is not founded on philosophical statements, which are then applied to the object, in this case the internet. We must begin and end with a big No. The very act of questioning is enough to generate interesting outcomes. The joy of reversal is real. That's why we call it Criticism.

—— 5 ——

MEDIA STUDIES: DIAGNOSTICS OF A FAILED MERGER

Am Anfang steht das Ende, sonst wäre das Neue das Alte.
[Every beginning starts with an end, otherwise the new would be the old.]
Editorial from *Radikal* 126/127, March 1984

The question of how to interpret the internet and new media is too important to be left to university course managers. Humanities-based "media studies" never had a grip on new media and internet education. Nor did it shape the new media field by being at the forefront of early-adopter waves. Via ineffective, calcified, and divergent combinations, the container concept "media studies" tumbles literature, film, radio and television, theater, design, visual and performing arts, and new media, into one jumbled, convoluted label. Humanities-based media studies did not position itself as an oasis of radical critique; nor did it make a case for dedicating itself to the past with the aim of further developing the "media archaeology" approach.

This dialogical manifesto intends to shuffle away institutional rubble. Needless to say, this is done with the interests of new media, digital culture, internet, and software studies in mind. The time in which we could have made a case for "the media" in general is well behind us. The term "media" has become an empty signifier. The same can be said of "digital media" since everything is digital anyway. In times of budget cuts, creative industries, and intellectual poverty, we must push aside wishy-washy convergence approaches and go for specialized in-depth studies of networks and digital culture. The presumed panoramic overview and historical depth suggested in the term "media" no longer provides us with critical concepts. It is time for new media to claim autonomy and resources in order to leave the institutional margins and finally catch up with society. There are at least three major obstacles to getting there: first, theory lags behind its subject and falls victim to its own general claims; second, media studies are still characterized by an awkward legacy within academia; and third, the new media landscape itself changes so rapidly it makes a slippery object of study. Let's go through these concerns before offering up some unlikely futures for the field.

When Theory Loses its Sting

During the first decade of the twenty-first century, media studies fought a losing battle to keep up with the pace of techno-cultural change. If we are to have any hope of catching up, we must consider the digital networked realm as a distinct sphere that demands its own theoretical vocabulary and methods. Digital media studies rarely have been much of a critical intellectual project. The maniacally impulsive culture of pop has proven to be a black hole for theory talent. Instead of generating concepts at a Twitter pace, most "new media" ideas are neutralized and flattened within a general atmosphere of budget cuts and slow change. Staff within higher education are tired of reform anyway. While struggling to distance itself from vocational training, academic media research has so far failed to develop appealing schools of thought. Faced with this ever-growing gulf between theory and practice, media studies staff can do little more than fight the bureaucratic monsters that breed in their unbounded meta-discipline. Media studies is presently an abandoned construction site, crumbling under its own neglect. Do we wilfully continue a failed project? Or should we acknowledge its growing cracks and celebrate its successes as we raze it to the ground and start anew? All too often the question is this: how do new media fit in? For pragmatic reasons new media scholars have thus far made a case that their field of study has an "elective affinity" with design, television, film, management, whatever ... but it never has. This strategy of disguise has now exhausted itself.

The reason for conceptual stagnation goes back to the very notion of media studies itself. Instead of synthesizing research methods and underlying theoretical concepts into an ambitious philosophical or theoretical unity, general media studies carry the weight of a heterogeneous bag of twentieth-century paradigms, ranging from hermeneutics, mass communication, feminism, and post-colonialism, to

77

visual studies, depending on the intellectual history of the specific country. If we look at textbooks, the canon has remained steady for the past 15 years, jumping from Benjamin and Brecht, via Innes and McLuhan, to Williams, Baudrillard, and Kittler, with personal tastes for Flusser, Virilio, Ronell, and Luhmann. While none of these thinkers directly deal with contemporary issues of networked digital environments, there have been enough conceptual splinters, or found footage, within these mostly general theories to satisfy young new media scholars. These so often negative visions worked as antidotes to the unreconstructed positivism of business gurus and consultants. As long as the theory toolkit remained useful, it yielded productive relationships. It was a powerful gesture to celebrate the end of the social, the political, and historical. This started to change around 2001 when the speculative years ended, after 9/11 and the dot.com bust. Slowly, theory became historicized. Theory is no longer a potpourri of living ideas but a fixed collection of twentieth-century canonical texts. The difference between media theory (as a concept pool) and "media archeology" started to dissipate. The humanities heritage, once seen as a rich source of weird (while irrelevant, nonempirical, and untimely) powerful insights, started to show its weak spot: the social. What had once been a liberating feeling – finally to avoid conventional topics of social theory! – returned with the rediscovery of social formations such as communities, mobs, tribes, and yes ... social networking sites.

Unfortunately, these concepts are ill prepared for the fluid media objects of our real-time era. Such analysis will by default favor visual representations (because this is what these scholars with their film, television, or art history backgrounds are trained to analyze) but neglect social and interactive dynamics. Do we truly expect to find exciting openings and applicable insights by "reading" YouTube under Spivak's guidance, and watching *Heroes* with Žižek in our favorite interpassive mode, flowing through the national libraries with Castells, understanding Google à la Deleuze, or interpreting Twitter via Butler? Not only are these "cultural studies" outcomes predictably inadequate, but the approach itself is flawed. Whereas this type of theory critique applies to many fields, it is also valid for media studies. The mechanical application of theory to the object (read X with Y), while abstractly subversive and innovative in moments, lost its critical edge some time ago. A principal function of theory – to foster socially crucial lines of questioning, while energizing and supporting those who do the theorizing – has been neutered.

Many media practitioners are unaccustomed to thinking within, much less playing around with, theoretical frameworks. US scholar Henry Warwick, who teaches new media courses at Ryerson University in Toronto, says:

> There is a consistent danger of being informed by an unthinking and uncritical acceptance of popular tropes, an empty and ignorant formalism [...] Digital media is seen from a non-theoretical framework and is implemented in an instrumental manner. Film departments often no longer focus on film, but in fact produce video. Illustration departments don't focus on watercolour, they teach Photoshop. [...] One economic example of the urgency of the contradictions created by this situation is indicated by the Canadian Television Fund, which changed its name to the Canadian Media Fund, and now requires applicants to submit online strategies with their television proposals even to be considered for funding.[1]

In a similar move, the Dutch Cultural Broadcasting Fund ("Stifo") was renamed as the Media Fund.[2]

The underlying problem of media studies is that "theory" no longer mesmerizes. It has lost its capacity to capture the collective imagination or to stimulate its core believers. Once progressive content simply no longer captivates audiences, especially younger ones. Some theories in certain decades were in sync with the zeitgeist. They seemed to talk to everyone's concerns in a miraculous way. Read them 20 years later and they're dead. Go back to them 50 years later and their weirdness is quaintly charming. These days, the holy scriptures of Parisian Theory are often perceived as indifferent text machines that exist for one sole reason: to legitimize academic positions. They're stating the obvious in a crypto-code that is meant for aliens. How did we end up in such a sorry state? Why is media theory a dead horse? Due to the drifting definition of media, "postmodern" theories have become outmoded very quickly. There is no sense in applying McLuhan or Derrida to Wikipedia for instance. In the past, media theory, when combined with speculative metaphysics and wide conceptual landscapes, provided a way out of the provincial atmosphere in English and German literature departments, but this is no longer the status quo that media studies must engage with. The out-of-context, speculative conceptualization that set apart these original text-based hermeneutics of literary theory have been replaced by neoliberal managers who tidily control research output through academic journals, thereby banning more experimental and speculative modes of writing such as essays that cross genres and disciplines.

79

Australian-US media theorist McKenzie Wark teaches at the New School in New York. According to Wark: "people will do some great work on few resources if they believe in it. And they will do better work. It's no accident our canon is full of people who were marginal: Marx, Benjamin, Debord, Baudrillard. They did not have NSF grants, they had passion. They had 'colourful biographies'."[3] Lev Manovich, working out of San Diego (US), where he heads a software studies centre, explains that theory of the 1960s–1980s is often not very relevant "because commercial culture and computers today run on many principles of this theory – from irony and the self-refentiality of advertising to 'rhizomatic' networks. So to use many of these theoretical concepts is to state the obvious."

Exodus from Media Studies

If the study of new media wants to mature and reach its potential to match the actual scale and diversity of its object of study, it must divorce itself from "old media" and go solo. We long ago passed the point where it's necessary to explain the use of the computer, what "digital" is, and the Net, to less technologically adept scholars. Instead of fighting over diminishing resources, it is time to throw caution to the wind and go for uncompromised growth. The grand synergies of the multi-, hyper-, and cross-media approaches may have worked as business concepts in hyped-up demo-or-die corporate culture, but in the publish-or-perish environment of academia, these synthesizing approaches have only delayed new media research. Hollywood films such as *The Lawnmower Man* and *The Matrix* never had much to say about the existing global new media culture. At best, they were interesting fantasies about how to escape the boring, busy, neo-liberal (There Is No Alternative) lives that people are caught up with. In retrospect, cyberculture has been a subcultural trap for those interested in body politics and visual representation, but a dead end for internet and new media theory. We need to say no to the "representation" school of media studies that reduces all issues to comparative aspects of imagery – not because we've resolved the media question and surpassed all of its issues, but because we need the speed and scaling-up that new independencies can grant.

For a proper study of the internet and other rapidly growing sectors such as mobile phones, geo-media and games, we must de-merge and liberate the "digital" from its confinement in general media studies.

Digital network education and research need to declare independence. We must leave behind the tired dialectic of old and new and
the dull atmosphere of competition with print and broadcasting.
Instead of negotiating to death over broad resemblances, we need to
define the specificities of these emerging platforms. Literary analogies
do not translate into topical knowledge that can be mobilized inside
the politics and aesthetics of the daily "protocolistic" fights that go
on around us. There is and always will be remediation, as it is implicit
in the digital realm. No one claims to start with a blank page; but
the age of infancy is over. Whatever constitutes the "death(s) of
cinema" or "the end(s) of television"[4] are other people's business. We
need to study in detail the specificities of digital, networked modes
of working, real-time pressures, and the mobile dimension of today's
media experience. It is time to take the internet, computer games, and
mobile phones, now loosely gathered under this broad umbrella
subject of "new media" on their own terms. Instead of wasting time
on the destiny of printed newspapers, our attention is urgently needed
in fields such as location-based services, cloud computing, search,
online video, and the "internet of things."[5] The debate about "free"
and sustainable models for the internet economy has reached mainstream audiences, yet there is very little theoretical grounding, be it
positive or negative, to help guide us through these fluctuating times.

Let's also look at the underlying metaphor that drives media
studies: the idea of the "merger," in this case of disciplines and platforms, driven by the multidisciplinary dream that "we are all working
on the same page anyway." CNET author Steve Tobak fittingly sums
up the fate of doomed mergers in the business world: "Some failed
so spectacularly that the combined company went down the tubes,
others resulted in the demise of the executive(s) that masterminded
them, some later reversed themselves, and others were just plain
dumb ideas that were doomed from the start."[6] So what's the destiny
of media studies? "A 2004 study by Bain & Company found that
70 percent of mergers failed to increase shareholder value. More
recently, a 2007 study by the Hay Group and the Sorbonne found
that more than 90 percent of mergers in Europe fail to reach financial
goals."[7]

One can reject the banal translation of business lingo to academia,
but why would this be so different in education? Due to constant
reshuffling, the programs and departments we're talking about here
are not exactly marriages (which have a failure rate of 40–50 percent
themselves). What if the supposed communalities and synergies
between old and new media simply do not materialize? Note how

Time Warner is undoing their merger with AOL, "allowing Time Warner to concentrate on creating television shows, movies and other content without having AOL hanging like an albatross around its neck."[8] With a push toward vocational training, a stagnation in cultural studies, and a distaste for theory in general, film and television studies programs can only make defensive gestures toward the ever-expanding digital realm. All is lost if this or that merger between disciplines and programs doesn't work out.

The future of media studies instead rests on its capacity to avoid these forced synergies toward "screen cultures" or "visual studies" and to set out on a path to invent new institutional forms that connect with the collaborative and self-organizational culture of teaching and research networks. Unless media studies makes such a move it will join the vanishing objects that it assumes as constitutive of media in society. What exactly would be lost by trying a new approach? Isn't it time to just say farewell and move on? Perhaps in some institutional contexts, a collapse of media studies, and media and communications, makes sense (even most insiders have no clue where the disciplinary boundaries between humanities and social science have to be drawn anyway). In other cases, it could be more interesting to merge with art and art history programs, thereby strengthening the still weak "technical" arm of visual studies. In rare cases, one could even think of moving new media into computer science, but there are no examples worldwide that demonstrate "cultural" approaches are welcome in that well-resourced (and therefore) introverted and self-satisfied context.

Unfortunately, there is an unspoken attitude of indifference, if not superiority, from contemporary cultural theory toward new media. Are we repeating the high–low divide yet again?[9] What is the price of ignoring the specific exigencies of a medium by heavy-handedly applying the works of Freud, Lacan, and Foucault to media products in desperate attempts to gain scientific recognition?[10] These uses of theory, practiced in cultural studies programs and art academies around the globe, can also be read as leftovers from the 1990s when there was an abundance of speculative theory and not enough empirical data and (digital) methods. A decade later, we have to renegotiate how much technical programming knowledge humanities researchers need as a basic skill. To what extent should you write software to be truly creative with digital matters? Should writing code be required in undergraduate media programs? Explain it to your nephew: media studies is not cultural studies, not visual studies, not communication studies. But what is it then?

A Blurry Heritage

Which brings us to the second problem, one that is implied in the first: media studies had little coherence as a field or a discourse from the beginning and have always been accused of faddishness and hot air even before taking off. What is lacking in media studies is a *Geburtsmythos* (birth myth).[11] As an academic genre, it sprang out of the heads of education consultants and bureaucrats and blended into unrelated departments and intellectual cultures, in order to scale-up output. Unlike cultural studies, which can claim its emergence from the social conflicts and confusion of the post-war UK, media studies have been a managerial construct from the beginning, a half-heartedly positioned, top-down merger between literature, theater, communication studies, and a handful of others, depending on the local situation.[12] Because of technology's maladroit initial phases, media studies was given second-class citizenship in the academic society: neither inside nor outside. It is vocational enough to play a role in the media business; tough yet not sophisticated when compared to philosophy. In retrospect it would perhaps have been a better proposition to situate media studies as an offshoot from literature studies (as still happens in certain places), which is the birthing ground of most media theory, from McLuhan to Kittler (and the subject in which I received my PhD at the University of Melbourne).

Media studies exist in a variety of precarious positions. This area is found nestled between media and communication programs with a social science emphasis, within fast-growing and economically successful vocational training at universities of applied science, due to the growing importance of MBAs in the recent reawakening of the social sciences, and inside the creative industries paradigm. Last but not least, there is computer science, which, despite declining student numbers due to the outsourcing of IT services to India and other countries, receives hundreds of millions of euros in funding.

This situation was made worse by the fact that very few people, if any, foresaw the ensuing IT explosion as software and its infrastructure imposed itself on all sectors of society. Instead of firing up debates and developing critical concepts, crucial time was wasted on the unproductive question of how "new media" could be integrated into "old media" departments.[13] The genealogy of the computer, rooted as it is in mathematics, the military, and cybernetics, still hasn't found an equivalent to the art history approach of visual studies, which collapses painting, photography, film, and the internet into one analysis. The visual studies perspective does not privilege the (technical) carrier concept as in media studies. The parallel histories of code and the image make it a difficult task to bring them together in one curriculum only to pretend to students that it's all one and the same, namely "media." Convergence, in its latest incarnation as "cross-media," "screen studies," and "trans-media," has always been criticized for its reductionist business approach. Not everything can, or should, be reduced to zeros and ones, much in the same way that human experience cannot be reduced to "visual culture." There is more to media than reception. As Matthew Fuller states: "If we instead emphasize production, whether this is as practice-based research, or a Deleuzian emphasis on expression, the problem of genealogy gains a different inflection."[14] Would any regular user of technological media consider it an astute decision to lump TV, radio, and fine arts alongside the mobile phone, Twitter, and Google? Users are actively participating and sharing on a daily basis. Where is such a classification in our highest educational institutions most likely to lead us: to the avant-garde edge of expertise or to some backwater thought-swamp?

Yet, compared to the growing demand in the labor market for new media expertise, the academic sphere's focus on and development of the new/digital media discipline has been startlingly negligent. Why would communication studies, literature programs, film, television, and cultural studies, themselves often only a few decades old, welcome an aggressive predator in their midst? Whereas on the technical-infrastructural level much has happened, the public perception of "old" and "new" media has only grown further apart. Throughout society, serious frictions and conflicts are on the rise around such notions as intellectual property rights, online language politics, and techno-libertarianism, yet the supposed new media intellectual experts play a very small role in such conversations. This is particularly distressing as arts and humanities departments face serious competition from anthropology, sociology, information studies, science-technology-society (STS) programs, and even management and organization degrees. It is time for the humanities' new media community to set off the alarms. There is a serious case to be made for approaches that are rooted in the history of ideas, for approaches that stress the importance of aesthetics and critical conceptual thinking to reflect the current state of affairs. Society is asking critical questions that land squarely at the feet of new media. What are the social implications for the production of online subjectivities? What are the politics of information visualization? How are

84

global relations and local cultures going to manage the information tidal waves? What effects can we expect from corporate walled gardens and national webs?[15]

The diminishing role of linguistic theory, along with the shrinking presence of humanities and stagnating staff numbers, doesn't help either. At this moment, we can look back on a decade of hard work by new media pioneers to set up programs that yielded only modest results. They started building a comprehensive body of critical concepts and related case studies, yet there is still a lack of classic texts produced between the years 2001 to 2009. Few books and art works can match the vital energy and speculative madness of the 1990s. Despite its shortcomings, Manovich's *Language of New Media*, first published in 1999, remains one of the few canonical texts known to outsiders. But even this text, in retrospect, tells us more about 1990s multimedia culture than the Google age of blogs, Twitter, and social networking sites. Also look at *The New Media Reader*, an otherwise quite useful series of texts, edited by Noah Wardrip-Fruin and Nick Montfort, that functions now as a historical reference. Why does this anthology end with the invention of the World Wide Web in the early 1990s? It is telling that my intellectual hero of the digital age is an urban sociologist, Saskia Sassen. The canon of critical internet studies has yet to be written, particularly as an academic textbook,[16] but *Mute Magazine*'s anthology, *Proud To Be Flesh*, is certainly a good start. Who is bringing into other contexts the radical critique of the networked world that has been developed over the past 15 years? In the end, will it boil down to the mainstream concern that our brains and our bodies can no longer cope, and that we risk collapse under the pressure of information overload?

In response to this dead-end situation, young and ambitious thinkers deliberately avoid media studies, be it in film, television, or new media. Careerwise, it's better to position one's CV inside visual arts, sociology, or philosophy, or to specialize straight away in the history and discourse of print, film, and television.[17] In this crisis era, the Green New Deal has taken over the role of future science from hardcore ICT that, at least in the West, has started to seriously suffer from outsourcing and a bad gender reputation. Research funds flow instead in the direction of electric cars, wind energy, and the like. Rather than being celebrated as a hotspot for the cool, media studies is seen as a dumping ground for scattered, overworked, mid-career academics who have many reasons to complain about lack of funding, inspiration, and lasting values. For many, its "nerd" image is no longer funny. For those positioned inside shrinking humanities faculties, there has been only one way to go – down a dizzying spiral into the maelstrom. The globalization of higher education and increasing competition between disciplines over diminishing funds and gifted students has only further exacerbated the sense of crisis in the adolescent years of new media education and research. In order to tackle these challenges, we need to develop an art of "collective assistance" for growth spurts, because the next metamorphosis of the new media field is imminent even amidst the danger of conceptual weakness and uncertainty. Are the new media players in this climate of stasis ready for the next Great Leap forward?

Keeping Up with the Googles

Apart from the difficult institutional politics of new media research, another more general problem is rearing its head. We come to the third element of difficulty characterizing the state of the art of new media within media studies: increasingly, new media research is running far behind the zeitgeist, and subsequently has the tendency to write history rather than form critical theory that can intervene in emerging processes. The timeline for academic research is so long and still so focused on book production that there is less and less room for real-time interventions, let alone contributions from the arts and humanities to co-design tomorrow's technologies and societies. Twitter easily outpaces CNN and other global news agencies, while social science and humanities research dropped out of the technological race long ago. What is research in a real-time society? We can no longer run away from this question, or sum up, yet again, all of the institutional restraints we're facing. Strategies used by hard sciences to acquire the largest investments in "fundamental research" are encouraging, but also wildly unrealistic, as they cannot easily generate immediate practical outcomes. Arts and humanities continue to suffer, while the hard sciences, on average, claim 85 percent of research funds. Facing such a radical imbalance, it is hard to collaborate on an equal basis. Have all the ethical problems of CERN, datamining, and biotechnology been adequately confronted? Do we simply want to leave it to governments and corporations to patrol themselves? In this climate, can theory and aesthetics regain leading positions as visionary activities, be they positive or negative? How ironic, that in times of much talk over the "creative city" and its "creative industries," the arts and humanities continue to be allocated less and less money. Perhaps these are not the right strategies to prove one's engagement and the urgency of the topic and of the approach. Wouldn't it be better to start doing untimely research?

In an email conversation, Toronto-based media theorist and music expert Henry Warwick noted the following:

> Literally hundreds of media departments all over the planet are dealing with a similar dynamic. The idea that the analogue/broadcast/fine art regime is the centre of the game clearly no longer obtains, for in fact it's all been "componentised" and each are simply particular stripes in the broad media flag. As a consequence, "disruptive" theoretical concerns are pushed aside, ignored, or punished. The resulting precarity is accepted as "part of the game" [...] Meanwhile what's going unnoticed is that the turn of media as a matter of computability – in the face of cheap storage and increased bandwidth – has enormous and far reaching theoretical, social, political, aesthetic (and a host of other) impacts and ramifications.

Talking to pioneers in new media education and research, one can witness a let's-wait-and-see attitude creeping in as Generation X comes of age; a culture of complaint infuses the conversation. The critique of neo-liberalism and free-market capitalism may be sharp and correct but underneath we hear tired voices. After 10–15 years of hard work spent building up digital and interactive programs, many have lost their vitality and are no longer capable of bold initiatives to break new ground. A defensive mode kicks in. Should one aim for greater institutional recognition or see institutionalization per se as a source of the stagnation? The system is crushing spirits that have only been rewarded with a few crumbs. The "digital" faculty is new, usually untenured, and not backed by professorships or PhD programs, and, as a consequence, the positions of lecturers are precarious. Built to flip, as might have been said in the late nineties. The underlying assumption is clear: newness will not last; as a fad, the digital will fade. The structural precarity that sets in as a consequence is threatening and unwelcome for those employed to lecture. What is lacking is a long-term vision that these fields might become powerful, an idea that is frightening. Neither going for the big ride on the back of capital, nor the radical refusal, new media artists, programmers, and critics are confronted with diminishing opportunities while the field at large expands far beyond their reach. What and where is the expertise? If we are to escape from this stagnation, we must locate the rotten, ineffectual parts and practices and cut them out before we open the collaborative wikis. It takes a radical change in culture to stop thinking as a default response in institutional terms.

Is theory itself, with all the baggage it entails as a term, a necessary core element of the work to be done?

Media Studies in the Netherlands

Let's zoom in further on the Netherlands, where the "new media" departments in Utrecht and Amsterdam are fighting uphill battles of their own. With few exceptions, the national academic research grant-giving body NWO has failed to earmark new media (from an arts and humanities perspective) as a priority. This is the main reason academic new media programs in the Netherlands remain tiny compared to the booming vocational schools within the universities of applied sciences (*hogescholen*), which were actively supported to start separate degrees aimed at high enrolment growth. Instead of expanding to match the pace of the growth of the internet (including games and mobile telephony), these academic new media initiatives had to push themselves into existing departments that were less than excited to support a competing program in times of shrinking opportunities.

The anthology *Digital Material*,[18] presented in May 2009 to celebrate the 10-year anniversary of media studies in Utrecht, doesn't claim to have a program either. It merely proposes a summary of the media question in the form of the pragmatic and rather artificial concept "digital materiality." Basically, the common point of differentiation is in the method and approach, not in the platform. Even the divergence of research is celebrated, much in the Rosi Braidotti fashion, as heterogeneous – keep in mind that there is no Utrecht or Amsterdam School of New Media Research. While some praise this lack of unity, others see it as a lost opportunity, in particular, for the countless students who must leave the country because the Netherlands still does not provide a new media PhD program or even a research masters degree. If one wants to keep new media small, then create multidisciplinary teams with dispersed interests – divide and conquer. What we now have is a slowly expanding, haphazard cloud of scholars, doing interesting but comparatively unsupported work in light of the magnitude and potential societal implications of the field. How will new media research leave this vicious circle and make the quantum leap to catch up with society?

What is lacking is the capacity, or the collective will, to set up bold and coherent programs, departments, and eventually entire schools based on future scenarios that could make an all-too-obvious claim:

all that is digital and networked is going to stay with us and will not disappear overnight. Nevertheless, if new media programs are to assume their critical function, we must demand a space to build up exactly such bold initiatives. We should note positively the increased interest in new media tools and methods (for instance, Richard Rogers's Digital Methods Initiative in Amsterdam, and Lev Manovich's Cultural Analytics in San Diego) but, in observing current technological development, this interest is hugely undernourished. Furthermore, the tools and methods used are a far cry from the vision that is so sorely needed in response to the question of where to take new media studies as a whole. The method is the message. So who knows? Let's turn now to proposals from within the field itself.

The Quantitative Turn

The "quantative turn," perhaps the most current and co-opted "best answer" put forth by media studies, does not present itself as a program; at best, it is a clever response inside digital humanities to understand and utilize the latest technological affordances. If we say "text has become searchable" and "images have become computable" it means that we can explore another layer of knowledge, namely, patterns that become visible in comparison to other works. This comparative approach puts the work in a larger context that transcends unique expression. The work of Adorno and Horkheimer shows that quantative research, such as the Princeton Radio Project, and qualitative analysis, such as the *Dialectics of Enlightenment,* can very well be done by one and the same person. There is no decision to be made here. While there is no obligation in cultural analysis to use tools (and it is even uncertain that the research results of data mining and info-visualization will be useful at all), we should note the process of tool development as cultural prototyping beyond good or evil. Many questions still remain. Do we need these tools to understand wider trends? Are there other ways to think globally? Why do we need large datasets and patterns in the first place? Is there indeed a crisis of the "readability" of society? Previous generations thought that they could decode the signs of the times through a single novel, film, or song, but is this method still valid? Hasn't it become too easy to instantly deconstruct the gender-race-class interest of the single-author work? It's just one opinion; why bother with only one judgment (or symptom)?

89

The uncertainty over the status of any single cultural expression in mass society has further fueled this trend toward "the larger picture." Says Alex Galloway:

> the crisis revolves around the social sciences and the collection of data, the so-called "quantitative turn." Scholars used to have a monopoly on the collection and interpretation of information. Today that job is performed by Google, Monsanto, and Equifax. Scholars today are outspent and upstaged by industry. Because of this, the very concept of media studies needs to be scratched out and rethought. The irony of course is that the universities are precisely the place where this will never happen, given the conservative nature of these kinds of institutions. It is the poverty of academic life. So shall we supersede the academy?[19]

Whereas in the roaring mid-nineties there was a glimpse of hope that a new media bohemia could take up the role that Galloway points to, the dot.com wave all but strangled independent theory production. In such an environment as exists now, how do we best utilize the ever-widening range of coding practices, from unconferencing to barcamps, from bricolabs to book sprints? Do we really accept that the highest levels of expertise are locked behind the doors of Google, Monsanto, and Equifax?

Can the quantitative or computational turn revitalize media theory? Lev Manovich:

> While I am certainly very excited about the range of new possibilities it offers, and that's why I was putting all my energy over the last two years into "cultural analytics," I am not sure about the answer to this question. First of all, it will be about ten years before people who study media will be ready to take up this approach. Second, it has to be combined with another major conceptual shift of the study of Culture as everything being created by everybody, as opposed to selected objects and people who are thought of as important for particular reasons. This is really a very big paradigm shift which I am not sure will happen. Without it, we will simply continue with digital humanities as they have been practiced in literary studies already for two decades – analysis of style and historical patterns but only in important "literary texts."[20]

Outlook Toward a New Program

Instead of time and again trying to enforce the paradigms of film and television studies onto new media, we could also turn to other disciplines that have been overlooked in the process. For some, that would be computer science and mathematics. For Lev Manovich, it is design:

> The key to development of self-sufficient theory of software culture, or whatever we want to call it, is taking design seriously. Since in general design is ignored, the academy leaves out something like 80% of contemporary culture. If the academy starts taking design seriously – graphic design, web design, interactive design, experience design, software design and so on – this can also lead to looking in detail at concrete hardware, software, and web apps – analyzing their details as opposed to seeing them through the glasses of "high theory."[21]

Also, instead of creating artificial mergers, Matthew Fuller and Andrew Goffey have proposed the intriguing "Evil Media Studies," not so much as a discipline, but as a "manner of working with a set of informal practices and bodies of knowledge" which they have characterized as "strategems."[22] They suggest the following possibilities: "Bypass Representation, Exploit Anachronisms, Stimulate Malignancy, Machine the Commonplace, Make the Accidental Essential, Recourse Stratagems, The Rapture of Capture, Sophisticating Machinery, What Is Good For Natural Language is Good for Formal Language, Know Your Data, Liberate Determinism, Inattention Economy, Brains Beyond Language, Keep Your Stratagem Secret As Long As Possible, Take Care of the Symbols, the Sense Will Follow, and The Creativity of Matter." These programmatic statements can be used to counter corporate literature, academic conventions, and other self-satisfied statements about how beneficial "media" can be (but actually aren't in the messy reality of everyday life).

Evil or not, it's time to leave behind academic constraints and open up collective imagination. It's time to cut back conversations on local limitations and see what the common goals are. There are more than enough tools and platforms available (though few know how to use them fluidly). All too often we constrain ourselves according to "their" rules in the naive belief that a positive attitude on our side will enlarge the room for negotiation. In no case is this clearer than when new media theorists, artists, and activists are faced with tight IP rules enforced by academia and the corporate publishing industry. What we see happening are subversive characters blindly signing away all their rights to SAGE, Elsevier Reed, and other giants. Why? With the Open Access movement gaining such momentum, there is cause to wonder when civil disobedience in this area will finally take hold and the cases of micro-resistance (which do happen) reach critical mass. It is time to say "no" to restrictive publishing contracts and organize ourselves. Let's stop complaining and develop another publishing culture, one that is more up-to-speed with the times, and update how we ourselves think about our field. While not completely relinquishing the "brand" of media studies, McKenzie Wark suggests an alternative perspective for locating the developments of the field within the spectrum of history:

> Having to always declare something is over is connected to refusing to historicize. There are two ways of situating media studies historically. One way is to see new media as add-ons or extensions of old media. Start with cinema, for example, and position the new as same-but-different within this space of thought and disciplinary organization. The other way starts with the phenomena before us – games, mobiles, internet – how do they call into being entirely new (long range) genealogies? How do they call us to reject or revise existing histories? It needs to be allied to three methodologies: the conceptual, the ethnographic and the experimental. The mere reading of "texts" does not serve us well at the moment.[23]

Over in New York, McKenzie Wark intends to revolutionize media studies: "I am inclined to think it is an intellectual struggle within that space. The age of infancy is over, yes, and with it our innocence. Positioning an intellectual project is about resources, about picking fights, about finding allies." As part of this dialogue, Toby Miller, chair of Cultural and Media Studies at University California-Riverside, sees media studies dominated by three topics: ownership and control, content, and audiences. "Media Studies 1.0 panics about citizens and consumers as audiences, whereas Media Studies 2.0 celebrates them. I would prefer a panic-free, critical, and internationalist Media Studies 3.0." According to Miller, the old versions of media studies are tied to nativist and imperialist epistemologies that must be transcended. He proposes a Media Studies 3.0 that will blend

> ethnographic, political-economic, and aesthetic analyses in a global and local way, establishing links between the key areas of cultural production around the world (Africa, the Americas, Asia, Europe, and the Middle East) and diasporic/dispossessed communities engaged in their own cultural production (Native peoples, African and Asian diasporas, Latinos, and Middle-Eastern peoples). Media Studies 3.0 needs to be a media-centred version of area studies, with diasporas as important as regions. It must be animated by collective identity and power, by how human subjects are formed and how they experience cultural and social space.[24]

We need a global perspective for media studies as a productive force that goes beyond a mere study of new media's impact in these places. New media should be seen as an integrated system where its users contribute to the vital core of the technology itself. This approach not only needs spiritual support but also needs to be implemented. The humanities perspective, for example, cuts deeper and addresses other registers. The critique here demands full autonomy (from BA to PhD programs, to put it in education-talk), before we can speak again of interdisciplinary collaborations. Another approach would be to develop new organizational forms altogether. What are the tactical resources necessary for contemporary "organized networks," distributed think tanks, and temporary media labs to do their work? Much of the technical infrastructure is already at our disposal – sometimes for free, and in other cases purchased for a handful of hard currency. Even though theory lays the foundation, this path can only be followed through with praxis. It's all about concepts, demos, betas, versions, and meeting face to face, the most precious and expensive part of the operation.

According to German media theorist Florian Cramer, who teaches and researches at the Rotterdam Piet Zwart Institute, it is one of the terrible legacies of media studies to play the prophecy/futurology game. Florian Cramer:

> People like Marshall McLuhan and Norbert Bolz had their side-careers as highly paid media industry advisors with their "visions" of a future communication culture. Media art as it's featured from Ars Electronica in Linz to STRP in Eindhoven still gets away with coloring rabbits or producing expensive, non-working tech art junk at art media labs because it somehow could be the vision of future media (although it never managed to be) and still claims national subsidies.[25]

What we really need, says Cramer, are critical studies of the contemporary uses and cultures of electronic and digital information technology.

Let's not call for Media Studies 2.0, or 3.0, for that matter. We're not talking about a next generation, let alone a mere upgrade of the current institutional set-up. The main players within media studies do not need to be informed about the potentials of Web 2.0; we have to presume they're well aware of the possibilities. This is not the time to put demands on the table of Those Who Rule. What we need to do is reimagine the social modes of philosophical enquiry itself. Too much energy has already been wasted on the question of how "new media" could possibly fit into institutional arrangements. An entire generation has lost the way in a confusing uphill battle through the institutions, while the world's frisky vitality has gone digital. What do we have to show for all this expended energy? Are computers and the internet absorbing so much creative libido that there is little left to change the bricks and mortar in which traditional life took place? What happens if we cultivate more self-awareness amongst new media theorists and practitioners? What happens if we place ourselves as actors in the new media saga and relate to neighboring media technologies in a frank and ultimately sovereign manner?[26]

— 6 —

BLOGGING AFTER THE HYPE: GERMANY, FRANCE, IRAQ

I am tempted to say that we must return to the subject – though not a purely rational Cartesian one. My idea is that the subject is inherently political, in the sense that "subject," to me, denotes a piece of freedom – where you are no longer rooted in some firm substance, you are in an open situation. Today we can no longer simply apply old rules. We are engaged in paradoxes, which offer no immediate way out. In this sense, subjectivity is political.

Slavoj Žižek, interview for *Spiked Online*[1]

Let's praise blogs. As successors of the 1990s internet homepage, weblogs create a unique mix of the private (online diary) and the public (PR-management of the self). Blogs were the software vehicle that turned the internet into a mass media culture beyond the utopian cyberculture of the 1990s. Blogs, and the social networking sites they both feed and pull data from, have made new media mainstream. Bloggers are the digital multitude. The relatively stable number of 150 million blogs that exist (according to 2010 figures), roughly 10 percent of the Net's population, find their unity at the technical level. Blogs zero out the twentieth-century centralized meaning structure found in newspapers, radio, and television by fragmenting audiences and attention. Bloggers are neither journalists nor geeks. More than anything else, they embody Web 2.0 culture.

To study blogs we must understand that it is not enough to measure the output of this or that application. Critical internet studies should instead start with the assumption that media do not merely report but play a key role in the circulation of sentiments. Users are caught in a web of stimuli and feelings that are channeled in specific ways. Every application informs us; it provokes us to say this and not that, and then it shapes and packages these sentiments in a new and different way. We need to develop an awareness about which emotional responses are addressed by the software itself. What social networking sites, MSN, Twitter, blogs, IRC chats, email, Usenet, and web forums have in common is that they are not taming the inner beast. Instead of explicitly "civilizing" its users, the internet lures them into an informal, grey space between public and private.

Some platforms are better at capturing, storing, and sorting human sensory output than others. Once typewriters were considered a precondition for inspiration, provided the writer had access to a (female) secretary to dictate the streams of his unconscious to. Today, the internet creates an endless flow of nervous responses. Email is considered more personal and direct compared to letters written on paper. On Facebook we try to be nice since we're amongst "friends." Blogging, on the other hand, starts off as a solitary exercise that is primarily focused on information processing and reflection, one that only rarely results in social exchanges even when others respond. Building on Nietzsche, who saw that "our writing tools are also working on our thoughts,"[2] we witness that each internet application addresses its very own set of human qualities.

Winer and the Blogging Individual

What makes a blog a blog? The entries are often hastily written personal musings, sculptured around a link or event. In most cases bloggers simply do not have the time, skills, or financial means for proper research. Blogs are not anonymous news sites; they are deeply personal, even if the blogger does not reveal his or her own name. The blog software does a wonderful trick: it constitutes subjectivity. When we blog we become an individual (again). Even if we blog together, we still answer the call of the code to tell something about ourselves as a unique person.

Blog pioneer and RSS feed inventor Dave Winer defines a blog as "the unedited voice of a person." It isn't so much the form or the content; rather it is "the voice" of an individual that characterizes the blog as a distinct media form. "If it was one voice, unedited, not determined by group-think – then it was a blog, no matter what form it took. If it was the result of group-think, with lots of ass-covering and offense avoiding, then it's not."[3] Winer does not believe that blogs are defined by comments from others. "The cool thing about blogs is that while they may be quiet, and it may be hard to find what you're looking for, at least you can say what you think without being shouted down. This makes it possible for unpopular ideas to be expressed. And if you know history, the most important ideas often are the unpopular ones." Whereas social networking sites and email-based mailing-list culture are focused on social networking and (discursive) exchange, blogging, according to Dave Winer, is primarily an act of an introspective individual who reflects on his or her thoughts and impressions. For this US techno-libertarian, blogs are expressions of free speech, of an individualism that believes each is entitled to his or her own opinion and should be brave enough to say it.

Dave Winer's definition is a good example of a particularly raw, Western, heroic individualism. "Me, I like diversity of opinion. I learn from the extremes."[4] The blogger is portrayed as a Western dissident: the loner who begs to differ. But there is nothing particularly courageous about expressing what one thinks on a blog. The medium knows this: what is encouraged and applauded, what gets the comments stirred up and starts a rash of cross-posting, is the outrageous, the beyond the pale, the extreme. It doesn't matter whether anyone actually supports the outrageous point of view – it can be said with zero effort just for jokes or kicks, for hits or attention.

This is why language games about definitions are so important. Winer's description leads us back to an experience at the very beginning of the Web in the late 1990s. What informed blogs was the initial arousal of the developers and early adaptors to go where others hadn't gone before, seeking the edges of ethics, freedom of expression, language, and publishing, and what is commonly accepted. Blogs were the final frontier where you could write whatever was on your mind. Users arriving a decade later rarely have this sensation. They see themselves confronted with an extremely busy social environment and are puzzled about fitting in. The challenge is not what to scream into the well but how to find our way through the busy ant farm called the "blogosphere." Am I a visual person attracted to Tumblr and Flickr, or hooked on the community aspect of blogging as facilitated by, for instance, LiveJournal and SkyBlog, or rather someone obsessed with the social noise on the micro-blogging service Twitter?

Despite the short time it takes to set up a blog and the easy-to-use interfaces, users need time to get accustomed to the rules of the game. Here it is not so much the self-referential moment of sitting down and writing up a story that matters. In Winer's ontology, the essence of the blog experience is the very start of the blog itself. It's not the software or the social buzz but the thrill of creating an account, naming your blog, and choosing a template:

> What's important about blogs is not that people can comment on your ideas. As long as they can start their own blog, there will be no short-age of places to comment. What there is always a shortage of, however, is courage to say the exceptional thing, to be an individual, to stand up for your beliefs, even if they aren't popular.[5]

For Winer, blogging is a brave act because he associates writing with authenticity – unedited and uninfluenced by a group. Somehow, writing is a pure expression of an individual (comments just dilute the purity and risk pushing the author to conform to group-think). Winer's emphasis on authenticity goes back to an old Romantic idea that has lost its currency in postmodern society in favor of repetition, mimesis, and, everyone's favorite, the big Other. Most of what we say and think is repetition of what we've read or heard (and we are aware of this). We are spoken through, rather than being autono-mous subjects creatively producing the new. This isn't bad or nega-tive or something to worry about – we can get over the fetishism of the new and leave that to consumer capitalism. Shifts and altera-tions, changes in ideas and thinking, occur more accidentally and retroactively.

Winer's understanding of authorial voice is in a sense different from the Slovenian philosopher Mladan Dolar, a Lacanian and author of *A Voice and Nothing More*. If we apply Dolar's notion to blogs we could say that the blog voice can emerge as an effect, acci-dentally; it can seep through the writing and not be produced delib-erately via the author's intention. We could think of this as the subjectivity of the blog or the persona of the blog (which has the benefit of bleeding toward impersonation). Winer's mistake could be associating this voice or persona with authenticity and courage. If we follow Dolar, it could be more convincing to associate the voice with the art of creating a persona. Blogging is by default a masquerade; it is impersonation, presentation, and a drive to be seen, present, acknowledged, recognized – perhaps a drive just to be, period.

To further nuance Winer's definition of blogs, we must understand that the blogger's voice also indicates a verbal turn gaining impor-tance in new media. References to Walter Ong and Marshall McLuhan are obvious in this context. Blogs are a digital extension of oral traditions more than they are a new form of writing.[6] Too often, blog postings are judged as pieces of creative writing, whereas they should be seen as recorded conversations (which are then, in the next round, commodified and traded as content). Through blogging, news is transformed from a lecture into a conversation. Blogs echo rumor and gossip, conversations in cafes and bars, on squares and in corridors. They record "the events of the day," as New York University journalism professor Jay Rosen defined blogs. Today's "recordability" of situations is such that we are no longer upset that computers "read" all our moves and expressions (sound, image, text) and "write" them into strings of zeros and ones. In that sense blogs are in accord with the wider trend in which all our movements and activities are being monitored and stored, yet in this case not by some invisible and abstract authority, but by the subjects themselves through recording their everyday life.[7] Much like the SMS language used in mobile phones, blogs "capture" the spoken word of the everyday and should not be judged as a degenerate version of official written languages found in literature, journalism, and academic texts. At first glance, this is a confusing observation. Aren't blogs all about the return of quality writing amongst ordinary citizens? Still, we need to see blogging's informal, unfinished style within a technological trend in which more and more devices are capturing speech, including, paradoxically, keyboards. Not everything that is new is news. What we need to reclaim here is the freedom to unfold untimely activities. Not every recently uploaded file wants to be categorized and colonized in the real-time economy.

As a secondary notation system, blogs should be positioned between officially sanctioned writing in books or newspapers by authors who are spell-checked and copy-edited, and the informal communication of email, text messaging, and, most obviously, chatting on MSN and in other chat rooms. Blogs are one step closer to sanctioned writing in that they are a form of publishing: we add a file to a database once we press the "submit" button. At the same time, this text-based talking to a screen is a personal way of storing communication that we have with ourselves (and with the machine). Chatting is talking, using the written word; whereas we communicate with another person through chats and emails, whom we address in blogs is often less clear. The mainstream media in particular have a hard time understanding the emergence of this new, in-between realm. As a consequence of these misunderstandings, bloggers are qualified as "secondary" participants in a competition they didn't sign up for in the first place.

Blogs are so 2004

Let's face it: the novelty of blog studies that mapped the early terrain is long over. The millions of weblogs that currently exist can no longer be explained by those who pioneered the field. The masses of blogs appearing and disappearing at an ever-increasing rate easily exceed the terms introduced to describe the A-list of American pundits, disaster and event blogs, and political swarms. What once started with the introduction of banners and Google ads ended up with AOL's acquisition of *The Huffington Post*. The trend toward centralized aggregation seems unstoppable worldwide. Given the remaining vastness of the blogosphere, and the variety of uses, engagements, attachments, performances, networks, and content produced through the practice of blogging, the lack of adequate theorization is palpable. The literature, most written between 2004 and 2008, features well-known bloggers and can only emphasize blogging's potential. Hardly any detailed discourse analysis has focused on individual blogs.

Again, the concern here is not with the (potential) relationship to the news industry but with self-expression in personal blogs. How does the unedited voice of the individual relate to the growing tendency facilitated by software to position the blogging subject in a web of users along with their links to documents and multimedia objects? For this, we should describe the blogger as having a "distributed subjectivity." If the blog is part of an existing social network, they are simply nodes created to store material (text, picture, profile). If the link list is absent or indicates that there are standard "elective affinities" with A-list bloggers and news media, we can guess that the blog has a predominantly reflective, introspective style. In the first instance, blogs position our "distributed subjectivity" within clouds of "friends," the latter being within pop media. As blog culture progresses into its second decade, we see increased pressure on the underlying software architecture to move away from the culture of insular retrospection toward this technical positioning of the blogger inside networks, a transition facilitated by search engines (read: Google). From now on, the machine automatically creates social relationships for us; we don't have to do anything ourselves, provided we feed the search engine with personal data. What we perceive as personal, the system has redefined as working for the engine.

Blogs validate and celebrate the personal, individual, and singular. They mobilize the personal as celebrity, championing the individual

100

even as good old liberal bourgeois rights are overwritten by neo-liberal capital and undermined, at least in the US, by enthusiasm for torture, security, and surveillance. In a way, blogs document a change in the status of the personal wherein the personal is both mobilized, and erased or flattened (erased insofar as blogging prioritizes display over introspection, documentation without reflection, and archiving without internalization). The personal that is produced for display uncouples from any supposition of a true or underlying self – that question simply isn't relevant. What matters is what appears. Communicative capitalism is not an identity container. Rather, people produce their identities through networked communications media. The internet is a medium for mass experience, but one that is highly differentiated and singularized. Blogging comes in as the technology of that experience.

That software produces and frames subjectivity and steers the user within its architectures is clear enough. I now want to add an additional layer to blog analysis by asking how mediated subjectivity is itself overdetermined by cultural differences. Go to Japan, for instance, and the trend is toward anonymity, while the US's blogosphere is very much about the cultivation and display of the true self. In other places, blogs are standalone features on web pages; elsewhere they dissolve into chats and rapid-fire social networks where the aesthetic renaissance of tumblr, for instance, emphasizes blogging's visual joys. If blogs play such a crucial role in bridging the internet and society, and spreading Web 2.0 values across the globe, then it is time to go beyond the well-covered US and investigate other blogospheres. I have selected three cases that I feel passionate about, and all three, for various reasons, spill beyond the nation-state borders: Germany, France, and Iraq.

Digression into the German Blogosphere

The great German negative bloggers are long dead and worked with paper: Friedrich Nietzsche, Walter Benjamin, Karl Kraus. Maybe a cheery nihilism prevails in the affirmation of negation and the joyful "rather not" of German blog culture. Many regard blogging as an effective way to grump and grouch – as yet another, though rather blunt, weapon in the arsenal of criticism.[8]

Pit Schultz

Few might have noticed, but Germany's passion for blogging has been remarkably low over the years. With German the most widespread language spoken in Europe and sixth online, this fact needs some explanation. While, according to statistics in mid-2010 that 75 out of 98 million German-speaking users (most of them in Germany, Switzerland, and Austria) were online,[9] estimations of the German blogosphere do not exceed the half-a-million mark. Blogcensus.de counted active German blogs, defined as those with at least a post every six months, and relied on manual inspection. Their February 2008 estimate was 204,500 active blogs. John Yunker of Byte Level Research bets this number is much too low. The German magazine *Focus* claims to have counted approximately 1.1 million German blogs, which, according to Yunker, is instead too high. Yunker:

> Technorati's State of the Blogosphere counted 50 million blogs in 2006 and claims that approximately 1% of blog posts were in German. With the bold assumption that the blogging frequency is the same globally, this would result in approxiately 500,000 blogs in German. This seems to me to be a more realistic estimate, in line with other guestimates of other sources.[10]

Yunker concludes: "In absolute and relative numbers the German blogosphere is very, very small."[11]

Distrust in Numbers

What makes blog software so unattractive to Germans? Put in other terms, is there a techno-cultural tendency or mode of subjectivization within blogging software that German speakers find particularly disagreeable? The answer to this question should tell us something about the character of blogs, not about the ethnographic characteristics of a few continental Europeans. Could this refusal to engage be a collective distrust toward providing authorities with personal data through the mechanism of the user profile? Upon registering a new blog, users freely dispense information about their music preferences, favorite films, and reading lists. Does blog software indeed invite the individual to say more than he or she wants? Or should German users participate in the cult of the celebrity, beef up their biography, and pretend they are an Ich-AG, as self-promoters are called in German (the I Ltd)?

When I contacted author and full-time blogger Oliver Gassner, he stressed distrust in public discourse, both politically and privately, as a likely explanation for the low number of bloggers. History proved to Germans that openly discussing one's point of view can have unforeseen consequences, and restraining from public speech stems from this experience. "Open," in the German context, has the connotation of being unprotected (against intrusions by the security forces or police state). There is also a tendency toward delegation. Professionals such as journalists, academics, and politicians are in charge of public opinion, not ordinary people, who are, rightly or wrongly, considered xenophobic and anti-Semitic. Oliver Gassner: "We're talking about a discipline that you practice in public. Debating is a widely spread practice but remains strictly within the realm of reason. The bottom line is that creativity and individualism are not to be expressed in the public realm." According to German law, a blog needs an "Impressum," where a person with a name and address admits that he or she is the publisher and is responsible for the content. This default device polices the borders of expression and makes them liable for perceived offence, preventing people from saying whatever comes to mind. Companies in Germany are afraid to enter the Web 2.0 era precisely because of such legal issues. Unsurprisingly, this code of conformity does not impress young people, who tend to babble in a seemingly open manner. However, according to Gassner, they are still affected by the legalistic culture in which they were raised.

Instead of trusting the limelight of blogs and social networking profiles, Germans feel safer in groups. This is why online forums are much more popular, though most of these are buried in the "long tail" of the Web. Unlike blogs, forums supply a ready-made audience and provide users with a clear point of entry, and culture of communication. Without creating a scene and laboring at establishing connections, you are already part of a social setting. Forums are not pre-programmed with social graphs ("the global mapping of everybody and how they are related"),[12] and they provide a more protected, anonymous look and feel. Media theorist Stefan Heidenreich calls this predetermined interface the "orchestra effect": expression within closed groups is the preferred option.

Florian Cramer, another Berlin media theorist working in Rotterdam, agrees: "The high profile German bloggers who identify themselves as 'the blogosphere' are caught in a typical German 'Vereinskultur,' or stamp collector mentality. It's no wonder the German blogosphere has the stuffy atmosphere of an old-fashioned Gentlemen's Club. It reminds you of the 1990s German 'hyperfiction' scene, which was just as self-absorbed, provincial and irrelevant."[13] In Germany, people are hesitant to express themselves in public using their own name and prefer to troll under pseudonyms. Does this tendency signal a subversive underdog mentality, or is it an instance of the perpetual fear of disclosure? Whatever the case, such user practices constitute new media's articulation of privacy law battles in Germany. As a continuation of the early 1980s census boycott movement, these choices reiterate the point that authorities are not to be trusted. Freedom of information in the German context, says Cramer, translates as the right to "prefer not to have" a public identity. This was proven in 2010 with the massive withdrawal from Google Street View, when Google had to process 300,000 requests to blur houses and apartments in Germany.

It's no wonder, then, that German blogs are embedded in forums (opinions) on the one hand, and news sites (information) on the other. When blogs work well, they continue the "extended conversation" of Usenet and web forums, though in a more decentralized and private manner. Instead of registering a response via the "reply" function, they adopt the link. With the correct algorithms, users can reassemble fragmented, interlinked posts, and the comment threads of singularly authored blogs into a subject-based forum format. At techmeme.com and its German epigone rivva.de, the statistical interlinkages around major headlines and cascading topics merely resemble a decentralized discussion forum.

The Frankfurt media theorist Verena Kuni, who tracks special interest blogs on art, media culture, science, video, and games, particularly from Switzerland, realizes that blog cultures in different countries vary enormously, even within the same language. What characterizes Germany, says Kuni, is the

> absence of the culture of sharing, a lack of openness when it comes to open publishing and knowledge sharing. The mistrust in the commons is real. These are not only personal observations. Sociologists looking at cultural sponsoring came to similar conclusions. This situation is made worse by a general fear to break the law in terms of copyright when reusing creative material of others.[14]

Anti-Nationalist Webs

Germans seem hesitant to establish a national culture, perhaps partly due to their awareness of the cultural attitudes around the "ugly German." The "anti-German" impulse even resonates in the "rational" business culture. Sure, there is a national market, but cultural producers prefer to identify themselves with their own region or city or to relate to international influences. Take this as a variation of Heimat-cosmopolitanism for creative workers. This mix of hyper-local village-like interrelations and international market orientation is typical of new creative industries such as electronic music, archi-tecture, and visual arts. The anti-national sentiment in turn slows down the emergence of an inward-linking German-language blog culture. Even if a branch of people specialize in "German jobs," they perceive themselves working with a local audience embedded within a European or global diaspora of German speakers. With often-specialized content, cultural producers must address an international niche audience out of economic necessity. In Berlin's start-ups and software companies, one will find that a good 20–50 percent of workers are non-German. On the other hand, hesitation toward a *Krautnet* should take into account small and medium German enter-prises, specialized, "anonymous" industrial culture, most of which you have never heard of because they produce the hidden elements and building blocks of system infrastructures. This "opacity" is shared by the arcane SAP enterprise software. SAP is known for the clumsy interfaces of its supply-chain software for supermarkets and airlines; it is the largest European software enterprise, and the third largest in the world, with headquarters in Walldorf, Germany.

Blogging follows a post-structuralist impulse. In this case the impulse is more American than French: career-oriented and ego-centred. Nevertheless, blogs display the regime of soft network power predicated on decentralization and heterogeneity to establish a spe-cific kind of hegemony, namely a market-oriented, competitive pro-duction of subjectivity. In the case of Germany, the rule of blogging is more Deleuzian: the "I prefer not to" mode. German users mostly contribute to the international traffic as readers only. US blogs serve as their primary source material since they typically appear in search-engine queries and are often employed as references. For German users, blogs are a mostly "passive" and indirect experience, and thus hold an affinity with the other US cultural products they consume. While German films are noticeably different from their Hollywood counterparts, it is quite difficult to adapt blog software. With closed parameters of customization, blogs prevent users from inflecting cul-tural difference and instead enforce a technics that reproduce the culture of origin. Whoever said that media-cultural imperialism was an outmoded condition?

The language setting of search engines is another foundational element of a linguistic ghetto. Many find it annoying that Google.de automatically searches in German. Users only need this for local searches of addresses, shops, and the like. It would be interesting to find out how many users actually employ the German language setting. Why aren't more German blogs in English? And why isn't there a more specialized German-speaking blogosphere? The answer could lie in blogs such as Riesenmaschine, Spreeblick, Netzpolitik, and Carta. These sites are deeply interwoven with broadcast media, aim at mainstream culture, and do not require specialized internet knowledge. Software alone is not at fault for poorly designed blogs.

The geographic diversity of German identity, the small scale of its regionalism, and its insider scenes, do not make blogs' open publishing approach an attractive option. Experience shows that if you start writing on a national level you quickly turn into an official figure, targeting a specific, yet large, media market. In response to this immanent danger (or opportunity, if you like), you will find social networks and forum culture fiercely reproducing the idea of hyper-locality, of cultural identity in a more or less decentralized federal state, thriving on the insider trading of events, language, jokes, and cult items.

High vs Low

Blogs also suffer from a lack of prestige, with no social pressure or economic incentive to create a thriving blog culture. There is a certain discursive German linguistic culture that relies on the polarity of authoritative texts and lengthy debates. The "light" and subjective-journalistic blog style simply does not resonate well with German textuality – which could be why, according to Florian Cramer, German blogs and German newspapers, particularly the cultural supplements called *feuilletons*, are in a mutual deadlock. The classic German cultural supplements are still hesitant to enter the blogosphere. The younger generation of the commentariat, insofar as they are commercially successful, run magazines such as *Monoton* or *Vanity Fair* and leave news writing to freelance academics desiring to establish themselves as public intellectuals.

Florian Cramer:

Papers like the *Frankfurter Allgemeine Zeitung* run rants against the internet and, particularly, blogging almost every day, blaming them for the doom of Western civilization, while the high profile German bloggers do almost nothing else but conversely criticise those rants, making

increasingly hollow promises of a citizen-journalism and thereby seriously buying into the Web 2.0 crap as a social movement.[15]

Cramer is unable to recall any interesting German blog at the moment:

> A reason for this is also that some German print publishers – above
> all, Heise with its heise.de and Telepolis website (plus associated dis-
> cussion forums), but also to a minor extent Spiegel Online, Netzeitung
> and Die Zeit – are doing a rather professional, and in the case of Heise,
> even decent job on the internet. As a result, there is less demand for
> bloggers to fill in niches.[16]

German print publishers have already integrated the German *blog-
dorf* prominent figures like Mercedes Bunz (Tagesspiegel Online),
Katharina Borchert (editor of Der Westen), and Katrin Bauerfeind,
the former moderator of the Videoblog Ehrensenf, who now moderates television shows.

The German blogosphere also places less emphasis on search and
algorithms and more on the cooperative manual labor of professional
editors. Perlentaucher.de, the daily aggregator of cultural supplements founded by two former journalists of the *Tageszeitung* newspaper, is a good example. Unlike Google News, which gives the
impression of being computer-generated, Perlentaucher provides the
reader with small, human-compiled reviews of the cultural supplements from German newspapers. This site, which usually arrives as
a daily electronic newsletter, looks almost like a paper-based equivalent of a well-organized RSS feed.

I asked media critic Mercedes Bunz, once editor of the Berlin
techno magazine *DE:BUG*, former chief of the daily newspaper
website *Tagesspiegel*, and now at the *Guardian*, what she liked about
German blogs:

> Perhaps not in quantity, but through quality, the German blogosphere
> strives to high standards, from the media watch blogs of Stefan Nig-
> gemeier[17] to the wonderful poetic observations of "Klage" written by
> the author Rainald Goetz[18] to the Hitler-Blog[19] of the young journalist
> Daniel Erk, to name but just a few. The postings of these blogs are
> awake and full of surprising observations, often initiating debates that
> later land in the feuilletons of German newspapers.

Still, the reputation of blogs is grossly underestimated in German
public opinion. Why? Mercedes Bunz:

107

Blogs are not considered as having a high cultural value because they are technology-focused. In Germany technology has a severe problem. Ever since the cultural theory of the Frankfurt School heavily influenced German thinking after the Second World War technology is suspect: it is the opposite of culture and authenticity. The lame debates about blogs follow exactly this structure. While journalism thrives for the ideal of the truth, blogging is only about being narcissistic, proclaiming rumors, in a desperate attempt for attention.

Toward German NetCulture

Like many other experts, Pit Schultz's analytical technique consists of observing and "studying." A freelance net critic, radio-maker, and programmer, Schultz is co-founder of nettime and a passionate Web 2.0 watcher. If you really want to join the game of scholarly legitimacy, you need to publish in English, an obligation that scientific publishing has long been aware of. Only then do you have any chance of becoming a registered expert in the English-centered economy of Net discourse. For Pit, this is a rather boring option. In Germany, research on network cultures and new media is predictably small. Nonetheless, at the level of popular culture, there is a "collective intelligence" involved in the production of what you could call the "German Web." Their speciality is niche applications, software, and infrastructure, localized for German speakers. This culture of tinkering expresses itself in "barcamps" and at other events with an engaged mentality that combine mainstream culture, politics, and business with geek-friendliness, all under the banner of Berlin's accessible image as the ultimate, cool low-cost destination for cultural tourism and clubbing.

The organizers of re:publica, the annual German blogger conference that has taken place in Berlin since April 2007, well understood the productive (yet incestuous) dialectics between established media and bloggers. Unlike Loïc Le Meur's LeWeb conferences in Paris ("#1 European Internet Event"), which solely attract business start-up crowds (attracting 3,000 plus visitors), re:publica is cultural in focus and does not market itself outside of the German-speaking world. The conference's successful, albeit slightly unfocused, formula mainstreams social media and deflects focus from hackers' issues, as showcased at the annual Chaos Computer Club Congress a few months earlier – though both events share a civil freedom agenda. Supported by both corporate sponsors and federal agencies, re:publica drew

2,500 visitors in 2010, though its bloggers-only label may as well be dropped.

Geared toward techno-cultural acceptance and widespread adoption, activities such as re:publica follow rather than define computer culture, Pit Schultz explains. The playing field for blog conferences and new media festivals increases if we zoom out to cultural production and pop culture in general, such as music, television, fashion, and popular writing. At this level, blogs in Germany play a surprisingly small role, even if they strive to be mainstream. The internet, new media, and computer culture are all still perceived by traditional German media as the domains of hobbyists, specialists, hackers, geeks, and artists, despite efforts at popularizing techno-culture. Even standard German blogger discourse has no interest in the insider topics of the Chaos Computer Club hackers' network, the media art of Transmediale, the established "minor" cultures in electronic music, the club scene, or the creative industry represented by Ableton/Native Instruments. Reports on *DE:BUG* magazine or Spex, or designers/ architects such as Graft, are nowhere to be found. Instead, TV culture and news sites, like Spiegel Online, dominate attention, creating a web sphere where those hesitant about their English end up.

Yet the idea of specialists mediating and studying subcultures that create "Net culture" or "media art" as a niche product has passed its use-by date. A decade after dot.com mania, the Web is now mainstream and indistinguishable from pop culture. In that sense there is no future for a "blogosphere" as a counter-culture distinguishing itself from commercial publishing. Just look at the engagement of German publishing houses in "Web 2.0." One of them, Holtzbrinck, bought StudiVZ, the German Facebook back in January 2007.

Despite these counter-forces, the German blogosphere nonetheless plays its own successful version of the Habermasian "public sphere" game. An example is the online activism and debate regarding new legal proposals on surveillance and online privacy, which were finally rejected by the federal constitutional court – partly because of heavy resistance as countless blogs and websites joined the campaign. The initiators and primary mobilizers were not considered "prominent leading figures." Chaos Computer Club and Netzpolitik are rather anonymous and collaborative ventures, acting below the radar, with the occasional brilliant publicity hack delivering an intelligent subversion of the "conversation" on surveillance and privacy. In the end the campaign aimed for recognition by mainstream media, which the handful of A-list bloggers eventually obtained, as actions, articles, and evening news features contributed to this strategy. While this doesn't mean there were no key names or cult of the author, the campaign resisted the celebrity logic. Writer Rainald Goetz, who, in the late nineties, wrote his *Abfall für alle* (*Garbage for All*) online diary, perhaps exemplifies how blogs could function in Germany. His current blog (funded by a big print magazine) celebrates Goetz's inability to write and amplifies his disgust about Germany's stagnant cultural climate.[20]

Germany's media culture is struggling to position blogs and Web 2.0 within the wider media landscape. Alternative projects and "citizen-journalism" do not reach a critical mass, while old media is quick to portray the blogosphere derisively. The internet doesn't integrate well into a culture obsessed with rules and regulations. The vast archives of the German public radio and television, for instance, cannot be accessed online. The federal and state laws are simply too complex – and altering them will take years, if not decades. On April 20, 2008, the *Süddeutsche* newspaper published a provocative article entitled "Local Party Politics instead of Blogs," in which Simon Feldmer complained about the absence of an engaged political blogger scene.[21] He claimed politicians have no clue regarding the internet, and bloggers speak only to their constituencies, and asked where are Germany's Daily Kos, Huffington Post bloggers, or Moveon.org? The political parties lack a basic internet strategy, says Feldmer. The German blogosphere was up in arms about the article, but this remonstrance only stresses the intimate, non-productive relationship between news media and blogs, yet another example of Germany's sophisticated culture of stagnation.

Celebrating the French Blogosphere

France is one of the leading "blogging" countries. According to the *International Herald Tribune*, "the French distinguish themselves, both statistically and anecdotally, ahead of Germans, Britons and even Americans in their obsession with blogs, the personal and public journals of the internet age."[22] Their relatively late internet adoption, compared to their early use of minitel and CD-ROMs, could be a reason. Instead of learning the mark-up language HTM, or even the command line operating system UNIX, the French skipped the homepage cult and immediately began blogs. A perceived distrust of printed media, radio, and television could be another reason, along with their familiarity with informal, expressive forms of communication. "It is clear that in France we have very large egos and love to speak about ourselves," said Loïc Le Meur, a pioneer French (video) blogger, LeWeb owner and dot.com enterpreneur.[23]

In mid-2006 CRM Metrix conducted a survey and found that over a quarter of French internet users visit a blog at least once a month; about 20 percent post comments on a blog; around 5 percent have created a blog, and the top three types of blogs in terms of popularity were news, music, and leisure. Blogs are first and foremost user-friendly applications; they are not French in nature, or Anglo-Saxon for that matter. Nonetheless, Language Log blogger noted:

> no one was paying any heed to the decision of *La Commission générale de terminologie et de néologie* at the French Ministry of Culture, back in the spring of 2005, that the correct French word for *blog* is "bloc-notes" (note pad), or "bloc" for those in a hurry. More pragmatically, Canadians have chosen to speak about "blogues" as a French alternative to English. In all the newspapers, as well as in the blogs themselves, the blogs are just "blogs."[24]

It's a quintessential blogging tendency to indulge in national stereotypes. In the same *Herald Tribune* article, Laurent Florès, the French-born, New York-based chief executive of CRM Metrix, stated: "French blogs are noticeably longer, more critical, more negative, more egocentric and more provocative than their US counterparts."[25] Loïc Le Meur: "The French have a long tradition of expressing themselves. We're the country of the revolution, look at how many cafés are full of people discussing politics and how many strikes we have. Blogs are a great way for the French to have an influence, they understood that."[26]

Economist Yann Moulier Boutang works at the University of Technology of Compiègne and is editor of the *Multitudes* magazine. He compares the French propensity toward blogs as a well-known indicator of sociability, or the number of associations to which the French are affiliated, which is the highest in the world. "What is called 'civil society' (unions, corporations, local authorities, political parties) is weak and State power is Jacobinist and centralised, much like the Roman Catholic Church. Before the digital era, associations were, and still are, perceived as a place for people to escape the institutional sphere." Users choose blogs, claims Moulier Boutang, because chats and forums were exhausting and did not provide a common space. A network of blogs flourished through syndication and links in a country where alternative places such as squats, cyber cafes, and bookshops, so frequent in Northern Europe, are underdeveloped. Yann Moulier Boutang:

as soon as journalists and politicians discovered that the blog sphere was growing exponentially they occupied the field. The newspapers immediately saw what this could bring them since the number of sold copies was going down steadily. A little later journalists opened their own blogs and newspapers integrated blogs in their websites.[27]

Paris philosopher Paul Mathias counters that there is indeed a tradition of gathering in France at the famous "bistrot" where rural and urban citizens congregate several times a day to discuss local and national issues:

> Think of the French "sacralization" of lunch time – people leave every-thing they do to eat, preferably in groups. I am thus inclined to believe that the success of blogs in France is not due to an alternative to the lack of places where to gather, but rather as a technological implemen-tation of very old cultural patterns, the famous French "crabby temper."[28]

In September 2007, Christophe Druaux published a "subjective map" of the francophone blogosphere.[29] Druaux put the blogs in categories such as youth, media, technorati, art, and women. The work was conducted entirely by hand. Christophe Druaux:

> On a global scale there is no reliable method to estimate the size of the blogosphere. I noticed that Technorati favours sites that are popular amongst bloggers, for instance those about marketing, geeks, techno, and Web 2.0. Only those that have a blog can link to another blog. I wanted to find a complementary evaluation method to bring out those blogs that have been forgotten in the statistics. I chose to focus on published comments. This formula of evaluation is more complex as it involves the frequency of blog postings and weighs them. If you publish three blog posts a day and get 100 comments per post it is not the same as having 100 comments on one blog post a week.[30]

Druaux finds that the French are amongst the most dedicated blog-ging internauts (according to the amounts of inhabitants). In France, the mainstream media cites blogs on a daily basis. Journalists do not hesitate to visit blogs for inspiration. In the same email interview, Christoph Druaux said:

> it might also be that blogs are the perfect vehicles for the grumpy temperament of the French that feeds the debates and in turn pushes up the stats. Another character of French blogs could be that blogs about cooking and comic books are amongst the most popular, both

in terms of the numbers of blogs and visitors. They are even published as books.

Skyrock is one of Europe's largest Web 2.0 platforms. Even though it is known outside France as a "social networking" website, this large collection of interrelated blogs certainly qualifies as a blog service. Skyblog, as it was first called, started out in 2002 as a blog server for the listener community of the French Skyrock FM radio station, founded in 1986 to target 15–25 year olds. Skyrock, the "Free People Network," is a simple blog service with advertisements that began syndicating blogs in March 2007. In May 2007, after abandoning the Skyblog.com brand, Skyrock.com launched as a full-scale social network,[31] an interesting case of how the blogosphere literally blends in with the social media paradigm. With the slogan "blog, profile, chat," Skyrock invites listeners to sign up, log in, chat, use its messenger and free ads service, or search profiles and leave comments (*lâcher vos com*). When I visited the site in February 2008, there were 5,275,173 profiles available with 14,784 girls and 17,330 guys online. Skyrock is now the most visited site in France with 160 million siteviews a month. Much like other social networking sites such as MySpace, it invites its users to "personalize the skin of your blog."

Skyrock dominates the French-speaking blogopelago. According to Wikipedia, people contest its status as a real weblog service because "Skybloggers" often use their account to publish photos, videos, and links without commenting. The majority of Skybloggers use the cryptic SMS language – known from cell phones, web forums, and chats – in their entries. For instance, they will spell "j'ai un chien" as "G 1 chi1." Skyrock is the French version of MySpace, LiveJournal, and Xanga, ranking as the twentieth most popular website globally, according to the global web-traffic ranking site Alexa. Skyrock Blog is also very popular in Quebec, Switzerland, Belgium, Morocco, and other French-speaking communities. The Skyrock blog platform is also available in English, German, Dutch, Italian, Portuguese, and Spanish.

According to Druaux, Skyblogs are actual blogs, but they remain situated within the context of a popular youth radio station. This explains why most users are of the same age and share the same interests (music, dance, cinema, and dating). A teenager blogging outside of Skyrock would be as lost and isolated as the adult running a Skyblog on literature. Says Druaux: "I didn't want to include sky-blogs on my map because they already occupy 75% of the blogs on

113

the map. To do it thoroughly one would have to make a map exclusively dedicated to Skyrock blogs."

I also contacted Laurence Allard of the University of Lille (France), author of *Mythologie du Portable*,[32] who analyzes wikis and blogs. In response to a few questions I sent her, she wrote:

> Skyrock was one of the first sources to give insights in the living conditions of migrants, out in the suburbs. Rap and R&B are popular genres on Skyrock radio. We should read the massive skyblog culture in the spirit of Paul Gilroy's study *The Black Atlantic*. We have to understand the way people are represented in rap music, both through lyrics and performance. This all made it possible for children and grandchildren of migrants living in poor suburbs to feel at home on Skyrock. There is a positive identification here, even though most French intellectuals have no idea how Anglo-Saxon post-colonial theory and cultural studies describe this relation between media, popular culture and identity. ... If there's something like a "French" blogosphere, it is closely tied to the French post-colonial situation in which there is no decision made between universalism and communitarianism, the two sides of the same problem. Skyrock blogs represent a "third space" as described by Homi Bhabha in his book *The Location of Culture*.[33]

At the time of the (mediatized) *banlieue* riots of November 2005, the Skyrock blogs became an interesting object of study revealing how the televised images of the riots were debated by this group. Allard:

> Skyrock became a place for discussion, but also for spreading rumors, inside a closed community, moderated by the 'skycops' team. Because syndication of content at the time wasn't possible yet, the Skyrock moderators were able to censor articles and comments. Nowadays users are much more in direct contact, but late 2005 many blogs were brutally deactivated.

In total, around 10 blogs a day were deleted and 6,500 comments reported to the police.

Allard, writing together with Olivier Blondeau, describes the conversations as "game talk."[34] The young people have a game literacy that implies they can playfully combine and switch between different platforms. Besides popular computer games there are the "serious games" that mix fiction and reality in a more subtle way.[35] Blog talk should be put in this context. The playful chatting should be seen as a product of a "detraditionalized society." What bloggers in this "expressive era" show is their "stylized existence." The compiled subjects display their very own *ars recombinare*, mixing MTV video fragments and celebrity iconography with pictures of themselves and friends taken with their mobile phones. Identity is not merely a question of ethnicity, language, and statehood, but is enriched and distributed by a fluid data collection, taken from games, music, television, and the internet. The heterogeneous identity is not merely fragmented but gives people the very possibility to easily connect to others. If identity elements are taken from the large but limited pool that pop culture provides us, it becomes easy to connect and create networks. This could be a reason for Skyblogs' huge success. Groups can quickly take shape around specific interests or events such as the November 2005 riots.

In a variation of Gayatri Spivak, Laurence Allard asks: "La racaille peut-elle parler?" ("can the rabble speak?"). Then-minister of the interior Nicolas Sarkozy used the derogative term "rabble" to stigmatize the rioting youth as scum that ought to be removed with high-pressure nozzles. We could clarify this: can the rabble speak through individual channels provided by a commercial media outlet? The "digital rabble" chatting on their Skyblogs are in a "do-it-yourself" opposition to the traditional media structures, in that they occupy and cultivate the blogs in order to engage in their own conversations. For Paul Mathias, this opposition between traditional, alienating media structures and liberating blog technologies is rather simplistic. "I would rather interpret the switch from traditional to networked media as an internalization of alienating processes. People are not alienated by pilot-driven machines like the 'anchor' of a TV network. They are alienated by self-driven computer programs."[36]

Demise of the Iraqi Blogosphere

The rise of the Iraqi blogosphere coincided with the "war on terror" after 9/11 and the US-led invasion in Afghanistan and Iraq. Many would have heard the word "blog" for the first time in the context of news reports about an anonymous blogger named Salam Pax, who first started writing personal entries in September 2002 under the regime of Sadam Hussein. In his English-language blog, Salam discussed the war, his friends, disappearances of people under the government of Saddam Hussein, and his work as a translator for a journalist. Salam Pax is arguably not only the first Iraqi blogger; he is also the role model and faithful figure in the story about the Iraqi bloggers in general. After a brief career as an international media star in the aftermath of the March 2003 invasion, Salam Pax discontinued his blog, then started another one and, bit by bit, Salam al-Janabi (his real name) disappeared to become one of the many knowledge migrants in the greater London area.

Salam Pax was part of a network of friends such as Abdul Ahad and Raed Jarrer, who were also first-hour bloggers. There was also Zeyad Kasin with his blog *Healing Iraq*, which still exists with the motto: "It is useless to attempt to reason a man out of what he was never reasoned into" (quoting Jonathan Swift). His younger brother also started a blog and during the play back of a Cat Stevens song, the music was interrupted by bullets – a blog posting many will not easily forget.[37] Another noteworthy blogger is Riverbend, *Girl Blog from Iraq*, a female computer nerd whose well-written postings in English were collected in two volumes and also adapted into a theater play.[38] Even though Salam Pax was in contact with her at the very beginning, up to this day her identity has remained a well-kept secret. She stopped blogging after she and her family fled to Syria in late 2007.

These blogs and others should be seen as the result of a language restriction; most international observers do not read Arabic and depend on the English language. This is the general situation even for international aggregation sites such as the irregular *Iraqi Blog Count*, initiated in Melbourne. Exceptions may be *Niqash*, a German-sponsored English-Arabic journalism website that specializes in international exchanges and has no specific focus on blogs, and *Global Voices*, where we can read English summaries of the Iraqi blogosphere.[39]

Writing about Iraqi blogs and the situation in Iraq after 2003 can easily make you depressed. After the extremely bloody 2006–07 period, the slightly calmer 2007–08 years showed a decline in car bombs and civilian deaths, but without a political solution in sight. The election of Barack Obama and the partial withdrawal of foreign troops in 2009–10 put the situation off the global news agenda. Only occasionally did we hear reports about never-ending coalition talks led by Prime Minister Nuri al-Maliki. Even now, it may be too early to write the history of the Iraqi wartime blogs. Let's anyway avoid reading the state of the blogs as a 1:1 mirror of the street violence. We should not forget the resilience, irony, and humor of Iraqi bloggers. It is this vital energy that makes reading and supporting these blogs worthwhile.

This case study tells the story of the daily (manual) aggregator Streamtime, a solidarity campaign from Amsterdam, edited by the Dutch investigative journalist Cecile Landman and initiated by radio activist Jo van der Spek, with technical support by FLOSS activist and artist Jaromil. Streamtime started off in early 2004 as a combined Web-radio-meets-free-software initiative, which over time became an international support campaign for Iraqi bloggers. Streamtime described itself as a "loose network of media activists dedicated to assist local media to get connected. We use old and new media for the production of content and networks in the fields of media, arts, culture and activism in crisis areas like Iraq."[40] Differing from the typically dry professionalism of NGOs, Streamtime adopted a poetic strategy. "Streamtime is first of all a gesture of solidarity: it may take the form of a campaign, a work of collaborative art, a current of unheard sounds, unspeakable words and unseen imaginations."

In retrospect, the first year after the 2003 invasion looked calm, even promising – particularly with regards to the media: the internet was becoming widely available, the print press blossomed, and there were plenty of international exchanges at the civil society level inside Iraq. This changed in the spring of 2004 when insurgency intensified with the (random) violence of the US troops searching for "terrorists," coinciding with the release of the Abu Ghraib torture pictures. This is the moment that Streamtime was launched (June 2004). It became clear that the recently gained media freedom was under pressure. Journalists were being kidnapped and killed. It was no longer safe for foreigners to visit the country. The first period of the invasion and subsequent protests against occupation were coming to a close. The dynamic became more violent. At first there were no noticeably significant drops in the blog population or postings. Then insurgent attacks increased in 2005 with 34,131 recorded incidents, compared to a total of 26,496 in the previous year.

In an interview with me from 2006, Cecile Landman described her daily exchanges with the Iraqi blogosphere as follows:

> When I first joined Streamtime in 2004 I followed a lot of Iraqi blogs and, more significantly, their comment sections. That seemed the place where it all happened back then. Comments on one posting could run into the hundreds. Daily. Or to be more precise: nightly. What was most striking were the violent tones and attitudes in those debates. I was flabbergasted, and at the same time most fascinated. Also horrified. I started to mingle and join these discussions, with the aim to promote Streamtime, get involved and make some waves. I stopped doing that, because most of the time this mode of interaction gave the feeling of being smashed on the head with a baseball bat. "It's masochism," Iraqi Raed Jarrar and his Iranian girlfriend Niki, both bloggers, said to me, when they visited Amsterdam in November 2004. However, I learned a lot from the comment sections of the blogs; and from there

117

I followed a lot of links, of which 75% were not interesting but the rest turned out to be useful.[41]

Contacts from the early days included Abu Khaleel (also known under his real name Ibrahim M. Al-Shawi), who ran two blogs, Iraqi Letters and A Glimpse of Iraq. Similar to Salam Pax and Riverbend, he also brought his blog postings together in a book that he self-published, using the Lulu print-on-demand website. The Iraqi Linux Group played another important role in the early days. They had already managed to break through the communication barriers during Saddam Hussein's reign, and though they had no direct connections with the storytelling bloggers, they were first and foremost the technicians who knitted together the infrastructure.

After 2004, the fragility of the Iraqi blogosphere became obvious. If we move to early 2006, we have to remember the publishing of the "Danish Mohammed-cartoons," a highly discussed subject on Iraqi blogs, where it was simultaneously debated if it should be discussed in the first place. Many bloggers in or from Iraq and Afghanistan and elsewhere wrote about the "Danish cartoons" with a lot of humor. Iraqi Konfused Kid wrote about the "Mohammed vs. Laudrup" case and fought Danish butter in his fridge. Saudi blogger The Religious Policeman wrote hilarious posts and created a monitor for "Muslim-offence levels."

The cartoon posts then intermingled with news about the bomb-blasted Askariyah shrine in Samarra on February 22, 2006, the incident that silenced the ongoing discussion over whether a civil war was yet being fought. This day would signal a harmful turning point for the US occupation – and also for the Iraqi bloggers. According to Iraq Body Count, deaths per day from gunfire and execution rose from 27 in 2005 to 56 in 2006. The figure of civilians killed rose to its highest level in 2006, approximately 26,000, then around 23,000 in 2007, with a total of over 100,000 civilians killed in the 2003 to 2010 period.[42]

At his Informed Comment blog, quoted on the Streamtime site, Professor Juan Cole summarized the wild mix of ferocious facts of that fateful day in an entry titled "Shiite Protests Roil Iraq":

The day started out with a protest by ten thousand people in the Shiite holy city of Karbala, against the Danish caricatures of the Prophet Muhammad. These days, Shiites are weeping, mourning and flagellating in commemoration of the martyrdom of the Prophet's grandson, Imam Husayn. So it is an emotional time in the ritual calendar when

118

feelings can easily be whipped up about issues like insults to the Prophet. An anti-Danish demonstration in Karbala is a surrogate for anti-American and anti-occupation sentiment. The US won't be able to stay in Iraq without increasing trouble of this sort.

Earlier that same day, guerrillas set off a bomb in a Shiite corner of the mostly Sunni Arab Dura quarter of Baghdad, killing 22 and wounding 28. Another nine were killed in violent incidents that day around Iraq. The attacks, said Cole, were "manifestations of an unconventional civil war." Then the day's real disaster struck. Militants blew up the domed Shiite Askariyah shrine in Samarra.

Average Iraqi blogged that day:

> I believe that the reason for such an attack is an attempt to stir up civil war, between the Shias and Sunnis. In addition, of course, Al-Sadr is not helping at all. His militias are already calling for revenge, and raiding Sunni mosques. Someone should tell him that Sunnis condemned these attacks, and that no one has claimed responsibility yet, why should he presume it is Sunnis.

Everyone was frightened. There were several more Iraqi blogposts about the bombing of the shrine, each one's tone heavy as lead. Average Iraqi stopped blogging soon after and ultimately left Iraq.

Blog posts and photos from Baghdad then began to testify about the "Men in Black," of whom Konfused Kid wrote: "Events have culminated in the emergence of the Men in Black with torn slippers driving pickups, who are purportedly Mahdi's army, but Moqtada Sadr denied their allegiance, the Men in Black have taken numerous mosques around the capital." An article in *The Independent*, dated March 6, 2006, by Patrick Cockburn, was titled "And Now Come the Death Squads." I could go on quoting the Streamtime site. Indeed the turbulent, ongoing "history making" of early 2006 faded away slowly, with constant heavy assault and numerous dead. The Iraqi history of daily terror became too much. A recurring subject in blogposts was the ever-growing exhaustion itself, from the continuous flow of bombs, killings, kidnappings, death-squads, electricity and petrol shortages, to the overall political idiocy with its immense mortal consequences.

So why haven't we heard much from the Iraqi bloggers since 2007? Only a few bloggers remained in Baghdad and Mosul and continued blogging, such as Sunshine in Mosul, a girl aged 15, and her mother. Or the very active Last-of-Iraqis in Baghdad, who gave several accounts of being so close to explosions that only a matter of seconds and meters prevented him from typing any more. A snapshot of post titles on the Streamtime site in late 2007 read: "US military dealings with Sunni Awakening movements; Civilians killed, wounded, in Turkish cross-border shelling; A small Eid-campaign for Iraqi refugees; Afghanistan: Foreign Troops Accused in Helmand Raid Massacre; F**k Alqaeda F**k Almahdy army F**k anyone responsible."[43]

The ongoing daily violence was so overwhelming that it's more than amazing that Iraqi bloggers still had the courage and energy to write down what happened around them. Streamtime was not alone; the project Alive in Baghdad brought weekly updates with original video content from Iraq, and sometimes from Syria or Jordan. Some Americans supported and trained local Iraqis in filming and editing. One of them was shot in Baghdad, in what looked like an execution in his own house where he was alone until the Iraqi National Guard "knocked" on his door, just before midnight. After they went away, at around 3 a.m., Ali Shafeya was found by his neighbors, shot with 31 bullets.

To continue blogging amidst all the attacks must have been an intense and exhausting but also numbing experience. The list of people who died in these bloggers' immediate vicinity could only have continued to increase. We all too easily forget the horrendous events that happened in Iraq because they went on and on. Cecile Landman:

> The level of ongoing violence is numbing, and incomprehensible, for us "outsiders," and for the people inside Iraq even more so. There's a lot of "volume" in the news on Iraq, but that did not necessarily pair with the quality-question. What is also a constant factor, time and time again stated in several reports, is that "the Iraqi person" remains (still) close to non-existent in the voluminous (and often mainly military) news about Iraq.

Chats and chat rooms played an important role in the Streamtime project. But, as blog readers, we only see the selected entries that Cecile chose to cover. Cecile:

> Without the chats with the bloggers I would never ever have been able to develop my knowledge about Iraq, or Streamtime as a contact network, and the special kind of Iraq-war-blog-archive that Stream-time has become too. My first chats with Iraqi bloggers date back to the end of 2004 and the beginning of 2005. Since the end of 2005 an Afghan blogger knocked on my chatdoor too. It is "normal" journal-ism as far as that exists. Journalists most of the time know more about

120

a subject than what can be mentioned in an article. This goes for blog-posts too. And journalists chat, or telephone with their editor about their subject, and the bloggers chat with me and others. So there's a lot more information behind what's being published. And in some cases I edit posts in English, which happens "behind the chat-doors" and before a post is published. I edit the English in a rough way for I don't want to change the tone of the post. Many times while chatting I am pointed to specific posts, and sometimes I post parts from chats on the site, never ever without asking permission to the person at stake though.

Did the writing style of Iraqi blogs change over the years? Cecile:

The quality of the writings on Iraqi blogs lowered, which is partly because the top quality "natural-born-blogger" Salam Pax stopped blogging about Iraq. Others with a more journalistic focus continued, but most of them went to study journalism in the USA, which eventually changed their focus on Iraq. Others blogged from Jordan or other places in the Middle East, but lost subjects to write about, which on the other hand made their blogs more personal. Blogging from Damascus comes with other troubles, like Google's blogger.com service being blocked. This means when you're in Syria you can't read Iraqi – or other – blogs. And you can't update your own blog. Outside Iraq there was more possibility to focus on their personal life. Taking into perspective the huge numbers of Iraqi refugees, it would have been a good idea if an exile bloggers scene would have established, but that didn't happen.

By mid-2009, Cecile had stopped contributing to Streamtime on a daily basis, but the site hasn't been discontinued as of the time of this writing. How Iraqi people discovered the internet in 2003–04 and perceived the possibilities of blogging remains a fascinating story that needs to be told. Cecile Landman intends to visit the main players to write a book about the destiny of all the characters, most of whom she hasn't met in real life, in the hope of recapturing that very special atmosphere. Cecile:

Blogs give a good insight into people's daily lives, but what happens when your living room is damaged regularly because bombs went off close to your house? What if electricity lacks for hours so that you have to write down all your thoughts by candlelight, planning to post your frustrations later on in the hope that someone will be interested in the desperate lives of the Iraqi people? Even though some things might have improved, the black humour is still there, as a blogger recently chatted: "Violence is so 2005!"

121

RADIO AFTER RADIO: FROM PIRATE TO INTERNET EXPERIMENTS

What is radio in the age of the internet? Does the interactive, live aspect of streaming define the online listening experience? Rather than discussing digital radio as broadcast content remediated from ether into cable, the question at stake is whether massively distributed online audio material should be considered "radio" at all. Will "radio" as a medium exist in a few decades? Some of us have an emotional and nostalgic investment in radio as a content delivery format, but does that matter? Would it be better to refashion the word "radio" as "social audio experience"? Why not look at the future of radio in relation to Skype, as peer-to-peer audio exchange? Or as a massive sharing environment, based on recommendation and rumors about the latest and coolest? Or is radio by definition a one-to-many channel? Not so, if we read Brecht's radio theory and consider early experiments with two-way systems. There have always been talk-backs and phone-ins. Instead of speculating about the future, this essay describes and reflects on the transition from analogue to digital and then online by way of the Amsterdam pirate radio scene.

Amsterdam Free Radio Techniques

Dutch radio culture always had its rough edges. The Netherlands has a rich history of pirate radio stations, from the early 1970s squatters' Radio Mokum and commercial radio ships such as Radio Veronica which broadcast off the coast in the North Sea, to free radio stations' multicultural, indie pop, and techno sounds, broadcasting from squats in the eighties and nineties when numerous more-or-less commercial dance and pop stations were also active. Although such local stations were everywhere, from Rotterdam and The Hague to Nijmegen and Groningen, this discussion is limited to the situation in Amsterdam for biographical reasons. One of various starting points is Radio De Vrije Keyser, which started broadcasting in the early 1980s from the barricaded historic building De Groote Keyser.[1] After a politically inclined activist phase, De Vrije Keyser brought about an extensive lineage of free radio stations, all characterized by a vast crusade to experiment with music styles and formats.

Discussing the future of radio as such in the Netherlands could quickly become arduous. Like everywhere else, the commercial, judicial, and political models are outdated, and, in response, podcasters claim victory over public broadcasting. Online radio enthusiasts claim the "death of radio" as a moment of liberation[2] – the democratization of the medium has finally arrived. But the institutional reality is different. There is no revolution, no deregulation of the airwaves, and no fundamental change in the financing of public broadcasting. Despite a crisis, everything somehow continues as before. Reasonable public debates about the rise of the internet and its impact on radio first summarize the pros and cons, then return to business as usual. Already, everyone can use the internet to listen to most radio stations. What else do you want?

The broadcast of existing signals through other channels does not rouse the radical imagination. Remediation is a dead-end street. Artists and geeks proclaiming internet radio as a mutual experience are less interested in the real-time aspect of Twitter and Facebook, and instead focus on the stretched-out time spectrum of this spheric medium. Despite the doom-mongering about its downfall, the promise of radio as local audio-ecstasy is still attractive. Imagine radio waves floating through the city sky, bouncing and dancing. A powerful image, but how does it translate into new media metaphors? During the past few decennia, this energy ignited a rich ecology of free radio stations that are now virtually extinct. What does it mean that we individually surf from one soundscape to another? Radio doesn't need friends, it needs new social structures in which upcoming radionauts can freely transmit. But what is radio after radio?

My own writings on radio began some time ago. After a crisis of existential proportions in the summer of 1987, during my fourth year of unemployment, I made the decision, regardless of the dire financial prospects, to follow my destiny and desire and proclaim myself a "media theorist." As a free-floating intellectual and activist mainly involved in writing and publishing, I purchased my first PC (9n 1BM clone with a 8086 Intel processor) and joined the Amsterdam free radio scene within the (declining) squatters' movement.[3] Collectively, Radio De Vrije Keyser, Radio 100, Radio Patapoe (first called Radio Death), and a few additional (ethnic) programs that were scattered across the legal SALTO cable and AM/FM frequencies formed a solid yet wildly diverse scene of around 120 to 150 radio-makers. All of those involved listened to each other's programs and refined the radio medium. In other words, after reaching a critical mass, a self-referential dynamic arose and turned into an integrated radio culture.

I started my own weekly show on Radio 100 called the *Adilkno Portrait Gallery*, in which radical and independent thinkers spoke about a topic for one hour, uninterrupted by questions. The explicit aim of the program was pedagogical: to regain confidence in public talk about all matters of theory and history and to overcome the dark and grim age of post-punk's anti-intellectualism. The call for action ("stop thinking, start doing") had led to blind activism and an unreflective continuation of social movements such as radical feminism, squatting, anti-militarism, anti-nuclear, and gay rights activism. As this was one of the few spoken-word programs, I wasn't too concerned over whether these discussions on topics such as Bataille and other French thinkers, the history of German fascism, Dutch architecture theory, or the archeology of "running amok" in Indonesia were fitting or not. Like my fellow pirate radio-makers, I explored the outer edges of the mediascape. My encounters with Toek, Reinout, and Chris of the DFM (DeForMation) group, captured in a series of radio interviews, stand out in particular. In 1990, I switched to the even more radical and obscure Patapoe station, where I hung around underground groups such as STORT, and audio personalities such as Evangelina, Agent B., and Wolf.

Sovereign Mixing

While computers had processed audio for some time, the Amsterdam scene of radio producers connected PCs to the telephone around 1990, in order to transfer files using bulletin-board software. The core mission of new media was clear from the start: to blow up the centralized and controlled mass-media system into "a landscape of 1001 blossoming antennas." The Amsterdam radionauts liberated themselves from the very notion of an audience and happily embarked on their futuristic mission to explore the frontiers of the audio universe.

124

I first published my thoughts on radio theory in the 1992 essay *The Theory of Mixing*, originally in Mediamatic's magazine.[4] My radio texts grew into a collection in the same year and were translated into German as *Listen or Die!*, the first book with my name on it. In these essays, I explained how the cut-up and live mix were characteristic of the Amsterdam sound. This technique was much more radical than the methods of mixing used by DJs in the club scene. Rather than inaudibly fading two tracks into each other and intensifying the sound with an electronic beat, the Amsterdam school of radio-mixing accentuated the rupture, the scratch, and the grinding contrast between musical styles: imagine Giuseppe Verdi smashing into Crass. The Amsterdam sound extended beyond music-mixing, toward remixing streams of information; its strength was in the "live" aspect and not in professional equipment or a journalistic approach.

Contrary to the time limit of the CD track, the free radio-maker takes her time. In particular, the late evening programs had an open end. Mixers create their own sound universes stretched infinitely in all dimensions, bobbing about in an ocean of spare time. Research on radical radioscapes eventually led to the Adilkno theory of "sovereign media" that was no longer focused on broadcasting the Truth or sending political messages with counter-information.[5] Rather than inform, enlighten, or entertain, sovereign media set out on their own journey – solocasters, free from any audience or target group, roaming around Chris Anderson's Long Tail.[6] The partiality for mixing signifies a transition from alternative media, which still hopes to fill a void in the existing repertoire, to sovereign media, which is disengaged entirely from its potential audience. Beyond media access and democratization, one enters the unexplored terrain of radio freedom.

By the late nineties, the Amsterdam free radio movement was past its prime. In the years from 1995 to 2001, the country experienced a level of economic growth not seen for many decades, with a government ruled by a one-off "purple" coalition of Labour and Liberal-conservatives. Neo-liberal market reforms now had a grip on the country. Coincidentally or not, this time also signaled the commercial breakthrough of the internet. The Dutch real-estate market took off and (youth) unemployment finally declined. Consequently, this meant less worry-free living on the dole and a rapidly declining stock of unoccupied houses. A study by UK scholar Lynn Owens chronicles the decline of the Amsterdam squatters' movement during this period when, toward the end, all three free radio stations were evicted.[7] Only Radio Patapoe managed to move to a new location and go on-air again, albeit with a much weaker signal.

125

Amsterdam radio fanatics cannot be accused of mono-medium fetishism. For them, radio was a tool, not a nostalgic medium. As early as the late eighties, they connected with hacker groups such as Hacktic and shared audio files through bulletin boards. Later, they experimented with internet plus radio, after the Real Player application launched in 1996, enabling people to listen to a radio station online. Where listeners once used point-to-point over a very expensive connection, the Real software inaugurated the age of "streaming." Dutch public broadcaster VPRO Digital was amongst the first to use RealAudio. One of the earliest internet radio webcasts happened during the tactical media festival Next Five Minutes 2, in January 1996, when a temporary crew from Radio 100, Patapoe, and Vrije Keyser produced live broadcasts from Paradiso and De Balie, parts of which were streamed through a RealAudio server, a technology that had been introduced the year before. At that occasion, Josephine Bosma remembers: "we used a dedicated server that only allowed five listeners to listen to the stream at one given time."

Supported by De Balie, xs4all, and De Waag, this technology became part of a solidarity campaign to migrate the Serbian radio station B92 onto the internet. In December 1996, with the help of xs4all, B92 created the internet provider OpenNet in Belgrade, a precaution in case Miloševic shut down the terrestrial station. The global campaign "Help B92" reached its height during the Kosovo war and the NATO bombings of Serbia in March–June 1999. Help B92 had its global solidarity headquarters in the attic of De Balie. A transmitter installed on the Waag building in the Nieuwmarkt broadcast the free internet data from Belgrade over the Amsterdam roofs. During those years, most computers were not yet capable of receiving streams, and the 14.4K modems were slow and unstable until early 2000 when ADSL and faster computers became more widespread. The limited capacity of the so-called streaming servers was another obstacle; if an online station could reach a few hundred listeners simultaneously, this was quite exceptional. B92 was indeed shut down several times by Miloševic and the internet relay successfully rebroadcast the signal throughout Serbia and overseas.

Vanishing Free Airwaves

Symbolically, the curtain fell for free radio in Amsterdam when technician Rob van Limburg passed away in July 2003. According to insider Mauzz, this all-rounder was about the only person who climbed up the wiggling masts of both the legal and the illegal radio stations without a hint of fear of heights, to place, fix, or replace antennas. During this time, Radio 100 lost their spot on-air after the redistribution of radio frequencies, and De Vrije Keyser lost theirs twice. Then the Radio 100 antenna was hit by a storm. De Vrije Keyser experienced a similar fate when commercial station 100% NL took their newly chosen radio frequency – interferences that occurred despite the Amsterdam free radio scene's own tenet never to disturb the radio frequency of other stations. The consequences when those involved do not share the same values, combined with a lack of technical expertise, were devastating. Mauzz: "The antenna always needs to be adjusted for a new frequency, and apparently no one in the decreasing group of volunteers had the expertise and guts to perform these kinds of stunts after all the hardship." The disappearance of this one-off radio culture coincided with the rise of right-wing populism in the Netherlands after 9/11, connected with the violent deaths of politician Pim Fortuyn and film-maker Theo van Gogh, and the emergence of anti-Islam/anti-migration politicians Rita Verdonk, Ayaan Hirsi Ali, and Geert Wilders.

By 2010, music had become a lifestyle business and lost all ties to counterculture. The atmosphere was one of nostalgia, not just for any type of music produced in the past 50 years but also for the true vinyl sound and other analogue experiences. Time for a free radio renaissance? De Vrije Keyser and Radio 100 maker Francois Laureys – now working for IICD in The Hague, a development organization that implements ICT projects in Africa – thinks that even though many creative people use audio/radio to express themselves, a collective movement will not naturally spring to life any more. "Back in the early 1980s, the scarcity of communication tools forced us to collaborate and get organized. Those Amsterdam-based stations that did not merge with WHS, Rabotnik, DFM, Radio Got and RVZ into Radio 100 were being hunted down by the investigation services."

Nowadays, anyone can produce podcasts and start his or her own web radio with hardly any budget. To create a community, however, you need meeting places such as a studio, office, or café. Former Patapoe radio-maker and net art critic Josephine Bosma agrees:

When Proeflokaal Marconi, later called Tesla, closed down, with it a meeting place for free radio-makers and audience, a place that created unity, disappeared. All of a sudden, this made radio invisible again: no longer did it have a direct connection to the audience. When cable radio became the standard, even before internet radio and MP3

127

downloads, people forgot how to find an on-air station. It is hard for average citizens to grasp that cable or digital brings about an entirely different new media landscape. Without the disappearance of the physical ties with the audience, the technical changes wouldn't have affected the landscape so drastically.

The same could be said about the wild Sunday evenings during the early nineties in Patapoe Bar, in a squat near the Zeedijk. These were events that kept Radio Patapoe together.

Free radio people are not very nostalgic by nature. We all produce for the Universal Archive. Still, it is no difficulty to observe that passion has, let's say, shifted, from the vanishing free airwaves' mad live mixing and babbling into the void, to the mindblowing global-distribution potential of the internet and its associated social rituals of networking. Amsterdam free radio culture around 1989 was a radical local situation: a one-directional gift to the inhabitants of the city in the spirit of Jean Baudrillard, without asking anything in return. Golden sounds for the big Nothing that nobody directly ordered. What remains is a box of cassette tapes and a folder of digital files. This state doesn't matter because radio is an evanescent, transitory medium. Josephine Bosma:

> What's left? Due to the rise of digital media, radio changed into a more individual experience. I deliberately do not use the word fragmentary, because I think it is too negative, and based too much on traditional power structures and the battle against them. In the Amsterdam scene, radio making had always been very individualistic and liberal. The reason I do not wish to speak of a fragmentary experience is that to me, radio is not about using one's voice to reach everyone, or to mobilise large masses. It is about a "media landscape" that contains – and preserves – multiformity. In that regard, nothing has changed. Today, the audience is not larger, but more scattered. We need to make sure that the audience remains, and that there will be new "radio-makers" and "audiences."[8]

For Bosma, making radio was, like art, expressive rather than communicative. That tendency to express persists, especially for Radio Patapoe, which still broadcasts but with a smaller range than before and an additional live stream on the internet. Bosma:

> They don't give a damn about having fewer listeners, they just go on. Patapoe is still making the same kind of programs and that is not just because they don't know what else to do, but because they have always

128

made radio that way: as a diary or a work of art. I now view the old situation (with large range and a bigger audience) as a kind of collection of "radio blogs" *avant la lettre*, a portal as such.[9]

Campfire Radio Online

The situation is different for the political activist-run radio station De Vrije Keyser.[10] Mauzz writes, "De Vrije Keyser was above all an alternative source of information for activists and the squatters' movement. The work has been continued on the internet on websites such as squat.net, kraken-post.nl, kraakforum.tk and especially indymedia.nl." According to radio-maker Lizet, who has been involved with De Vrije Keyser since 1986, opportunities to produce radio have only increased. "Since the internet, working in a collective is no longer essential. Sporadically, AM/FM radio projects exist, with a diverse character and often for a small audience, such as Radio Rietveld."[11] Lizet points out a different trend: leaving the studio and doing live broadcasts on location, for example, during the yearly anarchistic festival Pinksterlanddagen.

> Other media collectives also used this method, such as Mobile Radio, Ascii and squat.Net, as well as ad hoc groups comprised of young radio-makers from all over the country who filled the air with information, music and soundscapes. Using radio and the internet, they reported "live" and "on demand." The radio broadcasts had the feel of a summary of the day.

Bosma observes that De Vrije Keyser's work is carried on by M2M (Migrant to Migrant) Radio, a tactical media project that proceeded from the protest after the devastating fire at the Amsterdam Schiphol Airport detention centre in October 2005 during which 11 migrants who were awaiting deportation died. M2M uses the Streamtime.org server. This server was also used for broadcasts from Iraq in 2004 when a live stream was transmitted from the museum of Halabja.[12] M2M is the perfect sovereign media example, although with a situational slant to it. The programs are made up of (live) jam sessions. M2M started as a "narrow casting" initiative to connect the survivors of the Schiphol fire. M2M radio-maker Jo van der Spek calls it "campfire radio."

> The motto is: "the meal is the broadcast." The static interview format is passé. What it is all about is conversation, dialogue, and cacophony.

M2M conspicuously tests the borders of what can still be called radio. The programs are best described as surveillance – we listen in on certain situations while the tape recorder is on and the live stream is up and running.

But should this be webcasted? What should we make of this informal talk? The fatherly medium that strictly addresses the submissive ear, meticulously monitored by government and Party, intrudes into daily life. Van der Spek: "The strength of live streams is that it makes visible the intimate environments that then broadcast to the world."

At the workshops hosted by M2M, no radio equipment is brought along. Van der Spek:

> People have recording devices right in their pocket, i.e. their mobile phone. Further investments aren't necessary. It's about the skills. Most mobile phones enable you to make recordings, in the strangest surroundings, wherever you are. Discover the potential of the hardware you carry around. For instance, I once recorded myself being arrested. That was at Schiphol Plaza. And now people can listen to that on their mobile phone, on the internet or as a downloadable podcast.

For M2M the basic material is not music, but the spoken word from the multilingual cosmopolitan fringes. Pocket-size MP3 recorders carried everywhere act as documentation equipment. We hear detained migrants make phone calls from their cells. M2M provides the phone credit and broadcasts from public locations in the city; for instance, artist residency Het Blauwe Huis on IJburg provided a radio café on Friday evenings. Later, the Wereldhuis on the Nieuwe Herengracht acted as the location for the radio café, and in between it was in the temporary social space Scub, next to Amsterdam Central Station.

Pirate Radio Goes Global

The disappearance of gathering places and the lack of larger radio-events cause an additional problem: knowledge about radio techniques is no longer passed on. Bosma:

> Fewer people are aware of the simplicity of making radio or sound-scapes, which results in less fresh blood and less innovation. The modernization has shifted to other areas, for instance, the dance and techno scene. That is where people are now tinkering with technology

and sound. In the Amsterdam radio scene a strong link to alternative musicians and labels such as Staalplaat always existed. Currently, music and new media platform Worm in Rotterdam has a program at Patapoe. However, in this scene there is hardly any focus on spoken word, be it journalism or literature. We should change that.

An audience still exists, judging by the fan mail in Patapoe's mailbox, but the audience is now scattered all over the world and classified as niche. It doesn't evolve around technology, which can always be adjusted. During times of past repression there was the cassette tape, handed from one person to the next (today's equivalents are podcast and MP3 collections on a USB stick). And while there is plenty of available free storage space and bandwidth, the missing link is the community. Bosma proposes to change this situation. "Large meetings, exciting events, radio-making as part of the curriculum, it is all possible. However, it can only be successful if it is truly inspiring. We need a new radio philosophy. I am not so keen on promoting radio entirely on its own, isolated from other media. That is really outdated." In a time of fewer social movements, little time spent on protests, and a shift to virtual means of organization, radio, already labeled as part of the "minor media," may struggle to reinvent itself. People no longer sit on the sofa to listen to the radio or watch TV; they tweet and multitask. Media are mobile and constantly interconnected. These new conditions need to be accounted for in order that an active community of radio-makers and listeners can develop. According to London-based Australian radio researcher and producer Anja Kanngieser, radio philosophy must incorporate new ways to think about radio geographies and new relational spaces and sites in which radio is made:

> How we make it and with whom, and new sonic geographies, are tied in to how we listen and where. This is a political as well as social reconfiguration, because it challenges our understanding of the relationships that underpin radio as a communicative and affective medium. It is also a reconfiguration that addresses the intersections between imaginaries and desires surrounding radio as a form, and the material technologies and forms of governance around transmission, streaming and podcasting, intersections that are critical to understanding the ebbs and flows of DIY radio-making.[13]

The group DFM (DeForMation) holds a special position within the Amsterdam radio landscape. In the Dutch newspaper *Trouw*, music critic and DJ Stan Rijven writes:

131

Not only was this station one of the first web radio stations in the Netherlands, it is also the only descendant of the alternative radio scene that was still prominent in the eighties. DFM returns the strength of what radio may be: illusionary theatre for the ears. Exactly that which our public stations have failed to do for years.[14]

Toek, who made radio in the early nineties, is the pivotal force behind DFM. After working for Radio 100 for years, he went on to successfully transform the DFM website into a global network of listeners and sound producers, connected via a chat room during webcasts. The community regularly donates small amounts of money to secure the (financial) independence of the project. No subsidies or commerce here.

Mauzz points out that traditional FM broadcasting has not yet been submerged completely:

> What may have slipped your mind is that in the western part of the Netherlands, apart from Patapoe, another station is active: Dance Radio 992, irregularly airing on FM 99.2 (very close to the 99.3 frequency that Radio 100 had to give up because SALTO was given the 99.4 in the frequency redistribution for the commercial radio spectrum auction). I regularly speak to the people behind this station through chat. They're not commercial, this is pure passion. They use the most ingenious technologies such as powerful Chinese "disposable transmitters" to broadcast from bizarre locations such as a power pylon in the middle of the IJ! The studio delivers the signals over the internet which is without risks. The transmitters can be enabled and disabled remotely.[15]

Mauzz discovered a niche in which radio makes a fresh start: the 3D internet environment Second Life (SL):

> People and scenes I never would have expected are into streaming and broadcast live MP3 streams from their house, café or party for a group of people sharing a virtual space in Second Life. Every area in SL can have its own MP3 stream. Moreover, virtual "radio players" (scripts in a 3D object) can be purchased which are used to tune into countless radio stations and to which your personal favorite stations can be added. Also, open source radio players are distributed free of charge and users are connecting to teach each other how to stream radio. The live aspect is of significant importance. It is about the shared experience and the interaction of listeners with DJs and other radio-makers. That interaction in SL is not just of a verbal nature, but is also nonverbal and visual.

132

DFM, for instance, is very active in Second Life. Media artist Mauzz has been researching Second Life for two and a half years and has collected numerous non-commercial live streams:

> There are various MP3 stream server hosting companies that allow the users to pay for their hosting expenses in Linden Dollars. New groups of musicians with geographically widespread members have formed such as cover group Virtual Live Band and the experimental Avatar Orchestra Metaverse, with whom I have collaborated a few times. They create, for example, virtual 3D instruments which they, and the virtual audience, can use for live jamming.[16]

Second Life is also a platform for activists such as the Second Life Left Unity who use virtual events to draw attention to world issues. During the well-attended marathon Virtual festival "Teknival," DJs played alternative techno for 66 hours on six different stages and used the event to focus on the Palestinian issue.

All this activity is not just the offspring of the radio medium. These bottom-up techno-politics are the special effects of developments in hardware, software, bandwidth, and the spectacular decrease of telecom bills, enabling us to move from the era of mixing audio to that of mixing media. For Jo van der Spek, radio is, in the end, everything you do with audio in a live setting. Radio invites unexpected disruptions in ordinary streams of music and information.

Strikingly, some technological crossovers are still unexplored, namely the use of Skype and other free online telephone services. Skype can be a free phone service for listeners contributing to programs. One can build up a network of Skype correspondents and enable conversations between four or five locations worldwide, a situation best described as many-to-many micro radio. This signal can then be broadcast as a live stream or through classic ether. Few know that the audio service of Linden Lab (the Second Life owner) is the second largest service available. It is also time to update our perceptions about collective telephony. Smartphones are called "witness" devices for little more than the built-in camera that uploads images and videos onto Flickr or YouTube. Just consider the tactical use of smartphones combined with free radio. Last but not least, we can squat soon-to-be-abandoned AM and FM frequencies. We haven't reached that point yet, and who knows if, when, and how digital radio broadcasting will really take over and what will happen then, but there is much empty spectrum to discover once technologies are forgotten.

133

— 8 —

ONLINE VIDEO AESTHETICS OR THE ART OF WATCHING DATABASES

The automatic carriage-return on the typewriter, electronic central locking of cars: these are the things that count. The rest is just theory and literature.

Jean Baudrillard

We no longer watch films or TV; we watch databases.[1] Rather than well-defined programs, we search one list after another and confront the limitations of our own mental capacity. Which search terms yield the best YouTube results? What was that title again? Does anyone know that director's name? Can you remember the name of that band? What category was it under? Was the reference blogged somewhere? Who would know the URL? Was it under pets or entertainment? This is the database turn. We escaped the mercy of cranky reviewers and monocultural multiplexes. Welcome to the snack culture of the multitasking prosumer: watch a clip and move on.

So far, the implications of database watching are somewhat uncertain. We're all too happy to integrate YouTube into our busy daily lives and ignore the implications of computer viewing 24/7. It's already a cultural fact that we take TV everywhere with us and watch a quick clip while waiting at the bus stop. What does it mean that our attention is guided by database systems? Is searching really more important than finding? Why has searchability become such an essential organizing principle? Why do we encourage a personal relationship with the relational database? Who will guide us to the keywords that will deliver interesting results? Are we really in dialogue with the Machine? Do we determine the answers to our questions democratically, as is often suggested, or are there editors in the background recommending the "most popular videos"? Cultural awareness of

134

how algorithms function is still a long way off. The technological character of the search process also deserves more attention, as the hunt for and among moving images is now just as important as scanning the search results.

We must investigate the myriad smartphones, notebooks, laptops, car LCD screens, flip-down monitors, portable video players, pocket PCs, and handheld TVs that allow us to simultaneously produce and consume moving images wherever we are. Italian artist Albert Figurt demonstrates this in his brilliant *Notre Cam de Paris* video.[2] Tourists walk through the Notre Dame Cathedral in Paris, filming and taking pictures. The video carefully observes the shooting laymen as their bodies adjust to the camera, moving and stretching their arms to zoom in or out of the sculptures or glass windows they aim to capture. Figurt not only exposes the mass production of visual material but the image condition as flexible techno-extension of the body and the compulsory nature of touristic image capture. Beyond the often moralistic critique of gadget fetishism and the praise of technology-free watching, we need to upgrade and focus our "ways of seeing" (John Berger) and ways of describing the composition of our contemporary culture.

After the Fall of the Grand Narrative

A baby boy dancing on YouTube has wound up tangled in a legal dispute with pop star Prince and one of the world's biggest record companies. Stephanie Lenz shot a video of her toddler bobbing to Prince's 1980s hit "Let's Go Crazy." In the video, the little boy is running around the kitchen while the song plays in the background. After shooting the video, Lenz uploaded it on to YouTube so that friends and family could see it.[3]

What's so surprising about this episode is not the copyright dispute but that we know this factoid in the first place. Why do we even bother with recorded triviality? This question is not posed out of arrogance or disdain but signifies the general online condition: why did I have to see this? How did I get here? Was it ontological serendipity?

YouTube commentary in old media extends no further than complaints about the Decline of the Occident in general and of copyright in particular. Cultural pessimists chime in all too gladly about the fall of the Grand Narrative. Not only do we read few or no books, but

135

we now also watch too few films and not enough TV. Like small children, we are unable to sit still and pay attention while Father Cinema reads us a story. During a feature film we have already tweeted our judgments. Freud's "modern neurosis" now manifests itself as our scattered attention in cyberspace. Attentive watching and listening give way to diffused multitasking. The moment we sit behind a computer, we are susceptible to ADHD. While watching online video clips, which last an average of two and a half minutes, we jump up and down, sing along, and play air guitar. We behave like hyperactive children receiving too little attention, and if we don't like something, we either fuss at the drop of a hat, or, according to psychologists who study online behavior, immediately turn to something else.

American NBC anchor Brian Williams once said:

> If we're all watching cats flushing toilets, what aren't we reading? What great writer are we missing? What great story are we ignoring? This is societal, it's cultural, I can't change it. Like everybody else, I can burn an hour on YouTube or Perez Hilton without breaking a sweat. And what have I just not paid attention to that 10 years ago I would've just consumed?[4]

What is to be done when the vernacular becomes canonical? We must take database-watching seriously, not just dismiss it as "consuming video clips." Watching videos online is how people occupy themselves. In 2010, every YouTube user spent 15 minutes a day on the service. And 35 hours of material is currently uploaded every minute. The interface inherently keeps us going and going, and the clip chain continues forever. Allowing oneself to be led by an endlessly branching database is the cultural constant of the early twenty-first century. The online dream trip must not end. The brevity of many online videos does not detract from this perpetual skipping. Their short-lived character suits the meager level of concentration people muster for the average media product. Why watch when we already know the message in advance? Hours of material may well be packed within a few minutes of video, and viewers could spend years deciphering their deeper meaning. However, Time is the message. As Maurizio Lazzarato writes in his *Videophilosophie*, "video and digital technology machines, like the spirit, crystallise time."[5] With online video we consume our own lack of time. Have fun decoding the images – but in fact no one will ever get around to that. In our haste to move on, we forget to click "clear viewing history."

Five years into YouTube, we witness its necessary mainstreaming. Both pundits and cultural elites have acclimatized remarkably fast to online video libraries containing millions of mini-films, and the total recordability of all situations has reached the most intimate and distant corners that cameras can reach. In our "whatever" culture nothing seems to surprise us. Staggering statistics of hyper-growth are no longer impressive. Massive usage is no longer an indication of relevance; nor does it automatically translate into well-funded research or critical art practices. The continuous technological revolutions have the dangerous potential to numb us. B-S-B: Boredom-Surprise-Boredom. Rather than an explosion of radical imagination we witness digital disillusionment – perhaps explaining why online theory had a somewhat unspectacular start. Is the study of online video doomed to remain a niche activity, like most new media topics, or will it take a conceptual quantum jump, in line with the billions of clips watched daily? The low quality of YouTube's most popular videos certainly indicates that this platform is not a hotbed of innovative aesthetics, and so far there is no evidence of a dialectical turn from quantity into quality. It is time to leave behind "reality video," which is the candid camera level of spectacular television, and move toward new and yet unexplored forms of dialogical visual culture.

Proactivity and Social Viewing

Even though video existed on the internet in 1997 with the launch of proprietary video format RealVideo, users only became familiar with small video screens around 2005 to 2006. The secret of YouTube's success is one of pure luck, an idea implemented when the circumstances were right. As internet start-ups accelerated again in 2005 and the number of users with a broadband connection grew, a combination of built-in video players inside browsers and a liberal attitude toward "sharing" (read: copyright violation of TV content) enabled YouTube to reach a critical mass of both content and users. At the tipping point, hyper-growth was unstoppable. Google bought YouTube for $1.65 billion in shares in late 2006. During the first years of online video research, most attention was dedicated to Henry Jenkins's uncritical appraisal of "participatory culture" and the cult of the amateur response. Despite the criticism of Sunstein, Keen, and Lanier, the "most watched" amateur content logic dominates the academic cultural studies approach. Instead of pitting pessimistic

137

judgments against optimistic marketeer talk, it is more interesting to investigate closely the messy, corporate online reality. In the early 1970s, Jean Baudrillard defined mass media as "speech without response." These days, messages only exist if they are indexed by search engines, retweeted with shortened URLs, forwarded through emails and RSS feeds, liked at Facebook, recommended on Digg, and, let's not forget, receive comments on the page itself. Media without response is now unthinkable.

Now that the entertainment-as-diversion phase is over, we are literally and figuratively diverting ourselves all over the Net. The *cinéma-vérité* generation's wish for the camera as *stilo* has come true: the billions are scratching away with abandon. Popular YouTube videos with their lame entertainment character are not simply random junk or a distraction from something important or more real; they touch the essence of the internet, playing what John Hartley calls a "bardic function": just grab the harp and sing![6] The core of the YouTube project lies in this invitational gesture. Though YouTube's slogan "Broadcast Yourself" is acted on by fewer than 1 percent of its users – most of whom simply share existing media material – the internet still operates as a mirror, and we must acknowledge the subtle play with affect. YouTube is a hospitality service, giving us the energy to express ourselves and the warm feeling that we exist, that at least someone cares. This added layer of social viewing is what makes video today different from the film and television age. To study online video is to study this intimate aspect of affect, not the theories of commercial repackaging that underlie common rhetoric about remediation. The social is the core constitutive element of contemporary video practice and not some leftover redundant noise surrounding audiovisual content.

As we watch YouTube material, other windows are naturally also open. One person is chatting or Skype-ing, sending an email or reading a blog; the other is tweeting, gaming, or talking on the phone. Cultural studies researchers established long ago that we daydream while we watch films and do the washing, or that we talk to a friend on the phone while the TV is on; the Total Attention ideal is achieved only in retirement homes. Online video incorporated this discovery into its architecture and increasingly lives off recommendation systems created elsewhere in the social media sphere. While we check out the latest status update on Facebook, a clip that one of our mates "liked" plays on the left, and "related videos" by the same uploader appear on the right. The computer interface is geared toward more of the same. Antagonistic or dialectical programming is still a long way off.

Similar to other social networks, online video sites assume that we have an incestuous desire to be just like our friends. The essential fact of postmodernity – namely that we seek difference, not similarity – has not (yet) persuaded the Web 2.0 entrepreneurial class.

The coded maxim is: I want to see what you see. What are my friends watching? What are their favorites? Let's browse through your lists. Look at this channel! Associative and search-driven surfing is out. Seeking depth is simply barking up the wrong tree. The many open programs signify intensive engagement, not signs of a misspent youth. Today multitasking is the essence of the media experience, rather than an unintended side effect. Instead of traveling to and from various visual experiences such as the cinema or the desktop PC, we watch a film in the subway, car, or airplane to kill time and intensify our everyday life. The *totale Mobilmachung* of visual culture predicted ages ago has now finally arrived. With the spread of videophones and MP4 players, the film-video-TV complex travels with us, becoming part of the intimate sphere of the Self. We wear the image devices in our pockets, close to our body, and watch them within close range of our face. The intensity of solitary watching while on the move, in bed, at the kitchen table, or the home theater plasma defines the online video experience.

In a macro-economic sense, online video concerns the millions of films watched every day, providing Google (YouTube's owner) with a treasure trove of user data. What is your "association" economy worth? Am I really aware of why I click one clip away to look at the next? If not, we can always reread our own history on YouTube. We can find everything – but in the end we will mainly find out more about ourselves. Then after a while we grow tired of the media savvy American college students with their mainstream rock 'n' roll tastes, so we click away again.

Finally, automatic infantilization occurs because Authority is nowhere in sight. Power exists but remains invisible and unnameable. Google permits everything, from porn to politically incorrect jokes; no one notices anyway (or so it seems, until the videos are removed). In this danger-free communication zone, itself barely out of diapers, we relive our childhood while aware that unknown companies watch over our shoulders. The controlling power is as anonymous as we believe we are. As long as we extend this naive phase and do not internalize the Network as authority there is no problem. This is the dilemma of radical YouTube criticism: why spoil the fun of millions of people who've long known they are intimately watched?

139

Online Video Criticism: Video Vortex

Soon after online video launched, students approached our Institute of Network Cultures to borrow books about YouTube. We might laugh at this demand for instant analysis, but the question is legitimate: would it be possible to develop a critical theory of current developments? How can artistic research and political use contribute to the further development of online video? Can concepts be developed beyond the uncritical fan culture promoted by Henry Jenkins, in order to question the corporate PR management rhetoric without downplaying online video's creative-artistic and social-political use? Will the looming cultural clash with the more established film and television studies disturb online video research? These questions fascinated both Seth Keen in Sydney and myself when we initiated the Video Vortex project in late 2006. Video Vortex became a lively research network of artists, activists, coders, curators, scholars, and critics at conferences in Brussels (October 2007), Amsterdam (January 2008), Ankara (October 2008), Split (May 2009), and again in Brussels (November 2009) and Amsterdam (March 2011): these events produced two anthologies, a website, a mailing list, and a number of exhibitions, with more to come.[7]

After the past decade's many changes, the question on the table is how to interpret the online Given. Moving on from justified excitement and the quick satisfaction of data porn ("May 2010: YouTube exceeds 2 billion views a day"[8]), serious research must commence. Let's dive into the wide range of questions raised by the Video Vortex network: What platform-specific concepts can judge the aesthetic, political, and cultural aspects of online video? Why do we "like" certain videos? What role do users play, whether through uploading, recommending and selecting, or commenting and tagging? Video Vortex's goal is to systematize further the work produced during the conferences and collected in the two INC Video Vortex anthologies (from 2008 and 2011) and *The YouTube Reader*, edited by Snickars and Vonderau in 2009.[9]

Video Vortex research seeks to understand, for instance, that YouTube's database style is a success not only because people like to browse short clips, but as a special effect of its early technical limitations. Consider its original three-minute upload constraint that produced the ongoing tendency to upload short and ephemeral content, or the fact that although video platforms allow users to create their own collections (called channels), they also have lesser-known, more-

or-less automated restraints. While YouTube established its reputation by encouraging users to "share" freely, it now intervenes more and more and has become very strict about nudity and copyrighted material. Soon it will begin organizing content around curated "channels" that aim to compete with television. How can a theory of filtering and flagging take shape, as first described by Minke Kampman?[10] What is the role of filtering bots or the "self-regulatory" model, also known as user-generated censorship? What do we make of the confusion caused by millions of incoherent tags? Will the Semantic Web solve these problems, taking into account that YouTube's search engine is the world's second largest after the Google search engine?

Among Video Vortex's early concerns were the selection, curation, and conservation of online video hosted on independent (art) servers. These issues are still important for both users and art professionals and are an extension of the worlds of video art and documentary film-making which have seen a progression from analogue to digital, as well as from VHS to DVD to online distribution. What aesthetic strategies do artists like Natalie Bookchin and Perry Bard[11] employ when integrating the "video of the crowds" into their work? Their question is strategic: how can user-generated content transcend the individualized level of the remixing citizen who reappropriates culture, and make sense of it as a co-created coherent artwork? If we agree that all artworks are collaborative, multi-authored efforts, how can they transmit a unique style and message? Bookchin's 2009 video installation *Mass Ornament* is paradigmatic here. We see teenagers who turned their homes into theaters, dancing alone but together. These solo acts, self-portraits that are exhibitionist in nature and processed by the digital craft of the artist, thus become part of a collective statement. "Beyond the fragments" was a demand formulated by UK socialist feminists Robotham, Segal, and Wainwright in the late 1970s during the rise of new social movements and the decline of unions and parties. This demand has now arrived in the context of digital culture. How can a patchwork of files be transformed into a lucid work of art?[12] How can a multitude of individualized expressions be brought together into a compelling zeitgeist image? We could ask the same questions of Lev Manovich's cultural analytics.[13] Can a multiplicity of data express the unity of art? How can we balance the individual voices with the general outcomes that are processed? Is there a place for anomaly and the casual witness? At what point does complexity turn into distortion? Or should we simply learn to read those "technical images" as coined by Vilém Flusser?

Video Foresight

Where will all this take us? In *Beyond Viral: How to Attract Customers, Promote Your Brand, and Make Money with Online Video* (2010), YouTube comedian aka marketeer Kevin Nalty, who claims to have made 800 videos that have been watched 160 million times, sums up the philosophy of the online video insiders who have understood how to play the rules of the game. The trick is to do aggressive marketing, and this starts with the realization that no one wants to get stuck in the Long Tail. The massively watched "funny video" genre is creating its own professionals. The future as seen by YouTube is cross-media, and driven by these aspirational professionals, supported by institutional arrangements through content deals and sponsorships. To the growing group of ex-amateurs ("weblebrity"), Nalty explains how to monetize your videos. According to Nalty, the first step would be to realize that "viral" is dead. The mouth-to-mouth strategy is simply too slow and doesn't bring in money. Fox Broadcasting, MTV, Logitech, Microsoft, Holiday Inn Express, Crowne Plaza, and Mentos started sponsoring Nalty's videos. The so-called "YouTube Next" initiative desires to go beyond the Long Tail to a form of cable television with a level of audience personalization that broadcast media could never achieve. However, it remains to be seen if YouTube is going to transform itself into a main player in the struggle to define what the future of television formats will be. Most likely YouTube will further explore and exploit ways of making money with other people's content by turning it into channels that run as part of a meta-channel, then share revenues with the "most viewed" players such as the comedy web series *Annoying Orange* (with more than 500 million views on YouTube alone).[14]

Can we speculate on a more interesting turn that involves online video's "live" element? Massive live streaming, though technically within the realm of the possible, has not yet taken off, which is surprising because distributed, real-time streaming was promised from the very beginning. We watch clips, reports, and movies in the time-space coordinates of our liking. Though video is viral, it has not yet deeply penetrated the social networking experience. Even embedded, video remains beyond what we recommend and "like." The worlds of user-generated content and video-over-IP have not yet met, even though hundreds of millions of users use both. The intimate banality of Chatroulette, Skype, and other webcam software is not yet perceived as a legitimate video input signal for film and television consumption. We could blame this on the poor image quality and the high dropout rate, but more likely the dominant single media ideology (in this case recorded video signals) prevents us from making perverse connections. These connections are also overlooked by the engineers and their business managers.

Will services like Seesmic (multi-user video dialogues) take off, or is it too early to fully integrate (live) video into the social media experience? In April 2009, Seesmic surprisingly suspended its innovative video service and replaced it with a social networking aggregator. The future of vlogs (video blogs used as diary devices) is equally unclear, having peaked at the end of the blogging wave in 2006. Even with the resolution of most technical problems, who feels the need to keep a video diary? Whereas more and more laptops, PC, and notebooks come with webcams, and phones have built-in cameras, the use of these video devices for public dialogue remains underdeveloped.

Was will das Medium? Should we champion user-generated content over remediated film and television material or vice-versa, or is it precisely the complementary viewing that defines the platform? Will online video remain a jukebox item passed from one social network to the next? Have we all switched from zapping to searching? Should we approach YouTube culture from the plasma screen angle? Is the final destination the living room, where the online video logic competes with cable and free-to-air television? Is online video liberating us from anything? Instead of merely measuring the ever-changing field we could also define future scenarios. Let's dig into the destiny of online video and discuss three possible directions:

1. Due to their financial and legal muscle, the television and film industries will create a coalition to marginalize online video platforms such as YouTube. They do this not by taking YouTube offline or through copyright court cases, but through designing appealing online viewing applications that link the comfort of the home theater with the mobility of smartphones. Easy-to-use payment systems and new models of advertising combined with fiber into the homes will do the trick. Online video as we know it is too closely tied to the multitasking practices of the PC-bound computer user, who, like a cybernetic commander, sits on a chair behind a desk. In this scenario, online video is a disruptive technology-in-transition, doomed because its values are too deeply rooted in a white male geek culture and also because it doesn't fit into the busy lives of the billions who demand seamless interfaces and easy access to instant infotainment.

143

2. Following the heroic rhetoric of Old battling New, many insiders believe online video will emerge as the great winner. Google, Facebook, and Twitter are the media companies of the Web 2.0 era. How will this corporate reality translate into future owner-ship of the visual? Cyber-evangelists emphasize the transition from dead content to interaction and aggregation, the clicking, linking, and liking, in short, "the social" that generates value. The more visual material aligns itself with users by facilitating "clouds of meaning" (as YouTube and Flickr do), the more they will dominate future media markets. The parasitic strategy that promotes "free" and "open" helps us navigate the plenitude of images, and it no longer matters whether content is old or new, as long as we exchange our micro-impressions.

3. The third scenario is in the midst of a Hundred Years War between platforms and corporations competing for the user's attention. As a never-ending event of non-compatibility and built-in obsolescence, this techno-media drama is an epoch without clear winners, unless the overall picture radically changes. Right now, growth in emerging markets in Asia, Africa, the Middle East, and Latin America guarantees market expansion in all directions. But this spectacular escalation might yet fool us. The attention war is real. We all participate through choices, and the contribution of our micro-data to online video (or not) is only one of many activities to which we dedicate our time. Online video is merely a manifestation of hardware, software, and network configurations, an endless helical chain of codecs, pro-tocols, and models generating their own "auto poetic" aesthetics. In that case a plethora of "new media" platforms (pads, pods, and smartphones) will coexist next to television and film for some time to come. Concepts such as cross, trans, locative, or geo media will be short-lived business memes. In this Machiavellian view, media do not have a "telos." This cynical play concerns power and resources that most idealistic and utopian new media actors do not want to know about, let alone respond to.

Regardless of the outcome, all three scenarios demand platform-specificity. How can we anticipate new forms of moving image pro-duction that will emerge under the "network condition"? What are the unique characteristics of online video? Are we open to the unfore-seen and the unexpected, or do we simply bet on the safe remediation thesis that claims that content always remains the same and simply migrates from one platform to the next? In *An Introduction to Visual*

144

Culture, Nicholas Mirzoeff asks: "Can the writing of the digital present and its implied futures only be accomplished by a counter history that refuses to tell a history of progress? How do we write a history of something that changes so fast it can seem like a full-time job keeping up, let alone learning the software?"[15] In an age that closes the gap between subculture and main street, can the avant-garde only respond to yesterday's pop culture?

9

SOCIETY OF THE QUERY: THE GOOGLIZATION OF OUR LIVES

A Tribute to Joseph Weizenbaum

With the rise of search engines, it is no longer possible to distinguish between patrician insights and plebeian gossip.[1] Both the distinction between high and low, and their co-mingling on occasions of carnival, are from bygone times and should not concern us. Nowadays, an altogether new phenomenon is causing alarm: search engines rank according to popularity, not Truth. Search is the techno-cultural code that governs contemporary life. We no longer learn by heart; we look it up. With the dramatic increase of accessible information we have grown hooked on retrieval tools. It is hard now to imagine a time without search engines. We look for telephone numbers, addresses, opening hours, a person's name, flight details, and best deals, and, in a frantic mood, declare the ever-growing pile of grey matter "data trash." Soon we will search and only get lost.

The specter of information overload haunts the world's intellectual elites. Ordinary people have hijacked strategic resources and are clogging up the once carefully policed media channels. Before the internet, the mandarin classes relied on the idea that they could separate "idle talk" from "knowledge." Not only have old hierarchies of communication imploded, communication itself has assumed the status of cerebral assault. Noise has risen to remarkable levels. Even the benign greetings from family and friends acquire the status of a choir expecting a reply. The educated class frets above all else that chatter has entered the hitherto protected domain of science and philosophy, when instead they should worry about who will control the increasingly centralized computing grid.

Ever since the rise of search engines in the 1990s, we've been living in the "Society of the Query," which isn't so far removed from Guy Debord's *Society of the Spectacle*. Written in the late 1960s, this Situationist analysis was based on the rise of the film, television, and advertisement industries. The main difference today is that we are explicitly requested to interact. We're no longer addressed as an anonymous mass of passive consumers: instead we are "distributed actors" present on a multitude of channels. Debord's critique of commodification is no longer revolutionary. Consumerist pleasures are so widespread that they've reached the status of a universal human right. We all love the commodity fetish and the brands, and bask in the glamor that the global celebrity class performs on our behalf. No social movement or cultural practice, however radical, can escape the commodity logic. No strategy has been devised for the age of the post-spectacle. Concerns instead focus on privacy, or what's left of it. Capitalism's capacity to absorb its adversaries is now so routine that it is next to impossible to argue that we still need criticism – in this case of the internet – until the day when all your private telephone conversations and internet traffic are becoming publicly available. Even then it will be difficult to make the case for critique when dispute takes the guise of organized complaint by a consumer lobby group; of this is "shareholder democracy" in action. Only then will the sensitive issue of privacy catalyze a wider consciousness about corporate interests, but its participants will be carefully partitioned. Entry to the shareholding masses is restricted to the middle classes and above. This only amplifies the need for a lively and diverse public domain in which neither state surveillance nor market interests have a vital say.

Weizenbaum's Islands of Reason

My interest in the concepts behind search engines developed while reading a book of interviews with MIT professor and computer critic Joseph Weizenbaum, known for his 1966 automatic therapy program ELIZA and his 1976 book *Computer Power and Human Reason*.[2] Weizenbaum died on March 5, 2008, at the age of 84. A few years before Weizenbaum had moved from Boston back to Berlin, the city where he grew up before escaping with his parents from the Nazis in 1935. Besides the 2007 *Rebel at Work* film documentary, produced by Peter Haas and Silvia Holzinger, which gives an overview of his life,[3] there are also a number of interviews conducted by Munich-based

147

journalist Gunna Wendt, which she put together in a book. Some Amazon reviewers complained about Wendt's uncritical questions and the polite, superficial level of her contributions, but this did not disturb me – I enjoyed the insights of one of the few insider critics of computer science. Especially interesting are Weizenbaum's stories about his youth in Berlin, his exile to the US, and how he became involved in computing during the 1950s. The book reads like a summary of Weizenbaum's critique of computer science, namely that computers impose a mechanistic point of view on their users, and that, as autonomous machines, they reject direct experience. Weizenbaum argues that there should be no elevation of calculation above judgment.[4] The "heretic" Weizenbaum shapes his arguments as an informed and respected insider – a position similar to the "Net criticism" project that I developed with Pit Schultz after we started nettime in 1995.

The title and subtitle of the book of interviews are intriguing: *Wo sind sie, die Inseln der Vernunft im Cyberstrom? Auswege aus der programmierten Gesellschaft* (literarily translated: "Where are they, the islands of reasons in the cyber flow? Ways out of the programmed society"). Weizenbaum's system of belief can be summarized as *Nicht alle Aspekte der Realität sind berechenbar* ("not all aspects of reality are calculable"). Weizenbaum's internet critique is general, and we must appreciate this. Skeptical of all computer idolatry, his remarks about the internet are nothing new for those familiar with his oeuvre: the internet is a great pile of junk, a mass medium that consists of up to 95 percent nonsense – much like the medium of television, which is the direction in which the Web is inevitably developing. The so-called information revolution has disintegrated into a flood of disinformation. A key reason for this is the absence of an editor or editorial principle. Yet the book fails to address why this crucial media principle was not built in by the first generations of computer programmers, of which Weizenbaum was a prominent member. The answer probably lies in the computer's initial employment as a calculator: techno-determinists insist that mathematical calculation remains the essence of computing. Crucially, mathematicians did not foresee the (mis)use of computers for media purposes. Why listen to records on a computer? If you want to see a film, visit the cinema. So today's clumsy interfaces and information management should not be blamed on those who designed the first computers. Once a war machine, the digital calculator took a long and winding road to repurpose itself into a universal human device that serves our endlessly rich and diverse information and communication needs and interests.

Putting Weizenbaum's info-anxiety aside, what makes the interview compendium such an interesting read is its insistence on the art of asking the right question. Weizenbaum warns against an uncritical use of the word "information." "The signals inside the computer are not information. They are not more than signals. There is only one way to turn signals into information, through interpretation." For this we depend on the labor of the human brain. The problem of the internet, according to Weizenbaum, is that we're invited to see it as a Delphic oracle. The internet will provide the answer to all our questions and problems. The internet is not a vending machine in which you throw a coin to get what you want. The acquisition of proper education and expertise to formulate the right query is essential. We do not reach a higher education standard simply by opening up the opportunity to publish. Weizenbaum: "the possibility for anyone to put something on the internet doesn't mean much. Randomly throwing in is as useless as randomly fishing out."[5] In this context Weizenbaum makes the comparison between the internet and the now vanished CB radio. Communication alone will not lead to useful and sustainable knowledge.

Weizenbaum relates this uncontested belief in search engine queries to the rise of the "problem" discourse. Computers were introduced as "general problem-solvers" and their purpose was to provide a solution for everything. People were invited to delegate their lives to the computer. "We have a problem," argues Weizenbaum, "and the problem requires an answer." He explains that personal and social tensions cannot be resolved by simply declaring them a problem. In place of Google and Wikipedia we need the capacity to scrutinize and think critically, which he sees as the difference between hearing and listening. A critical understanding requires that we first sit down and listen – then we not only hear but learn to interpret and understand.

The Semantic Web, or Web 3.0, is heralded as the technocratic answer to Weizenbaum's criticism. In place of Google's keyword-based algorithms and outputs structured by ranking, we will soon be able to use the next generation of "natural language" search engines, such as those initiated by Powerset (quickly bought and neutralized by Microsoft)[6] and WolframAlpha. However, we can already guess that computational linguists do not favor the question–answer approach and will be cautious about acting as a "content police force" that decides what is and what is not truth or trash on the internet. The same applies to Semantic Web initiatives and similar artificial intelligence technologies. We are stuck in the age of web

149

information retrieval. Whereas Google's paradigm is link analysis and page rank, next-generation search engines could, for instance, become visual and start indexing the world's images, not based on the tags that users have added but on the quality and characteristics of the image itself. Welcome to the hierarchization of the Real, where the next volumes of computer-user manuals will introduce programmer geeks to aesthetic culture 101. Camera club enthusiasts turned coders will be accused of being the new polluters of "good taste."

On a number of occasions I have formulated a critique of the "media ecology" approach that aims to filter "useful" information for individual consumption. Hubert Dreyfus's 2001 book *On the Internet* is one of the key culprits here.[7] I do not believe that it is the choice of any professor, editor, or coder to decide for us what is and what is not nonsense. This should be a distributed effort, embedded in a culture that facilitates and respects difference of opinion. We should praise richness and make new search techniques part of our general culture. One way to achieve this is to revolutionize search tools and increase the general level of media literacy. If we walk into a bookstore or library, our culture has taught us how to browse through the thousands of titles. Instead of complaining to the shop owner or librarian that they carry too many books, we ask for assistance or figure it out ourselves. Weizenbaum would like us to distrust what we see on our screens, be it television or the internet, but he fails to mention who is going to advise us on what to trust, on whether something is truthful or not, and on how to prioritize the information we retrieve. In short, the role of mediator is jettisoned in favor of cultivating general suspicion.

The Aggregation of Everything

What today's administrators of noble simplicity and quiet grandeur can't express, we should say for them: there is a growing discontent with Google's flagship and the way the internet organizes information retrieval. The scientific establishment lost control over one of its key research projects: the design and ownership of computer networks now used by billions of people. How did so many people end up so dependent on a single search engine? Why are we repeating the Microsoft saga once again? It is dull to complain about a monopoly in the making when average internet users have such a multitude of power-distributing tools at their disposal. One possible way to overcome this predicament is to positively redefine Heidegger's *Gerede*.

150

Instead of a culture of complaint dreaming of an undisturbed offline life and radical measures to filter out the noise, it is time to openly confront today's trivial forms of *Dasein* in blogs, text messaging, and computer games. Intellectuals should no longer portray internet users as secondary amateurs, cut off from a primary and primordial relationship with the world. The greater issues at stake require venturing into the politics of informatic life. It is time to address the emergence of a new type of corporation rapidly transcending the internet: Google.

The World Wide Web, which should have realized the infinite library described in Borges's 1941 short story *The Library of Babel*, is seen by many of its critics as nothing but a variation of Orwell's *Big Brother* from 1948. The ruler in this case is not an evil monster but a collection of cool youngsters whose corporate responsibility slogan is "Don't Be Evil." Guided by a much older and experienced generation of IT gurus (Eric Schmidt), internet pioneers (Vint Cerf), and economists (Hal Varian), Google has expanded so fast, and in such a wide variety of fields, that there is virtually no critic, or academic or business journalist, who can keep up with the scope and speed of its development in recent years.[8] New Google applications and services accumulate with increasing regularity like unwanted Christmas presents: the free email service Gmail, the video-sharing platform YouTube, the social networking site Orkut, GoogleMaps, GoogleEarth, AdWords' pay-per-click advertising, the sponsored links of AdSense, and office applications such as Calendar, Talks, and Docs. Google not only competes with Microsoft, Apple, and Yahoo, but also with entertainment firms, travel software makers, public libraries (through its massive book-scanning program), telecom firms, and, last but not least, their social media competitors Facebook and Twitter. After the development and successful implementation of its Android open-source operating system for mobile devices, rumors about Google's next step vary from the rolling out of its own smartphone (competing with Nokia and Apple's iPhone) to its ambitions of becoming a telecom giant like AT&T, Verizon, T-Mobile, and Vodafone. If we add all cell-phone related activities, it is not hard to portray Google as an evil genius planning world domination and the control of the full spectrum, from cloud computing to data storage, wireless infrastructure to apps, and operating systems to the chip architecture of the devices themselves. Not to mention notebooks and e-tablets which utilize Google's Chrome browser, replacing the multipurpose but heavy Windows or Linux operating systems.

151

Every week we see the launch of yet another Google initiative. Even for informed insiders, it is next to impossible to reveal a master plan. Who remembers the Google App Engine, the "developer tool that enables you to run your web applications on Google's infrastructure"? App Engine allowed start-ups to use Google's web servers, APIs, and other developer tools as the primary architecture for building new web applications. As Richard MacManus in his 2008 article "Google App Engine: Cloud Control to Major Tom" remarks, "Google clearly has the scale and smarts to provide this platform service to developers. However, it begs the question: why would a startup want to hand over that much control and dependence to a big internet company?"[9] Computing infrastructure is rapidly turning into a utility, as the Google App Engine illustrates. MacManus ends with a rhetorical question: "Would you want Google to control your entire end-to-end development environment? Isn't that what developers used to be afraid of Microsoft for?" The answer is simple: it is the developers' not-so-secret wish to be bought by Google. Millions of internet users are participating in this process, willingly or not, by freely providing companies like Google with their profiles and attention – the currency of the internet. In 2008, Google patented a technology that enhances its ability to "read the user." The intention is to decipher which page regions and topics the viewer is interested in, based on the viewer's behavior *after* they have arrived at a page – one example of the many analytical techniques the media company is developing to study and commercially exploit user behavior.

One of my less geeky family members said she heard that Google was much better and easier to use than the internet. The mistake sounded cute, but she was right. Not only has Google become the better internet; it is taking over software tasks from individuals' computers so that one can access data in the "cloud" from any terminal or handheld device. Google actively undermines the autonomy of the PC as a universal computational device and brings us back to the dark days when IBM's Thomas J. Watson predicted a world market for five computers. Nerds have always made a joke about the wrong-headedness of megalomaniac bureaucrats attempting to predict the future, but if we update this image to one large Google data centre on each continent we're not that far away from Watson's estimation. The majority of users, as well as universities and NGOs, are happily abandoning the power to self-govern their informational resources. Conspiracy or not, Google is moving into nuclear energy and wind turbines. Time to get concerned? Human rights activist, hacker, and TOR developer Jacob Appelbaum, who is also involved in WikiLeaks, says it like this: "I love Google and I love the people there. Sergey Brin and Larry Page are cool. But I'm terrified of the next generation that takes over. A benevolent dictatorship is still a dictatorship. At some point people are going to realize that Google has everything on everyone. Most of all, they can see what questions you're asking, in real time. Quite literally, they can read your mind."[10]

Grumblings from Europe

Already, in 2005, the president of the French Biliothèque National, Jean-Noël Jeanneney, published a booklet in which he warned against Google's claim to "organize the world's information."[11] He argued that it was not the job of any single, private corporation to assume such a role. *Google and the Myth of Universal Knowledge*, translated into English by the University of Chicago Press, remains one of the few early documents that openly challenge Google's uncontested hegemony. Jeanneney targets only one specific project, Book Search, which scans millions of books from American university libraries. His argument is very French-European: because of the unsystematic and unedited manner by which Google selects the books, the archive will not properly represent the giants of national literatures such as Hugo, Cervantes, and Goethe. Google, with its bias of English sources, will therefore not be the appropriate partner to build a public archive of the world's cultural heritage. According to Jeanneney, the choice of the books to be digitized will be impregnated by the "Anglo-Saxon atmosphere."

While in itself a legitimate argument, the problem is that Google doesn't intend to build and administer an online archive in the first place. The aim of Google is to make profit, not to build sustainable (public) archives. There have already been numerous occasions when companies like Google have literally overnight closed down valuable online services. As a for-profit entity, they have a right to such decisions. Google suffers from data obesity and is indifferent to calls for careful preservation or naive demands for cultural awareness. The prime objective of this cynical enterprise is to monitor user behavior in order to sell traffic data and profiles to interested third parties. Google is not after the ownership of Émile Zola. Its intention is to lure the Proust fan *away* from the archive. Perhaps there is an interest in a cool Stendhal mug, the XXL Flaubert T-shirt, or a Sartre purchase at Amazon. For Google, Balzac's collected work is abstract data junk, a raw resource whose sole purpose is to make a profit, whereas for the French it is the epiphany of their language and culture. It remains an open question if the proposed European answer to Google, the multimedia search engine Quaero, will ever be operational, let alone embody Jeanneney's values. By the time Quaero launches, the search-engine market will be a generation ahead of Quaero in media and device capabilities; some argue that Mr Chirac was more interested in defending French pride than in the global advancement of the internet.[12]

Studies on Google in the first decade of its existence can be divided into three categories. First are the easy-to-overlook computer manuals, from *Google for Dummies* to *Search Engine Optimization: An Hour a Day*. The second genre is corporate porn, written by over-enthusiastic IT evangelists such as John Batelle, Randall Stross, David Vise, and Jeff Jarvis. The third category is the odd European complaint about the Behemoth, warning against the latest incorporation of Big Brother. We could mention a few German titles. Gerard Reischl's 2008 *The Google Trap: The Internet's Uncontrolled World Power* claims to be the first European book critical of Google. Reischl plays with the fear amongst Germans of (American) corporations and their hunger for private data – much like the Gestapo and the Stasi, Google knows everything about you.[13] The 2009 title *Klick, Strategies against Digital Stupidity*, from journalist Susanne Gaschke, has a more general approach à la Carr, warning against computers, the internet, and their corporations taking over our lives (and particularly our children).[14] In *Google's Copy-Paste Syndrome*, also from 2009, Austrian media scholar Stefan Weber warns against the rise of plagiarism in classrooms and academic publishing, the decline of writing skills, and "the googlization of education." Why learn by heart if you can search for it in seconds?[15]

North American Search-Engine Critique

Despite the few grumblings from Europe, most of Google's critics are North Americans. So far Europe has invested surprisingly few resources into conceptually understanding the culture of search. At best, the EU is the first adopter of technical standards and products developed elsewhere. What counts in new media research is conceptual supremacy. Technology research alone will not do the job, no matter how much money the EU invests in future internet research. As long as the gap is reproduced between new media culture and major governing culture, or between private and public cultural institutions, we cannot establish a thriving technological culture. In short, we should stop seeing opera and the other *beaux arts* as a form of compensation to the unbearable lightness of cyberspace. Besides imagination, collective will, and a good dose of creativity, Europeans could mobilize their unique ability to gripe into a productive form of negativity. Their collective passion to reflect and critique can be used in a movement of "critical anticipation" to overcome the outsider syndrome felt by those in the roles of mere user and consumer.

Jaron Lanier wrote in his Weizenbaum obituary:

> we wouldn't let a student become a professional medical researcher without learning about double blind experiments, control groups, placebos and the replication of results. Why is computer science given a unique pass that allows us to be soft on ourselves? Every computer science student should be trained in Weizenbaumian skepticism, and should try to pass that precious discipline along to the users of our inventions.[16]

We must ask ourselves: why are most of the intelligent Google critics Americans? We can no longer accept the argument that they are better informed. Two examples of critics walking in Weizenbaum's footsteps are Nicholas Carr and Siva Vaidhyanathan. Carr has an IT business background as former editor of *Harvard Business Review* and has developed himself as the perfect insider critic. Carr's *The Big Switch* describes Google's strategy to centralize, and thus control, the internet infrastructure through its data-center.[17] Computers are now smaller, cheaper, and faster. This economy of scale makes it possible to outsource storage and applications at little or no cost. Businesses are switching from in-house IT departments to network services. Instead of further decentralizing, internet use is now concentrated in a few extremely energy-demanding data-centers.[18] Lanier: "what the fiber-optic internet does for computing is exactly what the alternating-current network did for electricity: it makes the location of the equipment unimportant to the user, allowing machines to operate together as a single system."[19]

Siva Vaidhyanathan's blog project, *The Googlization of Everything*, ambitiously synthesized critical Google research into a book published in early 2011.[20] In it, he covers issues such as Google Street View, Google Book Search, and the company's relation to China. His conclusion that we trust Google too much is surprisingly un-American: "We should influence – even regulate – search systems actively and intentionally and thus take responsibility for how the

Web delivers knowledge. We must build the sort of online eco-system that can benefit the whole world over the long term, not one that serves the short-term interests of one powerful company, no matter how brilliant."[21] Meanwhile, an informal group of critical search investigators gathers now and then under code names like Deep Search, Society of the Query, and the Shadow Search Project.[22] These initiatives do not get stuck in a moralistic critique of Google as an evil corporation ("Caesar-style" as Vaidhyanathan coins it), but actively promote alternative search engines, even going beyond the "search" principle itself. There is a collective need to develop radical algorithms, combined with a critique of our algorithmic techno-culture, such as the one formulated by the Italian Ippolita collective. According to Siva Vaidhyanathan, this loose coalition aims to beat Google at the level of its origin, through knowledge produced in and outside of universities, created and influenced by mathematicians, artists, activists, and coders.

Not only is there discontent toward an unaccountable data-hungry corporate giant, but also strategies to "uncool" Google are becoming visible. The capitalist answer is to to let the market do its work. The rise of Facebook is an interesting case of a competitor on the same level of Google's attention economy, yet arguably an even worse case in terms of privacy violations. It shouldn't be too hard to "uncool" the brand image. Kids running from power-hungry monopolies prob-ably provide the most effective political action. It might also be effec-tive to start calling Google an advertisement firm – which they are, if you look at their revenues. Regulations from Brussels will come a decade too late. Nationalizing parts of Google, for instance, its Book project, is still a very disruptive proposal in every debate, although there are moves afoot to hand massive book-scanning efforts over to public libraries and archives.

Criticizing Google in public debates and applying Jeff Jarvis's "publicness" strategy to the company itself still have a future, since much of what Google does is secretive in nature – for instance, its data-centers, energy policy, data policies, search ranking, and col-laboration with secret services. In the case of Google Books, the for-profit use of the public domain is so clear that it is time to stand up and reclaim the commons. Much of what Google develops should in fact be public infrastructure, and could have been if only universities and research institutes had better understood their public duties. Imagine Google as a non-profit global knowledge source. Looking at Wikipedia, this is not so utopian at all.

Returning to search, we are obsessed with the unsatisfactory answers to our queries but not with the underlying problem, namely the poor quality of our education and the diminishing ability to think in a critical way. How will future generations relate to – and design –Weizenbaum's "islands of reason"? A reappropriation of time is necessary. Currently our "culture of time" says we can no longer stroll around like a *flâneur*. All information, including any object or experience, must be instantaneously at hand. Our techno-cultural default is temporal intolerance. Our machines register software redundancy with increasing impatience, always demanding the update, and we are all too willing to oblige, mobilized by the fear of slower performance. Usability experts measure the fractions of a second in which we decide whether the information on screen is what we are looking for. If we're dissatisfied, we click away. We could start praising random query outcomes but hardly practice this virtue ourselves.

Serendipity requires a lot of time. If we no longer stumble onto islands of reason through our inquiries, we may as well build in this capacity ourselves. I argue that we need to invent new ways to interact with information, new ways to represent it such as techniques pioneered by Lev Manovich's cultural analytics, and new ways to make sense of it. How are artists, designers, and architects responding to these challenges? Stop searching; start questioning. Rather than trying to defend ourselves against information overload, we can approach this situation creatively, as an opportunity to invent new forms appropriate to our information-rich world.

— 10 —

ORGANIZING NETWORKS IN CULTURE AND POLITICS

The Master's Tools Will Never Dismantle the Master's House.

Audre Lorde

The important thing is not to be better armed but to take the initiative. Courage is nothing, confidence in your own courage is everything. Having the initiative helps.

The Invisible Committee

The dark periods of human history were, for Voltaire, simply not worthy of the attention of intelligent men. The purpose of history is to impart truth, not to satisfy idle curiosity, and this can only be done by studying the triumphs of reason and imagination, not the failures.

Isaiah Berlin

Today, we can claim that activism not only employs the internet as a tool, but that the internet has also started to shape the organization of social movements themselves. In the 1990s, the internet was used internally to network existing groups and NGOs, while the general populace was not yet privy to its utilities and organizing logic. This has all changed with the rise of "user-generated content." More than merely a coordinating mechanism, the internet's networking capabilities shape the very structures of activism and political activity today. It both mobilizes and accelerates awareness of issues. As well, there is an increasing turnover of campaigns asking for our time and resources. Every newspaper poses the question whether Facebook and Twitter can cause the fall of authoritarian regimes. When popular writers such as Malcolm Gladwell warn that the "revolution will not be tweeted,"[1] we know that we have ended up in a state of whirlpool dialectics in which the real and the virtual have gone out to play their own seductive game of attraction and distraction.

Wait a minute. How did we get here? Since when has internet activism been so *en vogue*? An influential factor is the decline of places to gather. Scarcity of urban space due to the rise of rentals and real-estate speculation has pushed activists further online, where dispersed people can find each other much faster. This social fact alone confronts us with the Web 2.0 question. The ruins of the industrial age have been recolonized and turned into valuable real estate. Squatting all the empty office spaces – symbols of the post-industrial era – has yet to take off and may never happen due to harsh legal and surveillance regimes. Even abandoned space itself has become scarce – except in the ever-expanding desert.

Criticism of this situation abounds. First, we need to be aware of a stricter separation between internal and external organization. Because of reduced privacy and increased surveillance, (militant) protest can no longer rely on electronic devices in either the early stages or during decisive moments of socio-aesthetic action. This is a problem because email, for instance, is still used as a tool for mobilization and internal debate, and mobile phones are employed for coordinating action on the streets. To decommission such tools at the right moment is an art in itself, comparable to the seventh sense one must develop to locate surveillance video cameras. Activism must, once again, become hyper-local and offline in order to strike its target effectively, a trend that might soon be adopted by larger NGO structures.

There is a perhaps unforeseen danger in Evgeny Morozov's justified critique of internet usage in authoritarian states such as Iran, Belarus, Russia, and Moldova.[2] While important to point out the failures of techno-optimism and the limits of the libertarian cyber agenda, this type of critique can also backfire on activists who run on empty due to apathy and indifference. RSS inventor and ur-blogger Dave Winer: "Technology is important because it empowers people. That's where you start. Not in novelty or neatness, not in the fact that it changes things, because it might change things by disempowering. Change is not in itself a valid reason for anything."[3] Change can end up in all directions, which makes the call for "change" such a potentially empty statement. The same can be said of the chatting-over-tea comment that technology in itself is not a force for liberation. Morozov's critique of cyber-utopianism with its naive belief in the emancipatory nature of online communication needs to be paired with detailed insight from the inside.[4]

159

In the end, Morozov is only concerned about US foreign policy, not the trials and tribulations of media activists. The insight that the internet can be used for both good and evil should never become our concluding remark, and there will be no return to old-school hard-core activism either. Even if we admit that a chain of offline incidents caused an event (such as the Tunisian street vendor who set himself on fire, causing the downfall of the Ben Ali regime in January 2011, or the Kifaya movement in Egypt), we should not fall back on offline romanticism. Instead we need to develop a long-term view on how networked technologies should and should not be embedded in political and cultural practices. We need a mix of long-term concerns and trial-and-error experiments. No matter how easy it is to use free corporate-owned "cloud" applications, we need to insist on building up and maintaining independent infrastructure combined with "crypto" awareness of how to protect privacy – not to mention the importance of free software/open source usage. If today's technologies scale up so easily, then why are so many activists still stuck in the margins? The questions are manifold. How can activists downplay hypes that will eventually backfire? How can we look beyond the widely covered street clashes to get a better understanding of why (open) conflicts arise in the first place? Is it enough to "reintroduce passion into politics" or to act on Slavoj Žižek's challenge to "bring together the rejection of a divine Otherness and the element of unconditional commitment"[5] by translating his call into network protocols?

Slacktivism

Regardless of urgent privacy concerns and our own user preferences (whether we say yes or no to Facebook), let us note that social media are playing an increasingly large role in the "organization of information" in general and that they compete with search engines, email, and web portals. Originally brushed aside as an ordinary online address book, generating meaning through informal chats amongst "friends," social media are now a prime news source for millions. This in turn affects the way we transform news items into issues that we act upon. How does this urgency occur? In order to answer this question, we need to distinguish between media activism that is "crystal" versus "mass" focused. Following Elias Canetti's *Crowds and Power*, we can look at how small-core units are formed, around which, often in the blink of an eye, they then swell into masses. In the heated debates about the "Facebook revolutions," it is essential to distinguish between how such core groups and organizational units come into being, and how they successfully communicate their message to mobilize larger events.

What counts in both cases is actual internet use, not how op-eds, columnists, talk-radio hosts – or book authors, for that matter – are framing the topic. Arts, culture, and political campaigning make highly strategic use of social media, from internal organization to mobilization and publicity. What looks like yet another layer of social fluff is much less informal and requires principled decisions. The moral debates that condemn Web 2.0 as short-lived hype and that call for exodus have so far not taken into account why the millions are flocking toward Facebook in the first place. From past experience, we know that easy-to-use, stable software with modest interfaces that do not overload the user with additional features are going to be successful. Time and again, the moral pressure to quit proves much less powerful than the drive to replace one desire with a more appealing one. The rushed critique of ideology also stops us from making careful observations. Social media are invading all aspects of life. From a traditional "underground" perspective, it may be inconceivable to use Facebook or Twitter, just as the Maquis communicated "breast to breast." Sure. Today's messy reality teaches us otherwise. Have you already tried not to use Google, Facebook, or your smartphone for a week? Like many before you, you're certain to fail that test.

The trouble with current media activist strategies in the age of social networking is not so much their ability to scale up, which they seem to manage quite well, but the absence of a painful set-back in the encounter with the powers that be. Cyber cascades à la Avaaz. org that organize online petitions with often millions of signatures create blips in mass awareness, but fail at resilience. Resistance means struggle-with-defeat as a real option – and this sounds profoundly uncool. There is nothing sexy about being told "no." Protesting today means party-time and jobs for event managers. Culture, marginal or mainstream, turns out to be less helpful in solving the organization question than most have thought. The vanishing point here is Heath and Potter's *The Rebel Sell, Why the Culture Can't Be Jammed*, from 2005. PR experts of the contemporary reformist movements, with Tony Blair as their guru, claim the moral high ground in their insistence on remaining positive, while militant fighters who defend rights, attack the system, and fight back are portrayed as twentieth-century losers.

161

In the past, hacktivist strategies have embodied certain elements of such radical negativity, with tactical media as its playful counterpart. For other models of inspired refusal, we could go back to the 1950s literature on the user as rebel (Albert Camus) and outsider (Colin Wilson). Today's protesting user is neither the perfect e-citizen nor a pathological, brain-damaged, white multitasking loner. Going post-pop, how would we define the aesthetics of online protest?

Bored with slacktivism, we know better: strong organizational forms, firmly rooted in real life and capable of mobilizing (financial) resources, will eventually overrule weak online commitments (I "like" your insurrection). Following market predictions, we design interfaces where the hyper-local and the global virtually intermingle, bootstrapping us to the next level of political commitment. As Malcolm Gladwell has already expressed in *The New Yorker*, Twitter alone will not bring about democracy.[6] Experienced campaigners will think: "nicely put, Malcolm, but how do we get there? It is no longer sufficient to deconstruct media hype: can you please come up with suggestions for what is to be done?"

Switching Offline

After slow food, eco marketers have discovered slow communication.[7] Will we soon get WiFi-free lounges in the name of leisure lifestyle? How about "calm" interfaces for hyperactive kids? What may be good for one's private health may not be in the interest of the commons. There is a lot to be said for increased information sharing and participation in important debates. In some cases we'll speed up; in others we'll slow down. Strong-willed (self-)mastery of technology will have an important social and educational component, and is miles away from the "info diet" motive. Going offline can balance one's body and soul, but it should not be promoted as the latest belief system.

The necessity for mobilizing struggles should therefore not be confused with ecological trends such as local-produce farmers' markets. The activist motive is an essentially different issue from New Age calls to have offline relaxation. The strategic move to disconnect (temporarily?) should follow the lines of danah boyd, who warns young people in particular of privacy issues on social networking sites.[8] Rather than using moralistic instructions to keep kids away, her method successfully studies the daily lives of teenagers in

162

order to help parents, teachers, and kids themselves reconcile their powerful desire to hang out with friends, with justified privacy concerns.

Luddite offline strategies are only effective if practiced collectively in the form of a general strike, detached from individual lifestyle design. After Facebook changed its privacy settings, the DigiActive website advised fellow activists to unfriend fellow activists and leave political groups. "Delete political status messages, notes, and links and do not add new ones, un-tag yourself from photos of you taking part in political activities or in the presence of known activists and remove any linkages connecting you to politically dangerous people, ideas, or organizations."[9] DigiActive continues:

> Activists need to create separate anonymous profiles for their political activities, which contain no accurate personal information and are completely unconnected to their real friends, affiliations, and locations. In some cases, it may even make sense to create a "throw-away account," much as activists use throw-away cell phone cards: create a fake account to do one sensitive action, and then never use it again. So that a single IP address cannot be connected to your activism account, you should access that account from different public computers in cyber cafes and never from your home computer.

One is never too young to learn to deflect deep package inspection by installing PGP (email), TrackMeNot (for browsers), or Tor Identity Cloakers (IP anonymity), or by buying a first crypto phone.

Activist committees no longer dream of having an invisible status because they are subjected to the same techno-surveillance as everyone else. In response, soft subcultures happily create websites, groups, and channels in the hope of being left alone as a community. Indeed, it can be quiet at the very end of the Long Tail.[10] But the masses have not yet discovered that demo-ing the latest cultural artefact is no longer hip either, and that there is no avant-garde outside the marketing realm. We have all understood the laws of cool, so how can we discard this logic altogether? It is not enough to "uncool" in a cool way (if we may summarize Adbusters like this). Can you ignore the iProducts? Social media promises to make unmediated, direct connections between people, and it is this utopian energy that drags us deeper into corporate media arrangements. Instead of making the simple call to reject such technologies once and for all, what is to be done?

Encounters with a Cause

That we are not all "friends" is a truism of the late Web 2.0 era, one that cuts off conversations rather than sparks the collective imagination to initiate "other networking." How then do we define contemporary relationships? How to design "sticky" relationships that matter, that go beyond the friend–foe distinction and symbolic representation of affective affinity? Let us dream up unlikely relations, spontaneous encounters (and how to solidify them), and technologies that actively derail everyday routines. Smart mobs were too innocent; 4chan has radical elements that bring us in contact with unknown online users, but after a few moments of excitement we are stuck in boring voyeurism. What would solidarity mean in the 4chan or Chatroulette way – getting matched with a global Southerner by the Machine as a peer-to-peer development-aid project of the post-NGO era?

There is a lot to learn from the Anonymous movement. Yet what is missing in this ironic Web 2.0 culture is the "sweet stranger" element,[11] in the vein of what Jean Baudrillard called "object strategies." Out there are random encounters with a cause. In order to be open to radically different possibilities, we need to say farewell to the "trust" paradigm that conceptually supports paranoid security systems and culminates in "walled gardens." The "risk" discourse should no longer only apply to entrepreneurs who are praised for their courageous risk-taking (with other people's money) while the vast majority of users remain locked into "trust" cages. Networks should not only replicate old ties. They have another potential. We need to abandon the "friends" logic and start to play with the notion of dangerous design.

In terms of activist strategies, let's jump over our own shadow to go beyond the turbulent-speculative 1990s' "tactical media" legacy.[12] A central concern is if and how social movements, art collectives, and cultural initiatives should make use of social media. It is one thing to make us less dependent on the Google cloud and Facebook's definition of social relationships. The real dilemma is how to approach the organization question. Žižek, Badiou, and Agamben as the next Marx, Lenin, and Mao (decide for yourself who is who)? These philosophers, no matter how interesting their work, are of little help as they fall back into outmoded Leninist nostalgia. Their collective refusal to discuss (new) organizational forms is telling. In the age of networked digital exchanges, the social is even more ambivalent than

164

ever. No longer a God-given, the protocols for human collaboration are up for grabs. This task is no longer exclusively in the hands of the Church, the village, the clan – or the Party, for that matter. Should we so uncritically put our faith in the hands of Palo Alto as the next Kremlin-Vatican?

In a discussion with Clay Shirky, Evgeny Morozov states: "I believe that a mass protest movement needs a charismatic leader, such as Sakharov, to really unfold its potential. I fear that the Twitter age will no longer produce a Sakharov."[13] This was obviously said before the celebrity cult formed around Julian Assange. Still, what Morozov views as lacking, we should see as a given: networks promote informal leadership that is hard to replace. The old-school masses on the streets once projected their desires onto a charismatic leader, but activists today confront the fact that new media both mobilize as well as deconstruct, disassemble, deschool, and fragment. The networked computer is a deeply postmodern, immobilizing Cold War machine. We are looking in vain for a way to reassemble the masses and use networks to build formal systems of representation. What Morozov suggests could also be read as a new starting point: there will be no masses as long as we sabotage the production of leaders in the first place. Instead of counter-power, we have dismantled power entirely. This implies that we have effectively reached – no, realized – the Foucauldian age. Autonomist strategies are less "utopian" in such conditions, which explains why we see mixtures of anarchists and techno-libertarians popping up everywhere.

A key moment for any social movement is the initial contact between two or more seemingly autonomous units. Call it the erotics of touching. Ever experienced the metamorphosis of weak links transmuting into revolutionary bonds? It is hard to imagine that this exciting phase will be removed from the digital equation. Creating new connections is pivotal in a political-artistic process. It is the moment of "change" when the desert of consensual hegemony turns into a blossoming oasis. Michael Hardt and Antonio Negri: "The kind of transition we are working with requires the growing autonomy from both private and public control; the metamorphosis of social subjects through training in cooperation, communication and organizing social encounters; and thus a progressive accumulation of the common."[14] This is nothing but the science of revolution: the ultimate object for organization studies and its underground cases.

If we want to get there, reading the zeitgeist correctly is not enough. We need to experiment with new forms of organization. Install, update, crash, restart, de-install. Academic revolutionaries' hearts may be in the right place, but their readings are straight-out retro and lack curiosity for contemporary forms of organization. Where are their trial-and-error stories? Web 2.0 puts the question on the table by asking how to organize dissent in the digital age. How do social movements these days come into being? If there is nowhere to hide, should we adopt the "open conspiracy" model? Do movements grow out of "mass crystals" as Elias Canetti framed it, those small and rigid groups that knew how to gather in crowds on the streets and squares? Is this why we are so fascinated with "viral communication"?[15] So far, curiosity has mainly expressed itself through the act of duplication and "going viral." Beyond weak forms of information dissemination, how can I call you to act? Are organized networks the "mass crystals" of the twenty-first century?

Orgnets in Practice

One of the few yet unexplored models left for new media culture is that of networking itself. If networks are here to stay, we must take them more seriously and radicalize their shape. Networks are still seen as secondary, informal platforms for interpersonal expression. Instead of focusing on the "network organization" – an instrumental view of networks as tools for organizations, social movements, or business to exchange information and experiences – we should gain a better understanding of "organized networks," a concept which I have developed with Ned Rossiter since 2005.[16] These emerging "organized networks" aim to cooperate in order to realize projects, write software, and, in short, produce cultural artefacts. Whereas network organizations are more loosely connected and form slightly noncommittal ties, aimed at "recharging the batteries" through information sharing and inspirational talks, the term "organized networks" is more transformative by moving the production of culture onto the Net, and so changing the very mode of organization itself. Active development of concepts like this respond to a lack of necessary terms. As Simon Critchley writes: "Politics is always about nomination. It's about naming a political subjectivity and organizing politically around that name."[17] According to Critchley, we should not pin our hopes on ontology but "[try] to conceive forms of gathering, coalition and association in relation to a more wild and formless social being." The nomination I discuss here comes from the world of network technologies. Why contemporary thinkers overlook this vital part of contemporary life is remarkable, but that's another matter.

166

Organized networks, or "orgnets," are new institutional forms of collaboration that arise after the process of digitization and informatization has reached completion. As an area of research it focuses on the potentially productive tension between decentralization and institutionalization. Much like the shifting relationship between social movements and NGOs 10 to 15 years ago, we see increasing tension between existing models of "cultural organizations" promoting new media, culture, and arts, and informal networks of individual artists. Unlike a decade ago, the cultural new media sector can no longer claim to embody an "avant-garde" position, because the avant-garde has been taken over by the market. This situation leaves a void: neither truly innovative nor particularly critical, new media organizations in the non-profit sector are confused. What direction should they take? If they are not conducting proper research considered useful by policymakers and academics, then what is their role? Now that the introductory phase of new media is coming to an end, should they simply do without public funding and disappear? The well-funded massive digitization of "cultural heritage" has proven useless for the new media sector and merely reproduces the existing, conservative cultural landscape dominated by museums, opera, and concert halls. The same could be said of "media wisdom" programs in the educational sector, which are merely run to "manage" (read: control) the already high computer literacy amongst youngsters as well as the ignorance and paranoia of parents and teachers.

Instead of aligning with the "creative industries" agenda, current organizational models must transform into facilitating hubs that empower organized networks. Rather than further exploring (and exploiting) weak ties, organized networks seek stronger bonds within smaller units that emerge out of peer-to-peer encounters. Instead of complaining about the decline of commitment, we'd better start designing tighter structures that can facilitate and coordinate collaborative work on cultural, political, and educational projects. In the same way, we should stop using volunteer labor and justify payment to (emerging) professionals by developing alternative revenue models and currency systems. What are the protocols that structure organized networks? What are the modalities of self-organization? How can organized networks scale up? And how sustainable are these networks, presuming that they will not, for the time being, have access to ordinary (financial) resources?

The orgnet concept stems from an active, dynamic environment that generates more questions than can possibly be answered. Activists organize transnational campaigns online, and Web 2.0 companies

167

profit from the free labor and attention provided by the networks of users. If we take these network technologies seriously, we have to ask ourselves: what's next after all the initial excitement? Will networking produce a dispersed, weak level of sociality or will relationships become more substantial? What long-term cultural transformations might emerge from networked interactions? How can networks maintain their critical edge, while aiming for professional status? Was the content produced in the context of "free culture" really meant to be distributed for no cost, or was this done because "free" was the only option? Will we return to our busy everyday life after the hype recedes or strive for an even deeper commitment to Social 2.0? As artists, researchers, activists, educators, and cultural workers are drawn into the network paradigm, it is urgent to collectively inquire into what happens when networks become the driving force of both work and leisure. Even if networks do not replace real existing office culture, how will they transform cultural organizations?

Instead, we propose to implement independent sources of income and types of organizations that reflect the "network condition" in which cultural workers find themselves. Living under the omen of neo-liberal capitalism, messy everyday life already offers us prefab ideologies, but we can also be open to new strategic designs. Network architectures express a freedom of choice, and their layout of the social aspects are vague possibilities to (re-)connect. The freedom to move from one city or professional field to the next is both liberating and distressing, implying both the risks and the pleasures of roaming. How do we balance the desire to move on with the justified struggle to defend rights and resources? The pressure to ruthlessly self-promote while practicing vulnerable "self-disclosure" on social networking sites is a similar dilemma. Subscribing to networks is no longer a choice. Many of the "precarious" culture workers feel they must sign up and join groups, lists, and professional networks, such as LinkedIn, since online social networking turns out to become a vital part of the reproduction of work. In this McJob era, artists and culture workers must prepare a range of parallel projects that may or may not become realized as paid labor. This is why it is not morally wise to dismiss participation on corporate platforms such as Facebook and Twitter – though a better idea is to actively promote distributed alternative social networking software based on free software and open-source principles.

One should recognize the actual force of the ideology of free and open as advocated by some in the "free culture" movement as a potential trap. Embrace Creative Commons, open content, free software,

168

and open access, but only if they become part of a larger movement that experiments with (alternative) revenue models. In this respect we also need a new notion of the public domain, and public broadcasting in particular, in which new media have an equal status with film, public radio, television, and print. Barcamps, unconferencing, book-sprints, hackathons, contentfests, and bricolabs are all manifestations of a thriving culture of temporary media labs. Rather than asking how these emerging practices might contribute to "policy," we should reverse this question: how can cultural policies strengthen networks? One of the steps we need to take is to understand networking as a cultural logic at odds with current democratic mechanisms. Networks start from a post-representational position. A network cannot claim to speak on anyone's behalf other than its own constituents.

Let's look at three cases of organized networks in action. As these are not religions, identities, or quality management systems, whether the subjects or institutions involved subscribe to the "orgnet" idea is irrelevant. At least in this initial stage, the idea of orgnets should first and foremost be seen as a proposal, a critical concept, and strange attractor harboring the potential to provoke events.

Case 1: Culturemondo

Culturemondo is a network of cultural web portals[18] that consist of researchers, including Taipei-based Ilya Lee, and Aleksandra Uzlac of CultureLink from Croatia; policymakers such as Frank Thinnes from the Luxembourg-based culture portal plurio.net and Jane Finnis from Culture24, UK; IT experts from museums, such as Seb Chan from the Powerhouse Museum in Sydney, Australia; and others in the cultural heritage sector. According to Ilya Lee, Culturemondo members recognize the value of peer sharing with like-minded people who want to increase influence and visibility for their work and spread literacy in progressive web development in their own fields. Ilya Lee: "They acknowledge that the internet promotes loose con-nections, not official global bureaucratic forms of organization. It is really important to coordinate and practice the value of collaboration in the cultural heritage sector." Amongst many topics, Culturemondo discusses how to ensure that culture and heritage policies are linked to digital policies and strategies. The 6th roundtable in Amsterdam, coinciding with PICNIC, was entitled "Bringing Practice into Digital Cultural Policy."

The Culturemondo network was founded by people from cultural web portals, who met in June 2004 at the Minerva International

Digitisation Conference in Dublin. Jane Finnis, of Culture24, and Vladimir Skok co-founded Culturemondo; Canada and the TELDAP program in Taiwan sponsored its first years. Culturemondo is not a global branch organization or a professional association, but an active, informal network that thrives on cultural differences and approaches. Rather than organizing conferences or annual meetings, it creates "round tables." Of note is its transdisciplinary attitude and the variety of professionals that it gathers: cultural heritage managers, cultural policymakers, web developers, designers, copy editors, and content producers.

Aren't web portals a residue from the dot.com nineties? They are not how content is distributed in the age of Web 2.0, which relies on recommendation, linking, and "liking." Culturemondo members are all too aware of this shift. The "cultural web portals" label is still used because funders and ministries understand this discourse. And, let's face it, the "cultural heritage" sector is notoriously sluggish. Culturemondo members talk about how to handle these traditional institutional demands. Over Skype, I asked Ilya Lee if he considers Culturemondo an "organized network." Lee:

> Culturemondo brings together policymakers and geeks. We emphasize the human dimension, informal exchanges and inward development of the network. Active members originate from 15 countries, with 250 collaboration organizations. We are turning Culturemondo into a real body where the local and global can meet. In that sense, one could say that it has "orgnet" characteristics.

Does Culturemondo subscribe to Creative Industry rhetoric? Lee:

> In terms of sponsoring, yes. But luckily there is a delayed pressure. As we speak, some of the programs and partners we worked with are forced to close down. The quest for business models is out there. This manifests itself concretely into pressures from the side of the creative industries to start developing apps for mobile phone in response to the "web is dead" rumors initiated by Wired editor-in-chief Chris Anderson. Institutions and commerce like their closed nature. Walled culture is growing. To counter this development, we have to discuss our core values. There is a need for theory. How can we introduce open-source practices into cultural policy? This goes back to the 1997 Amsterdam Practice to Policy agenda and it would be good to write the history of these efforts.

Culturemondo can easily get 5,000 "friends" on Facebook and bring in hundreds of new members, but what's the point? In December 2008, I spoke at the 4th Culturemondo roundtable in Taipei on the issue of organized networks in relation to the social media hype.

My presentation contrasted the exploitation of "weak ties" by social networking sites such as Facebook and MySpace and the urge felt by users to collect more and more "friends" (an effect provoked by algorithms), with the tendency to strengthen existing – but also very virtual – ties inside networks which themselves seek intense exchange and collaboration. The unease with Facebook's blunt privacy policies prompted artists, activists, and hackers not only to protest against Facebook with actions such as the Web 2.0 Suicide Machine (developed by the Rotterdam Moddr lab), but also to develop alternative social networking software such as Crabgrass, Diaspora, Appleseed, and GNUSocial. Blogging followed a similar path, evolving from a centralized, corporate, and proprietary platform (blogger.com) to open-source software that everyone can download and install on their own servers (Wordpress). Apart from cool and innovative user interfaces, the "open graph" principle could help make the latter initiatives successful by allowing you to migrate all your "friends" from one social network to the next.

German theorist Soenke Zehle spoke at the 6th PICNIC Culture-mondo roundtable in Amsterdam. I asked him how he would describe the network.

Culturemondo attracts people who no longer wonder whether networks will transform the way they operate but have the (conceptual and technological) competencies to actively shape the institutional transformation of the cultural sector. The stakes of such shifts in the dynamic of institutionalization will remain high as long as the museum remains the telos of cultural production. Culturemondo is neither the only nor the first effort to call into question the ways in which the borders of the cultural field are determined, but it is well positioned to explore corresponding transformations of its respective publics, as online portals are by definition located at the institutional margins, offering a new milieu for ethico-aesthetic experimentation, not least because here the interface itself has become the main concern. Which is why, above and beyond their concrete networking activities, such an ensemble of efforts, sustained by collaborative research as much as events, offers a logic of interstices and iteration rather than institutions – and therefore a much-needed disruption of the way the making and making-public of culture is organized.

Case 2: Winter Camp 09

In March 2009, the Institute of Network Cultures organized Winter Camp 09, a weeklong event in which artist and activist networks were invited to come to Amsterdam to work on the very issue of how to "organize" their network.[19] The aim was to connect the real and the virtual to find out how distributed social networks can better collaborate. The more people work together online, the more urgent the question of sustainable network models will become. Usually it is very expensive for (virtual) networks to meet up. Their members are spread across Europe or the globe, and if they meet it is for quick coordination sessions in the margins of a conference or festival, which is why larger players in the field should host such workshops. The 150 Winter Camp participants from 12 networks included programmers, activists, academics, writers, designers, cultural workers, and artists. A few of the 12 participating networks emerged within the context of the INC, such as MyCreativity, from the creative labor context. Others were already established (Dyne.org and Upgrade!), or on the verge of becoming a network (Bricolabs). The networks ranged from the highly informal (Goto10) to the more formal (blender.org, FreeDimensional) with participants from mainly Western Europe, North America, and a smattering from other parts of the world.

The Winter Camp format was a mix of largely improvised, conference-like presentations and working sessions that emphasized getting things done. The outcomes varied from research proposals to code, and sought to find a balance between the intense sessions of groups, plenary sessions, and mid-size meetings, while leaving ample opportunities for informal interactions. A "meta-group" was responsible for the programming and production details of the event and acted in close collaboration with a group of bloggers. The meta-group also conducted interviews – all available online at Vimeo – with almost 30 members across the networks, focusing on concerns such as the tension between informality and formality, financial and material resources, and relationships to other networks and groups. At Winter Camp, groups exchanged experiences of which I highlight three elements:

Growth: Sometimes, for no obvious reason, networks remain too small or grow too fast. Is there an ideal size? Research has shown that a network with 50–150 active members can go on for many years. Is expansion always the answer to a stagnated network? Are networked conversations in which more than 500 users participate doomed to fall apart, as stated in the past? Would "small is beautiful" be an apt response to the Facebook masses?

Conflict: Networks often get caught up in recurring instances of conflict between participants (flamewars, trolling, territoriality),

172

which can lead to the larger network's collapse. Is it enough to let time pass and bring in new people, in the hope of overruling ongoing differences? What role might codes of conduct or other procedures play in mitigating these interpersonal conflicts? In this era of "trust" between "friends," it is so easy to walk away, unsubscribe, filter out people you do not like, ignore emails, and leave networks. Networks are often transnational, and with this come vast cultural differences over how to negotiate the site or event of conflict most effectively.

Software and the technology fix: There are tons of suitable tools for collaboration. What are the limits of current communication protocols (email, mailing lists, web pages, social media, Skype) and are there alternative tools available that might enhance independence? Are there ways to reduce complex procedures and potential info overload? How does a network of non-experts learn programming and to handle non-mainstream software? Is technology an opportunity to expand and experiment with the network, or rather a buggy nuisance that scares off newbies?

Case 3: RIXC in Riga

The last example is a meeting that directly addressed issues of cultural sustainability with a focus on networking. A training program for cultural network management called Organized Networks took place in Riga, Latvia, in December 2009.[20] The event brought together representatives from over 20 cultural organizations, new media centres, and networks from the Baltic, Nordic, and other European regions, as well as Caucasus countries. The training program was organized by RIXC, the center for new media culture in Latvia, with partners from Finland, Norway, Iceland, Sweden, Denmark, Lithuania, Latvia, the Netherlands, Armenia, and Georgia. According to the organizers, networks are not only virtual structures: "there are people and real technical infrastructures behind them, and our network cultures also are facing the same sustainability issues."[21] The central question was how to work out new strategies and methodologies to improve and develop a more sustainable translocal cooperation practice. How do we develop new network-based models that will facilitate both individuals and local cultural organizations? How do networks and nodes relate to each other? Much like Culturemondo, the training program had a transdisciplinary approach, as artists, new media activists, renewable technology researchers,

173

social software developers, open-source activists, and designers of autonomous and alternative infrastructures discussed how to deal with sustainability issues. While sustainability is typically a metaphorical buzzword, here we witness the literal transference of sustainability concepts from the context of natural resources to the cultural sector.

Over Skype, in November 2010, I asked Rasa Smite, the organizer of the Riga event, if "organized networks" in fact exist, or if they remain a useful yet not very realistic construct:

> In comparison to the wild 1990s we've experienced that a network no longer grows by itself. Maybe we're no longer that idealistic? We just don't see the rhizomes growing all around us. But there is still the myth of self-organizing surrounding networks while the reality is quite different. There is simply no continuity. We at RIXC had to readjust ourselves to this new situation and start testing better network models. Nowadays, we do not expect a lot from other network participants, which turned out to be a liberating moment. And that is where the orgnet idea came in. The model means taking full responsibility – and then it really starts to work.

The Peer-to-Peer Foundation, coordinated by Michael Bauwens, is a source of inspiration for Rasa. In the good old days from 2006 to 2008, before the financial crisis hit Latvia particularly hard, RIXC employed eight staff members. In late 2010, they were back to three, the two founders plus a producer. In the meantime, Rasa Smite finished her PhD research on the early days of creative network communities. In order to survive, the RIXC founders incorporated a for-profit company and now run both a non-profit organisation and a commercial venture.

Maybe the question is not how cultural policies can strengthen networks. In the short term this might be the case. But soon the borders of cultural and political organization will become even more fluid. Right now, networks depend on existing bricks-and-mortar institutions to escape the virtual and claim legitimacy. But what if the tables are turned and an overwhelming majority of the players are self-employed "precarious" freelancers? Perhaps networks will soon be able to incorporate as virtual entities, managing their own legal and financial matters without having a base in a particular country. This is when self-organization, free cooperation, and distributed resources will no longer be marginal and knocking on the thick doors of walled culture, but will transform from secondary entities into cultural agents.

Making steps in the right direction, Slavoj Žižek declares:

> Countering the devastating world-dissolving effect of capitalist modernization by inventing new fictions, imagining "new worlds," is inadequate, or, at least, profoundly ambiguous: it all depends on how these fictions relate to the underlying Real of capitalism – do they just supplement it with the imaginary multitude, as the postmodern "local narratives" do, or do they disturb its functioning?[22]

Conceptual knowledge is embedded in software, and concepts such as "organized networks" will have the task, to put it in Žižek's words, "to produce a symbolic fiction (a truth) that intervenes into the Real, that causes a change within it."[23] Can organized networks play a role in overcoming the (leftist) fear of confronting direct state power? The orgnet practices discussed here directly address what Žižek, in dialogue with Hardt and Negri, poses: "What kind of representation should replace the existing liberal-democratic representation state?"[24] If the network form is rapidly becoming the de facto expression of the social, then we must insert "no networks without organization" into the debate of the Critchleys, Mouffes, and Badious, and ask whether "no governing without movements" (Negri) should also be countered with "no movements without governing" (Žižek). Rather than repeating twentieth-century debates about the vanguard Leninist party model vs vitalist anarcho self-determination, we should further experiment with new institutional forms that emerge out of the current phase of internet development when social media mature and reach their full potential.

— 11 —

TECHNO-POLITICS AT WIKILEAKS

This is the first real info war, and you are the soldiers.

John Perry Barlow

Disclosures and leaks have featured in all eras, but never before has a non-state or non-corporate affiliated group done anything like WikiLeaks.[1] Founded in late 2006, WikiLeaks gained global notoriety throughout 2010 in four waves: the first in April was the release of a video from a US helicopter's cockpit recording the killing of Iraqis (entitled *Collateral Murder*), followed by the *Afghan War Logs* (91,000 files), and then the *Iraq War Logs* (391,000 files), all of which were finally eclipsed in the fourth wave by the publication of 250,000 United States diplomatic cables. With Cablegate, millions of documents online morphed from a quantitative leak into a qualitative one. Never before had a Net activist initiative been responsible for the sacking of ambassadors and ministers worldwide.

When WikiLeaks hit the mainstream in April 2010, there was little knowledge of things to come. Its network, composed of a handful of core members surrounded by dozens of loosely connected supporters, was without a bricks-and-mortar office. It had just recovered from major internal restructuring in late 2009, when it had to take servers offline and face near bankruptcy. During this growth spurt, or perhaps we should say crisis, the "wiki" aspect was dropped and WikiLeaks started to centralize around the personality of its founder, the Australian hacker and internet activist Julian Assange. This chapter examines the organizational implications of decisions made at this moment, in the calm just before the media storm, arguing, to rephrase the anti-globalization movement's slogan, that Another WikiLeaks is Possible.

176

By way of digging into strategic issues concerning WikiLeaks in particular, I will present a techno-materialist reading of leaking electronic documents in the late Web 2.0 era.

The Power of Puny Players

WikiLeaks' disclosures are the consequence of the dramatic spread of IT use due to plummeting costs, which can be broken down into three elements: chips and hardware, bandwidth, and, most striking of all, storage.[2] We do not need to be members of the Ray Kurzweil ("singularity is near") cult or buy into George Gilder's conservative agenda to understand the importance of the ever-growing speed of semi-conductors, cheap bandwidth, and stunning storage capacities of small hard drives and USB sticks that all the while keep dropping in price.[3]

Also contributing to WikiLeaks' activities is the reality that safekeeping state and corporate secrets – never mind private ones – has become difficult in an age of instant reproducibility and dissemination. Not only are classified embassy documents proving hard to protect, but an overwhelming portion of leaked material is raw data, messy collections of folders with countless versions, missing emails, downloaded PDFs, Excel sheets and power-pointless presentations. A new branch of science called e-discovery, or digital forensics, has developed expertise on retrieving, opening, and classifying a growing variety of digital evidence.[4] WikiLeaks is symbolic of this transformation in the "information society" at large, a mirror of things to come. So, while one can look at WikiLeaks as a (political) project and criticize it for its modus operandi, it can also be seen as the pilot phase in the evolution toward a far more generalized culture of anarchic exposure beyond the traditional politics of openness and transparency.

For better or worse, WikiLeaks skyrocketed into the realm of high-level international politics. Out of the blue, it became a full-blown player both on the world scene as well as in the national spheres of certain countries. Small player as it is, by virtue of its disclosures WikiLeaks appears on a par, at least in the domain of information gathering and publication, with governments or big corporations. At the same time, it's unclear whether this is a permanent feature or a temporary, hype-induced phenomenon – WikiLeaks appears to believe the former, which is more and more likely the case. A puny non-state and non-corporate actor, WikiLeaks nonetheless does not believe it

177

is punching above its weight in its fight against the US government and has started behaving accordingly. One might call this the "Talibanization" stage of the postmodern "Flat World" theory, when scales, times, and places are declared largely irrelevant.

What counts and disturbs to the point of boredom is the celebrity momentum and intense accumulation of media attention. WikiLeaks manages to capture that attention by way of spectacular information hacks, where other parties, especially civil society groups and human rights organizations, are desperately struggling to get their message across. Thanks to Cablegate documents, items that have simmered in the margins for years such as Shell's role in Nigeria (in terms of the human rights situation and pollution), suddenly make front-page headlines. While civil society tends to play by the rules and seek legitimacy from dominant institutions, WikiLeaks' strategy is populist insofar as it taps into public disaffection with mainstream politics. WikiLeaks bypasses this old-world structure of power and instead goes to the source of political legitimacy in today's info-society: the rapturous banality of the spectacle. WikiLeaks brilliantly puts to use the "escape velocity" of IT, using IT to leave IT behind and rudely erupt the realm of real-world politics. Political legitimacy for WikiLeaks has not been graciously bestowed by the powers that be.

In the ongoing saga called "the Decline of the US Empire," WikiLeaks enters the stage as the slayer of a soft target. It would be difficult to imagine it inflicting quite the same damage to the Russian or Chinese governments, or even to the Singaporean – not to mention their "corporate" affiliates. In Russia or China, such disclosure would first need to surmount huge cultural and linguistic barriers, not to mention purely power-related ones. In that sense, WikiLeaks in its present manifestation remains a typically Western product and cannot claim to be a truly universal or global undertaking.

Beyond the Conduit/Content Debate

A central difficulty in defining WikiLeaks is whether the organization operates as a content provider or as a simple conduit for leaked data – a question that is unclear even to the WikiLeaks people themselves (the impression is that they see it as either/or, depending on context and circumstances). This, by the way, has been a common problem ever since media moved online en masse and publishing and communications became services rather than products. Assange cringes every time he is portrayed as an editor-in-chief, yet WikiLeaks says it edits material before publication and checks documents for authenticity with the help of hundreds of volunteer analysts. Content versus carrier debates of this kind have been ongoing for decades among media activists, with no clear outcome. Instead of trying to resolve the inconsistency, it might be better to look for fresh approaches and develop new critical concepts for a hybrid publishing practice involving actors far beyond professional news media. This might be why Assange and his collaborators refuse to be labeled in terms of old categories (journalists and hackers, for instance) and claim to represent a new *Gestalt* on the world information stage.

The steady decline of investigative journalism caused by diminished funding is an undeniable fact. Journalism these days amounts to little more than outsourced PR remixing. The continuous acceleration and overcrowding of the so-called attention economy ensures that there is no longer enough room for complicated stories. The corporate owners of mass-circulated media are increasingly disinclined to see the workings and politics of the global neo-liberal economy discussed at length. Many journalists themselves embrace the shift from information to infotainment which makes it difficult to publish complex stories. WikiLeaks enters this state of affairs as an outsider enveloped by the steamy ambiance of "citizen journalism," DIY news reporting in the blogosphere, and ever-faster social media like Twitter.

What WikiLeaks anticipates, yet has so far been unable to organize, is the crowd sourcing of interpretation of its leaked documents. Since mid-2010, that work has been done by journalists from a few "quality" news media, who further investigate selected cables, working to a deadline. Later, academics might pick up the scraps and tell the stories outside of the closed gates of publishing stables. But where is the networked critical commentariat? Certainly, we are all busy with our minor critiques, but the fact remains that WikiLeaks generates its capacity to irritate the big end of town precisely because of the transversal and symbiotic relationship it has with established media institutions. There's a lesson here for the multitudes – get out of the ghetto and connect with the Oedipal other. Therein lies the conflicting terrain of the political.

Traditional investigative journalism once consisted of three phases: unearthing facts, cross-checking them, and backgrounding them into an understandable discourse. WikiLeaks does the first, claims to do the second, but omits the third entirely. This is symptomatic of a particular brand of the open-access ideology in which content production itself is externalized to unknown entities "out there." Were the crowds perhaps wise enough this time to bail after their first

179

experiences with the "complex" personality of the leader? Wikipedia shows that it is possible to work with thousands (if not millions) of volunteers, but that it also takes time, including necessary conflicts, to develop a "culture of collaboration" based on trust and mutual understanding. This process includes decision-making structures specific to working online, with clear divisions of labor between those who make simple edits, expert editors related to specific sites and entries, and officials who are often only affiliated with national chapters.

From detailed news stories, we know that the collaboration between WikiLeaks and the *Guardian* (but also *The New York Times*) didn't quite work out smoothly either. Apart from a clash of the main players' personalities, incompatible value systems emerged between the hacker ethics of Assange and the journalistic common sense of mainstream news organizations.[5] The crisis in investigative journalism is neither understood nor recognized. How productive entities are to sustain themselves materially is left in the dark: it is simply presumed that analysis and interpretation will be taken up by the traditional news media. However, crowd-sourced analysis does not happen automatically. The sagas of the *Afghan War Logs* and Cablegate demonstrate that WikiLeaks must approach and negotiate with well-established traditional media to secure sufficient credibility. At the same time, these media outlets proved themselves unable to fully process the material and, inevitably, they filtered the documents according to their own editorial policies.

Figurehead Politics

WikiLeaks is a typical SPO (Single-Person Organization) or UPO (Unique-Personality Organization). This means that the initiative-taking, decision-making, and execution is largely concentrated in the hands of a single individual. Like small and medium-sized businesses, the founder cannot be voted out, and, unlike many collectives, leadership does not rotate. This is not an uncommon feature within organizations, irrespective of whether they operate in the realm of politics, culture, or the "civil society" sector. SPOs are recognizable, exciting, inspiring, and easy to feature in the media. Their sustainability, however, is largely dependent on the actions of their charismatic leader, and their functioning is difficult to reconcile with democratic values. This is also why they are difficult to replicate and do not scale up easily. How independent media projects structure their internal decision-making procedures is a matter of style and personal choice. The problems start if the hierarchies are not clearly communicated and agreed upon internally.

Sovereign hacker Julian Assange is the identifying figurehead of WikiLeaks, and the organization's notoriety and reputation merges with Assange's own. What WikiLeaks does and stands for becomes difficult to distinguish from Assange's rather agitated private life and his somewhat unpolished political opinions. The memoirs published in early 2011 by WikiLeaks' second man and spokesperson in the years 2008 to mid-2010, the German hacker Daniel Domscheit-Berg, are a painstakingly detailed account of how amateur-like the "office-free organization" was up to the moment in September 2010 when Assange "fired" Domscheit-Berg, even though he was not his boss, legally speaking. The collectives of self-managed projects in the 1980s which ran on the basis of consensus and equality might have been outdated and annoying back then, but the chaos inside WikiLeaks, in terms of its own lack of transparency (even for its own members!), unclear financial situation, and utter lack of internal democracy, is yet another extreme – so bad that Domscheit-Berg accused the paranoid, persecution-obsessed founder of running "his" WikiLeaks like a cult and was told: "Do not challenge leadership in times of crisis."[6] Domscheit-Berg disliked being spoken of as an "asset." When Assange fired Domscheit-Berg, he accused him of disloyalty, insubordination, and destabilization: military terms used when spoken about traitors. Assange, who threatened to publish compromising material about Domscheit-Berg, wrote in a chat: "If you threaten this organization again, you will be attended to. You are a criminal. (...) Our duties are bigger than this idiocy."[7] And, last but not least: "I'm running out of options that don't destroy people."[8] Instead of setting up his organization OpenLeaks, Domscheit-Berg might have been better discussing the proposal to "fork" WikiLeaks – meaning copy-pasting the entire project and going separate ways, as suggested by another WikiLeaks' core member named "the Architect" in Domscheit-Berg's book – as a serious option.

The Post-Representational Network

WikiLeaks raises the question of what hackers have in common with secret services, since an elective affinity between the two is unmistakable. The love–hate relationship goes back to the very beginning of computing. One does not need to be a fan of German media theorist

Friedrich Kittler or of conspiracy theories to acknowledge that the computer was born out of the military-industrial complex. From Alan Turing's deciphering of the Nazi Enigma code to the first computers' relation with the atomic bomb, from the cybernetics movement to the Pentagon's involvement in the creation of the internet, the correlation between computational information and the military-industrial complex is well established. Computer scientists and programmers have shaped the information revolution and the culture of openness; but at the same time they have also developed encryption ("crypto"), closing access to data for the non-initiated. What some see as "citizen journalism," others call "info war."

WikiLeaks is also an organization deeply shaped by 1980s hacker culture, combined with the political values of techno-libertarianism that emerged in the 1990s. The fact that WikiLeaks was founded – and to a large extent still run – by hard-core geeks is essential to understanding its values and moves. Unfortunately, this comes together with a good dose of the less savory aspects of hacker culture. Not that WikiLeaks doesn't lack idealism or the desire to contribute to making the world a better place: on the contrary. But this brand of idealism (or, if you prefer, anarchism) is paired with a preference for conspiracies, an elitist attitude, and a cult of secrecy (never mind condescension). This is not conducive to collaboration with like-minded people and groups who are relegated to the simple consumption of WikiLeaks' output. The missionary zeal to enlighten the idiotic masses and "expose" the lies of government, the military, and corporations is reminiscent of the well-known (or infamous) media-culture paradigm from the 1950s.

Lack of commonality with congenial "Another World is Possible" movements drives WikiLeaks to seek public attention by way of increasingly spectacular and risky disclosures, thereby gathering a constituency of often wildly enthusiastic but generally passive supporters. Assange himself stated that WikiLeaks deliberately moved away from the "egocentric" blogosphere and assorted social media, and nowadays collaborates only with professional journalists and human rights activists. Yet, following the nature and quantity of WikiLeaks' exposures, from its inception up to the present day, is eerily reminiscent of watching a fireworks display, including a grand finale in the form of the so-called doomsday-machine: the yet-to-be-unleashed "insurance" document (known as ".aes256"). This raises serious doubts about the long-term sustainability of WikiLeaks itself, and possibly also of its model. WikiLeaks operates with a ridiculously small staff – probably no more than a dozen people form the core of

182

its operation. While it proves the extent and savviness of WikiLeaks' tech support by its very existence, WikiLeaks' claim to several hundred volunteer analysts and experts is unverifiable and, to be frank, barely credible. This is clearly WikiLeaks' Achilles' heel, not only from a risk and/or sustainability standpoint, but politically as well – which is what matters to us here.

WikiLeaks has displayed a stunning lack of transparency in its internal organization. It is not enough to say something along the lines of "WikiLeaks needs to be completely opaque in order to force others to be totally transparent." Do that and we beat the opposition but in a way that makes us indistinguishable from it. Claiming the moral high ground after the job is done is not helpful – Tony Blair, too, excelled in that exercise. As WikiLeaks is neither a political collective nor an NGO in the legal sense, and is not, for that matter, a company or part of a social movement, we need to discuss what type of organization we are dealing with. Is WikiLeaks a virtual project? After all, it does exist as a (hosted) website with a domain name, which is the bottom line. Does it have a goal beyond the personal ambition of its founder(s)? Is WikiLeaks reproducible? Will we see the rise of national or local chapters that keep the name? What rules of the game will they observe? Should we see it as a concept that travels from context to context and that, like a meme, transforms itself in time and space?

Maybe WikiLeaks will organize itself around its own version of the internet engineering task force's slogan "rough consensus and running code"? Projects like Wikipedia and Indymedia both resolved this issue in their own ways, but not without crises, conflicts, and splits. Global NGOs like Greenpeace, Amnesty, and Soros' Open Society foundations all have their experiences with less successful national chapters. Even bottom-up organizations without a central global brand collaborate internationally. This critique is not intended to force WikiLeaks into a traditional format; on the contrary, it is to explore whether WikiLeaks (and its future clones, associates, avatars, and congenial family members) might act as a model for new forms of organization and collaboration. As we speak, WikiLeaks is anything but an "organized network." Perhaps WikiLeaks has its own ideas about the direction it wants to take. But where? Up to now, we have seen very little by way of an answer, leaving others to raise questions, for example, about the legality of WikiLeaks' financial arrangements (such as *The Wall Street Journal*'s front-page headline of August 23, 2010: "WikiLeaks keep funding secret").

We cannot flee the challenge of experimenting with post-representational networks. As ur-blogger Dave Winer wrote about the Apple developers:

> it's not that they're ill-intentioned, they're just ill-prepared. More than their users, they live in a Reality Distortion Field, and the people who make The Computer for the Rest of Us have no clue who the rest of us are and what we are doing. But that's okay, there's a solution. Do some research, ask some questions, and listen.[9]

The New Whistleblower Paradigm

The widely shared critique of Julian Assange's self-inflicted celebrity cult invites the formulation of alternatives. Wouldn't it be better to run WikiLeaks as an anonymous collective or organized network, a concept discussed in the previous chapter and that is now out-of-beta and starting to get real? Some wish to see many websites doing the same work as WikiLeaks. The group around Daniel Domscheit-Berg that launched OpenLeaks learned from previous experiences "that they did not scale very well."[10] Easily overlooked in the calls for WikiLeaks' proliferation is the amount of expert knowledge required to run a leak site where whistleblowers can submit their material in a secure way. We need an ABC toolkit of secure submission software. When all the media and legal dust has settled, who knows whether WikiLeaks retrospectively will turn out to be the prototype for an entirely new family of whistleblower software.

Perhaps paradoxically, there is much secrecy in this way of making-things-public. Is it realistic to promote the idea that ordinary internet users will be able to download the OpenLeaks software kit and get started? WikiLeaks is not a plug 'n' play blog application like Wordpress, and the word "wiki" in its name is misleading. Contrary to the collaboration philosophy of Wikipedia, WikiLeaks turned into a closed shop that was managed by a handful of people. The thousands of volunteers whom the organization in 2009 and 2010 claimed to have were illusory and the step to work with the *Guardian* and other newspapers was in fact a necessity, due to the total absence of its own network of friendly editors and researchers.[11] One is forced to acknowledge that the know-how necessary to run a facility like WikiLeaks is pretty arcane. Documents not only need to be received anonymously, but also to be further anonymized before they are released online. They also must be edited before being dispatched to the servers of international news organizations and other trusted parties such as NGOs and unions. It is questionable if such sensitive tasks can be "outsourced" to the crowds. What WikiLeaks in this respect teaches us is how *not* to organize collective editorial flows.

WikiLeaks has built up much trust and confidence over the years and newcomers must go through that same, time-consuming process. The principle of leaks is not the hack (into state or corporate networks), but to facilitate insiders from large organizations to copy sensitive, confidential data and pass it onto the public domain while remaining anonymous. If you are aspiring to become a leak node, you'd better start acquainting yourself with processes like OPSEC, or operations security, a step-by-step plan which, according to Wikipedia, "identifies critical information to determine if friendly actions can be observed by adversary intelligence systems, determines if information obtained by adversaries could be interpreted to be useful to them, and then executes selected measures that eliminate or reduce adversary exploitation of friendly critical information."[12] The WikiLeaks slogan says: "courage is contagious." According to experts, people who intend to run a WikiLeaks-type operation need nerves of steel. So before we call for one, 10, many WikiLeaks, let's be clear that those involved run risks. Whistleblower protection is paramount. Another issue is the protection of people mentioned in the leaks. *The Afghan War Logs* showed that leaks can also cause "collateral damage." Editing (and eliding) is crucial – not only OPSEC, but also OPETHICS. If publishing is not carried out in a way that is absolutely secure for all concerned, there is a definite risk that the "revolution in journalism" and politics unleashed by WikiLeaks will be stopped in its tracks.

Let us not think that taking a stand for or against WikiLeaks is what matters most. The WikiLeaks' principle is here to stay, until it either scuttles itself or is destroyed by opposing forces. Our point is rather to (try to) assess and ascertain what WikiLeaks can, could, and maybe even should do, and to help formulate how "we" could relate to and interact with it. Despite all its drawbacks and against all odds, WikiLeaks has rendered a sterling service to the cause of transparency, democracy, and openness. The quantitative – and what looks soon to become the qualitative – turn of information overload is a fact of contemporary life. The glut of disclosable information can only be expected to grow – and exponentially so. To organize and interpret this Himalaya of data is a collective challenge, whether we give it the name WikiLeaks or not.

If we look again at the big picture, we are dealing here with a shift from hacking to leaking, both as IT tools democratize beyond the geeks and hackers, and with a growing crisis in legitimacy due to financial scandals, the economic crisis, and widening gaps in society. Disenfranchised individuals who recently were fired feel they have nothing to lose and will overcome their fear and expose the hidden communications of authorities. Platforms come and go but what remains of the WikiLeaks saga, no matter how banal its poor inner life, is the outing of the very idea of leaking. Will leaks turn into cascades?

NOTES

INTRODUCTION: CAPTURING WEB 2.0 BEFORE ITS DISAPPEARANCE

1 Dean, Jodi, Anderson, Jon W., and Lovink, Geert (eds), *Reformatting Politics: Information Society and Global Civil Society*, New York: Routledge, 2006.
2 Oliver Burkeman, "SXSW 2011: The Internet is Over," the *Guardian*, March 15, 2011: <http://www.guardian.co.uk/technology/2011/mar/15/sxsw-2011-internet-online>.
3 See: <http://techcrunch.com/2009/02/21/andreessen-in-realtime/> and <http://www.roughtype.com/archives/2009/02/the_free_arts_a.php>.
4 See his March 2006 lecture in Vienna in which Habermas makes the observation/judgment that the internet is a secondary form of publicity: <www.renner-institut.at/download/texte/habermas 2006-03-09.pdf > (in German).
5 See Bernard Stiegler, *Taking Care of Youth and the Generations*, Stanford, CA: University of Stanford, 2010, and *For a New Critique of Political Economy*, Cambridge: Polity, 2010. Both books contain sections and references to the extensive use of games and the internet in relation to the depressed mindset of the young in what Stiegler calls the "battle for intelligence." Stiegler calls for a fight against infantilization and argues in favor of a reintroduction of the minority status of children. Only long-term attention produces retention of cultural memory.
6 Andrew Keen, *The Cult of the Amateur: How Today's Internet is Killing Our Culture and Assualting Our Economy*, London: Nicholas Brealey Publishing, 2007.
7 Nicholas Carr, *The Big Switch: Rewiring the World, From Edison to Google*, New York: W.W. Norton & Company, 2008.

8   Frank Schirrmacher, *Payback*, Munich: Blessing Verlag, 2009.

9   Jaron Lanier, *You Are Not a Gadget: A Manifesto*, New York: Alfred A. Knopf, 2010. See also: <http://www.edge.org/discourse/digital_maoism.html>.

10 Lanier, *You Are Not a Gadget*, p. 45.

11 Thierry Chervel, "Fantasie über die Zukunft des Schreibens," at: <http://www.perlentaucher.de/blog/134_fantasie_ueber_die_zukunft_des_schreibens#521>.

12 These are three net critics whose titles came out during early 2011: Siva Vaidhyanathan's *The Googlization of Everything (and Why We Should Worry)*, Los Angeles, CA: University of California Press, 2011; Sherry Turkle's *Alone Together: Why We Expect More from Technology and Less from Each Other*, New York: Basic Books, 2011; and Evgeny Morozov's *The Net Delusion: The Dark Side of Internet Freedom*. New York: PublicAffairs, 2011.

13 Says Steve Gillmor, TechCrunch, February 2, 2009; at: <http://techcrunch.com/2009>.

14 See my chapter on internet time in *Zero Comments*, New York: Routledge, 2008, which also appeared in Robert Hassan and Ronald Purser (eds), *24/7, Time and Temporality in the Network Society*, Stanford, CA: Stanford University Press, 2007.

15 <http://en.wikipedia.org/wiki/Google_Wave>. In late 2010, the project was transferred to the Apache foundation which renamed it Apache Wave.

16 In this context the web videos on intelligence dashboards, news radars, and information filters from Howard Rheingold are instructive: <http://vlog.rheingold.com/index.php/site/video/infotention-part-one-introducing-dashboards-radars-filters/>. For Rheingold, these are essential literacy tools for the twenty-first century. Dealing with info overload requires more than one type of literacy. It is not only important to know what information to block out but also what to let in. For Rheingold, "mindful infotention" (a term he came up with) is part attentional discipline and part technical skill.

17 Eva Illouz, *Cold Intimacies: The Making of Emotional Capitalism*, Cambridge: Polity, 2007.

18 Tiziana Terranova, "Another Life: The Nature of Political Economy in Foucault's Genealogy of Biopolitics," *Theory, Culture & Society* 26/6 (2009): 234–62. See also Tiziana Terranova, "New Economy, Financialization and Social

Production in the Web 2.0," in Andrea Fumagalli and Sandro Mezzadra (eds), *Crisis in the Global Economy: Financial Markets, Social Struggles, and New Political Scenarios*, trans. Jason Francis McGimsey, Los Angeles, CA: Semiotext(e), 2010, pp. 153–70.

19 An example: "DASHlink links to websites created and maintained by other public and/or private organizations. This link may be provided by a community member or the NASA DASHlink Team; however, the presence of a link is not an endorsement of the site by NASA or us. When users follow an external link, they are leaving DASHlink and are subject to the privacy and security policies of the owners/sponsors of the outside website(s). NASA and DASHlink are not responsible for the information collection practices of external sites."

20 See <http://www.malcolmcoles.co.uk/blog/links-banned-2011/>.

21 Nicholas Carr: "Links are wonderful conveniences, as we all know (from clicking on them compulsively day in and day out). But they're also distractions. Sometimes, they're big distractions – we click on a link, then another, then another, and pretty soon we've forgotten what we'd started out to do or to read. Other times, they're tiny distractions, little textual gnats buzzing around your head. Even if you don't click on a link, your eyes notice it, and your frontal cortex has to fire up a bunch of neurons to decide whether to click or not. [...] The link is, in a way, a technologically advanced form of a footnote. It's also, distraction-wise, a more violent form of a footnote." Carr calls the book an experiment in delinkification. See: <http://www.roughtype.com/archives/2010/05/experiments_in.php>.

22 Quote from an email, January 10, 2011. See also Anne Helmond and Carolin Gerlitz, "Hit, Link, Like and Share. Organizing the Social and the Fabric of the Web in a Like Economy," paper presented at the DMI mini-conference at the University of Amsterdam, January 24–5, 2011. Available online: <http://www.annehelmond.nl/2011/04/16/paper-hit-link-like-and-share-organizing-the-social-and-the-fabric-of-the-web-in-a-like-economy/>.

23 David A. Vise, *The Google Story*, New York: Pan Books, 2005, p. 37 (both quotes).

24 See: <http://www.becker-posnerblog.com/archives/2009/06/the_future_of_n.html>.

25 At: <http://www.techcrunch.com/2009/06/28/how-to-save-the-newspapers-vol-xii-outlaw-linking/>.

26 At:<http://www.annehelmond.nl/2008/09/23/blogging-for-engines-blogs-under-the-influence-of-software-engine-relations/>.

27 See: <http://wiki.digitalmethods.net/Dmi/WebCurrencies>.

28 At: <http://www.wired.com/threatlevel/2008/05/leaked-cisco-do/>.

29 The Invisible Committee, *The Coming Insurrection*, Los Angeles, CA, Semiotext(e), 2009, p. 131.

30 Reference to the famous internet Engineering Taskforce phrase that is part of its founding beliefs, described in its "tao" document as: "the IETF runs on the beliefs of its participants." One of the "founding beliefs" is embodied in an early quote about the IETF from David Clark: "We reject kings, presidents and voting. We believe in rough consensus and running code." Another early quote that has become a commonly held belief in the IETF comes from Jon Postel: "Be conservative in what you send and liberal in what you accept." URL: <http://www.ietf.org/tao.html>.

CHAPTER 1: PSYCHOPATHOLOGY OF INFORMATION OVERLOAD

1 A North American male writes to me: "I'm marking 163 papers for theory, 25 final projects in digital media and 48 grades for 4th year final projects. I'm half dead right now. [...] I am not very good at multitasking. I'm a bit OCD (obsessive-compulsive disorder) about my output – I'll do one thing, and do it fairly intensively. As an artist I was always striving to be in 'the Zone' – that creative space where time melts away and at the end you have a finished (or more fashioned) work. Between fulltime work, dissertation and family I'm already tasked out. There are only so many hours in a day. But If I set goals and fix them, I can usually meet them."

2 Franco "Bifo" Berardi, *The Soul at Work: From Alienation to Autonomy*, Los Angeles, CA: Semiotext(e), 2009.

3 Franco "Bifo" Berardi, *Precarious Rhapsody*, London: Minor Compositions, 2009, p. 44; see also pp. 69–71 and 143.

4 Ibid.

5 Like other unattributed quotes in Berardi's essay, this statement comes from an interview with the author, recorded at his home in Bologne, May 2010.

6 Mark Fisher, *Capitalist Realism, Is There No Alternative?* Winchester: Zero Books, 2009, all quotes from pp. 21–3.

7 At:<http://www.framemag.com/news/1255/My-Phone-is-Off-for-You-by-Ingrid-Zweifel.html>.

8 "The Slow Media Manifesto": <http://www.slow-media.net/manifesto>.

9 Ronan McDonald, *The Death of the Critic*, London: Continuum, 2007, p. ix.

10 Michael Newman, in *The State of Art Criticism*, New York: Routledge, 2008, p. 43.

11 About Frank Schirrmacher's (German) book *Payback*, published in 2009, see Matthias Schwenk's blog posting: <http://carta.info/18537/algoritmenstuermer-schirrmacher-payback/>.

12 "The Datadandy," in Adilkno, *The Media Archive*, Brooklyn, NY: Autonomedia, 1998.

13 See: <http://blip.tv/web2expo/web-2-0-expo-ny-clay-shirky-shirky-com-it-s-not-information-overload-it-s-filter-failure-1283699>.

14 Nicholas Carr, *The Shallows: What the Internet is Doing to Our Brains*, New York: W.W. Norton, 2010, p. 141.

15 Ibid.

16 Quoted in Nicolas Carr, *The Big Switch: Rewiring the World, From Edison to Google*, New York: W.W. Norton, 2008, p. 227.

CHAPTER 2: FACEBOOK, ANONYMITY, AND THE CRISIS OF THE MULTIPLE SELF

1 Jeff Kinney, *Diary of a Wimpy Kid*, New York: Amulet Books, 2007.

2 Max Blecher: "The terrible question 'Who exactly am I?' dwells in me like an entirely new body, having grown in me with skin and organs that are wholly unfamiliar to me. The answer to it is demanded by a deeper and more essential lucidity than that of the brain. All that is capable of stirring in my body writhes, struggles and rebels more vigorously and more elementarily than in everyday life. Everything begs a solution" (*Occurrence in the Immediate Unreality*, Plymouth: University of Plymouth Press, 2009, p. 26).

3 "Kwetsbaarheid is niks voor mij," interview with Rineke Dijkstra by Hans den Hartog Jager, *NRC-Handelsblad*, December 7, 2010.

4 Promotion phrase of Flipboard for iPad: "your personalized, social magazine."

5 See, for instance, Michael Zimmer: <http://michaelzimmer.org/2010/05/14/facebooks-zuckerberg-having-two-identities-for-yourself-is-an-example-of-a-lack-of-integrity/>, and danah boyd: <http://www.zephoria.org/thoughts/archives/2010/05/14/facebook-and-radical-transparency-a-rant.html>.

6 *Wall Street Journal*, October 11, 2010. Another example can be found in the LEGO ID terms of service: "As a LEGO ID owner, you agree that you will not create more than one user account, and that you understand that the use of an indecent screen name, profanity, and language and/or images that are considered obscene and generally improper will not be tolerated. You will not use or manipulate the game, chat or mailing areas of LEGO. com in inappropriate ways, and will not alter any LEGO.com software or code."

7 Both quotes from Zadie Smith, "Generation Why?," in *New York Review of Books*, November 25, 2010, pp. 57–60; available at: http://www.nybooks.com/articles/archives/2010/nov/25/generation-why/.

8 A good introduction to this self-management thesis is given by Ramon Reichert, in *Amateure Im Netz*, Bielefeld: Verlag (transcript), 2008.

9 Both quotes here are from Eva Illouz, *Cold Intimacies: The Making of Emotional Capitalism*, Cambridge: Polity, 2007.

10 Barbara Ehrenreich, *Bright-sided: How the Relentless Promotion of Positive Thinking Has Underminded America*, New York: Metropolitan Books, 2009, p. 5.

11 Bernard Stiegler, *For a New Critique of Political Economy*, Cambridge: Polity, 2010, p. 41. In the current interactive dialogue systems, it is Twitter and Facebook that ask the questions: "What are you doing?", "What's happening?". Brian Solis criticized this: "Nobody cares what you are doing right now. Drinking a cup of coffee? Going to bed? Getting up? Keep it to yourself! The question you should answer is: What inspires you? or What did you learn today?'" At: <http://www.briansolis.com/2009/11/on-twitter-what-are-you-doing-is-the-wrong-question/>. Instead of coming up with alternatives we should, in the spirit of Joseph Weizenbaum, reverse the process itself: it should be the users who start questioning.

12 Zygmunt Bauman, "The Self in a Consumer Society," in *The Hedgehog Review* (fall 1999): 35.

13 Clive Hamilton (with Richard Denniss), *Affluenza: When Too Much is Never Enough*, Sydney: Allen & Unwin, 2005, p. 3.

14 Elizabeth Farrelly, *Blubberland: The Dangers of Happiness*, Sydney: University of New South Wales Press, 2007, p. 9.

15 Ibid., p. 136.

16 Shelley Gare, *The Triumph of the Airheads and the Retreat from Commonsense*, Sydney: Park Street Press, 2006, p. 11.

17 Ibid.

18 The 14 theses, in German, are available at: <http://netzpolitik. org/2010/14-thesen-zu-den-grundlagen-einer-gemeinsamen-netzpolitik-der-zukunft/>. An English translation of a related speech can be downloaded here: <http://ec.europa.eu/justice/ news/.../bundesministerium_des_innern_1_en.pdf>. An interview with him by the *Spiegel* magazine, in English, is available at: <http://www.spiegel.de/international/spiegel/0,1518,702465,00. html>.

19 See: <http://groups.dowire.org/groups/newswire/messages/topic/ 6Qhy7BTkLXGXAr16uCarxs>; accessed 7 March, 2011.

20 See: <http://en.wikipedia.org/wiki/Thermidorian_Reaction>; accessed March 7, 2011.

21 See: <http://www.netforttechnologies.com/>; accessed December 28, 2000.

22 Jay Hathaway, "WikiLeaks Infowar Update – Assange Bail Stalled by Swedish Appeal, Anonymous Prepares for Arrests," posted on December 14, 2010. At: <http://www.urlesque.com/2010/12/ 14/WikiLeaks-infowar-assange-bail-anonymous-arrests/>.

23 In an online Q and A chat with readers of the *Guardian*, WikiLeaks founder Julian Assange wrote: "I originally tried hard for the organization to have no face, because I wanted egos to play no part in our activities. This followed the tradition of the French anonymous pure mathematicians [*sic*], who wrote under the collective allonym, The Bourbaki. However, this quickly led to tremendous distracting curiosity about who we were and random individuals claiming to represent us. In the end, someone must be responsible to the public and only a leadership that is willing to be publicly courageous can genuinely suggest that sources take risks for the greater good. In that process, I have become the lightning rod. I get undue attacks on every aspect of my life, but then I also get undue credit as some kind of balancing force." At: <http://www.guardian.co.uk/world/blog/2010/ dec/03/julian-assange-WikiLeaks>

24 See: <http://neteffect.foreignpolicy.com/posts/2010/12/16/should _we_ban_sit_ins_because_crazy_people_can_abuse_them_too>.

25 Tiqqun, quoted in Andreas Broeckmann and Knowbotic Research (eds), *Opaque Presence, Manual of Latent Invisibilities*, Edition Jardin des Pilotes, Zurich: Diaphanes, 2010.

26 Afterword of Andreas Broeckmann and Knowbotic Research (eds), *Opaque Presence, Manual of Latent Invisibilities*, Edition Jardin des Pilotes, Zurich: Diaphanes, 2010, p. 148.

27 Ibid., p. 44.
28 See the Tele_Trust project by Dutch artists Karen Lancel and
    Herman Maat, in which the artists walk in a (networked) burka.
    The project wants to discuss how we can trust each other as
    networking bodies. "Do you need to see my eyes to trust me?
    Do we need to touch each other?" At: <http://www.v2.nl/archive/
    works/tele_trust>.

CHAPTER 3: TREATISE ON COMMENT CULTURE

1 Geert Lovink, *Zero Comments*, New York: Routledge, 2007.
2 Clay Shirky, *Power Laws, Weblogs, and Inequality*, February 8,
   2003. At: <http://shirky.com/writings/powerlaw_weblog.html>.
3 An example: "Over the past fifty years, artists have increasingly
   engaged the presence of the audience in the conception, production, and presentation of their work. Without You I'm Nothing:
   Art and Its Audience comprises works drawn from the MCA's
   Collection that demonstrate a cultural shift towards a greater
   engagement for the individual in the public realm." This show
   at the Chicago MCA shows artists "whose multidimensional
   work invoked the interaction of the audience to reflect the
   manner in which architecture and internet technology have
   encouraged a more networked social sphere. In recent years,
   even artists working in film and video, such as Aernout Mik,
   have rejected the idea of theatrical spectatorship, framing their
   cinematic narratives within architectural and sculptural presentations that the viewer must walk around to fully appreciate."
   E-flux, December 25, 2010.
4 T. Adorno, *Jargon of Authenticity*, Evanston, IL: Northwestern
   University Press, 1973, p. 5.
5 Bob Stein, posting at the if:book blog, November 10, 2010. At:
   <http://www.futureofthebook.org/blog/archives/2010/11/what_
   ive_learned_since_posting.html>.
6 Measured on December 27, 2010.
7 Taken from George Monbiot's blog, February 23, 2011. At:
   <http://www.monbiot.com/2011/02/23/robot-wars/>.
8 "Discover the Bot that is bringing in hundreds, even thousands
   of unique visitors daily. With the YouTube Comment Poster Bot
   one will definitely get the attention they seek and desire. By

working together with some of the top internet Marketing Gurus and Super Affiliates in the business today, we have finally found an easy solution for flooding your websites with targeted traffic." At: <http://youtubecommentposterbot.com/>.

9 Jan Assmann, in his introduction of *Text und Kommentar*, Munich: Wilhelm Fink Verlag, 1995, p. 10.

10 Hodegetics teaches the theory of study to students who are not yet capable of studying on their own, and the teacher then assists by commenting on the text. Hermeneutics, on the other hand, is the art of solitary reading. Assmann concludes his introduction as follows: "Commentary develops as written codification from earlier given oral explanations in transition to solitary reading" (p. 31). It thus becomes clear why Assmann relates hodegetics, hermeneutics, and deconstruction as three stages to deal with a text.

11 At least, until Seesmic's introduction of video threads, for instance, on vlogs (video blogs), in which users send in their responses through webcam or their smartphone camera.

12 Philip Ajouri, Jost Philipp Klenner, and Cornelia Vismann (eds), *Kommentieren*, *Zeitschrift für Ideengeschichte*, *Heft III/1*, Munich: C.H. Beck Verlag, Frühjahr 2009, p. 4.

13 See Hans Ulrich Gumbrecht, *The Powers of Philology*, Urbana, IL: Illinois University Press, 2002.

14 This undertaking could start with an update of the virtual intellectual, an imaginary figure presented at Documenta X, July 1997 (<http://www.thing.desk.nl/bilwet/Geert/100.LEX>). See also the nettime debate from the same period over the issue of how "collaborative filters" could be invented in order to make sense of this poly-authored world (for both texts, see my book *Dark Fiber*, Cambridge, MA: MIT Press, 2002).

15 DMS, love it or hate it! According to the Wikipedia entry, "decision-making software is a term integrating decision analysis tools to facilitate a person's decision-making process, which results in a choice of a course of action or a variant among several alternatives. DMS belongs to the class of Decision Support Systems used to structure information, identify and solve problems and make decisions. DM-software is based on multi-criteria decision analysis (MCDA) and its varieties: Analytic Hierarchy Process (AHP), Analytic Network Process (ANP – extension of AHP), PROMETHEE, Multi-Attribute Value Theory (MAVT), Multi-Attribute Utility Theory (MAUT),

Multi-Attribute Global Inference of Quality (MAGIQ), Potentially All Pairwise RanKings of all possible Alternatives (PAPRIKA), etc."

16 See: <http://networkcultures.org/wpmu/query/2009/11/13/yann-moulier-boutang-asks-are-we-all-just-googles-worker-bees/>; and his upcoming book *Cognitive Capitalism*, Cambridge: Polity, 2011.

17 All quotes in this paragraph are from Leo Strauss, *Persecution and the Art of Writing*, Chicago, IL: University of Chicago Press, [1952] 1988, p. 25.

18 "Barack Obama fought hard to keep his BlackBerry when he became president, but with only 10 people authorised to email the super-encrypted device, he admitted that it is 'no fun' because they think that 'it's probably going to be subject to the presidential records act, so nobody wants to send me the real juicy stuff,' Obama said." The *Telegraph*, July 29, 2010. At: <http://www.telegraph.co.uk/news/worldnews/northamerica/usa/barackobama/7917368/Barack-Obamas-BlackBerry-no-fun.html>.

19 Michel Foucault, "The Order of Discourse," in Robert Young (ed.), *Untying the Text: A Poststructuralist Reader*, London: Routledge, 1981, pp. 52–64.

20 Paul Ricoeur, *The Conflict of Interpretations*, London/New York: Continuum, 2000, p. 4.

21 Günter Figal, *Der Sinn des Verstehens*, Stuttgart: Reclam, 1996, p. 7. Significant here is a reference to Walter Benjamin who said: "Ausdauernd hebt das Denken stets von neuen an, umständlich geht es auf die Sache selbst zurück. Dies unablässige Atemholen ist die eigenste Daseinsform der Kontemplation." (Persevering always lifts the process of thinking, elaborately it traces back to the thing itself. This relentless taking of breath is the most peculiar form of existence of contemplation.) How to transform this into software?

22 Figal, p. 18.

23 Used here is the German translation: Hans Ulrich Gumbrecht, *Die Macht der Philologie*, Frankfurt: Suhrkamp, 2003, pp. 85–6.

24 Bodo Plachta, "Philologie als Brückenbau," in *Zeitschrift für Ideengeschichte*, Marbach am Neckar, pp. 25–6.

25 See <http://www.futureofthebook.org/commentpress/>.

26 All quotes from Susan Sontag, *Against Interpretation*, New York: Dell Publishing, 1966, pp. 3–14.

CHAPTER 4: DISQUISITION ON INTERNET CRITICISM

1   Interview with Alexander Kluge by the German weekly *Freitag*, December 24, 2009. English translation at: <http://www.signandsight.com/features/1990.html>.
2   Arguments against negative critique and seeking another style can, for instance, be found in Rosi Braidotti, *Op doorreis, nomadisch denken in de 21ste eeuw*, Amsterdam: Boom, 2004, pp. 7–9.
3   Ronan McDonald, *The Death of the Critic*, p. ix.
4   Michael Schreyach, in *The State of Art Criticism*, New York: Routledge, 2008, p. 3.
5   John Sutherland, *Sunday Telegraph*, November 12, 2006; quoted in Ronan McDonald, *The Death of the Critic*, p. 6.
6   Ronan McDonald, *The Death of the Critic*, p. 36.
7   James Elkins, in Elkins and Newman, *The State of Art Criticism*, New York: Routledge, 2008, p. 12.
8   Ibid., p.11.
9   Ibid., p. 56.
10 See: <http://we-make-money-not-art.com/>.
11 See my blog posting on the event. http://networkcultures.org/wpmu/geert/2010/01/20/state-of-the-art-critic.
12 More on this notion can be found in Jean Baudrillard's *Fatal Strategies*, Brooklyn, NY: Semiotext(e), 1990.
13 In his review of Axel Honneth's *Pathologies of Reason: On the Legacy of Critical Theory* (2009), Barret Weber comes to a similar conclusion. In Adorno's work, there is "a lack of any recognizable sociological basis or location for critique. Against Adorno's best intentions to the contrary, critique itself becomes abstract in his work, and thus not situated in any recognizable sociological location. [...] Honneth's critique of Adorno begins with a consideration of how the project of 'Critical Theory', now as a proper noun once Adorno's project rose to prominence, was decisively rejected by the '68 student movement and eventually everyone else thereafter. In Honneth's view, this is why the classical project of the Frankfurt School cannot be continued today either: its foundations remain too abstract and dogmatic; it can't account for practice nor distinguish itself clearly from the other critical projects." (at: <www.long-sunday.net>; accessed July 14, 2009). This renders useless the argument that, first, we have to go back to Adorno, before we can properly embark on a critical project.

14 Manuel Castells is proud not to be a theorist. In an interview
    with *Occupied London*, he writes: "I find it essential not to build
    closed theoretical systems with the only purpose to win a share
    in the intellectual market of social theory. I always go back to
    the drawing board. It is so much more fun to try to understand
    new social forms and processes than to play with words. Theorists
    are usually very boring chaps. Do not fall in such a trap. Live
    in your practice, not in your books. Stay close to the facts, ask
    your own questions, and build your own conceptual systems
    with whatever is useful to your work. Ignore words or concepts
    that even their authors only half understand. Escape from theory
    courses, the last refuge of the intellectual gentry. Look around
    you and try to understand the world as it is, your world. And
    keep changing. The day you stop changing you are basically
    dead. Life is change." He also says: "You do not need fancy
    words. Make things simple, they are usually more simple than
    our concepts. Some social scientists use abstraction to enhance
    their status rather than their knowledge." While this call may
    sound sympathetic, bordering on anti-intellectual resentment,
    what Castells ignores is where the key concepts of networks
    originate. There is no intellectual history here, no role for debate,
    and thus also no understanding of how new concepts come into
    being – other than studying social reality. The world cries for
    critical concepts, including the further development of Castell's
    own "network society." Whether this essential work is done in
    an open or closed fashion, and in a boring way rather than an
    exciting way, is entirely in the hands of the author.
15 See Adilkno, *The Media Archive*, Brooklyn: Autonomedia, 1998,
    and Geert Lovink, *Dark Fiber: Tracking Critical Internet Culture*,
    Cambridge, MA: MIT Press, 2002.
16 Operating within the century-old art discourse, Irit Rogoff dis-
    tinguishes between criticism, critique, and criticality. In the
    rather rogue and primitive internet context, this may not be very
    useful. What I do like is Rogoff's emphasis on unlearning:
    "'Criticality' as I perceive it is precisely in the operations of
    recognising the limitations of one's thought for one does not
    learn something new until one unlearns something old, other-
    wise one is simply adding information rather than rethinking a
    structure" (p. 99). The unlearning in this context would be to
    merely complain and contemplate. What the internet invites us
    to do is to constantly give input, become active, respond – what
    Henk Oosterling coined as "interpassivity."

17 Gail Pool, *Faint Praise: The Plight of Book Reviewing in America*, Columbia, MO: University of Missouri Press, 2007, p. 4.
18 Ibid., p. 56.
19 Ibid., p. 123.
20 Ibid., p. 125.
21 See: <http://www.smith.edu/library/libs/rarebook/exhibitions/penandpress/case15a.htm>.
22 See George Steiner, *Real Presences*, Chicago, IL: University of Chicago Press, 1991.
23 Gail Pool, *Faint Praise*, p. 124.
24 L. E. Sissman, "Reviewer's Dues," in Sylvia Kamerman (ed.), *Book Reviewing*, Boston, MA: The Writer, 1978, pp. 119–25.
25 More on this in Richard Rogers, *The End of the Virtual*, Amsterdam: Vossius Press, 2009.
26 I am paraphrasing Irit Rogoff here, and her essay, "What is a Theorist?," in James Elkins and Michael Newman (eds), *The State of Art Criticism*, pp. 107–9, in an attempt to show that there are certain similarities in the agendas of critical internet studies and visual culture.

CHAPTER 5: MEDIA STUDIES: DIAGNOSTICS OF A FAILED MERGER

1 Private email conversation, June 6, 2009.
2 See: <http://www.mediafonds.nl/page.ocl?mode=&version=&pageid=10&MenuID=0>.
3 Private email conversation, June 6, 2009.
4 Title of a UvA Media Studies conference. At : <http://www.mediastudies.nl/vv-conferenties/conferenties-organisatie2006/End%20of%20television.html>.
5 University of Utrecht Media Studies teacher Mirko Tobias Schäfer disagrees: "Serious scholarship would concern itself with analysing the metaphors. I am afraid that the constant attempts to keep up with the 'marketing machinery' produces poor research, and will identify wrong, inappropriate objects of research" (email correspondence, September 18, 2009).
6 See: <http://news.cnet.com/8301-13555_3-9796296-34.html>; accessed October 12, 2007.
7 See: <http://edition.cnn.com/2009/BUSINESS/05/21/merger.marriage/>, May 22, 2009.
8 See: <http://www.tvweek.com/blogs/tvbizwire/2009/05/time_warner_to_undo_aol_merger.php>.

9   Florian Cramer, in an email response, September 16, 2009: "This is already happening. If you are a scholar and you only publish online, you're lowbrow; if you publish books, you're highbrow. If you are a film-maker and you have a theatrical release on 35mm, you're highbrow. If you release on YouTube, you're lowbrow."

10 This is the thesis of Jordi Wijnalda's "What is Film? Manifesto for a New Film Analysis," in *Xi* # 17/4: 6, the student quarterly of Media Studies at the University of Amsterdam, April 2009 (in Dutch). Wijnalda rejects "grand theories" and calls for more selection in the choice of theoretical frameworks. She calls for a renaissance of film aesthetics, against one-dimensional approaches that reduce film to text. In short, critics need to show more respect for their object of study. Film speaks a different language, set apart from other art forms and media.

11 An alternative history of media studies would point to the Macey and Bateson conferences and other sources from the history of cybernetics. However, written media archaeologies have not yet sufficiently incorporated these sources, and media studies is more often perceived to derive from 1970s film and theater efforts (to leave aside the social science references of media and communication).

12 The Wikipedia entry on media studies is an interesting case that illustrates how poorly defined media studies is at the moment: <http://en.wikipedia.org/wiki/Media_studies>.

13 In his pamphlet *Media Studies* 2.0, David Gauntlett observes how, amongst media studies, 1.0 programs are a "vague recognition of the internet and new digital media, as an 'add on' to the traditional media (to be dealt with in one self-contained segment tacked on to a Media Studies teaching module, book or degree)." At: <http://www.theory.org.uk/media studies2.htm>; see also his forum at: <http://twopointzeroforum.blogspot.com/>.

14 Private email correspondance, June 30, 2009.

15 Florian Cramer, in an email response on September 16, 2009: "The problem is that the humanities, in their orientation towards canons, are never interested in producing short-term input or knowledge. If you write a Ph.D. dissertation or monograph, you will, as a scholar, always choose a subject that will ideally ensure your eternal reputation and yield "timelessly" valid criticism. This is true for all the landmarks of modern criticism, from Walter Benjamin to Auerbach's "Mimesis" to Northrop Frye,

Harold Bloom etc. With that goal, you will never write a book on Twitter – every professorial advisor would warn you that it would be outmoded when it's done and ruin your career. This is why the humanities are structurally conservative and not interested in cutting edge cultural issues."

16 In his email response, Mirko Tobias Schäfer emphasizes the need to call bad research, poor teaching, and incompetent administration by name, and not to blame media studies as such for the current situation. "Students are taught poorly; TED talks all of a sudden are mistaken for an academic conference; blog posts are quoted as if they were papers and comments are over-estimated as peer review. Visibility and attention become the new academic merits. Checking the blog-roll of so-called academic blogs is interesting; they are full of popular and admittedly witty conference speakers, but links to First Monday, Arxiv or others are rare" (September 18, 2009).

17 Florian Cramer, in an email response, September 16, 2009: "If I had happened to father a child at age 21, it would graduate from high school right now, and I would – if asked – give her or him the strong advice to study, rather than media studies, philosophy combined with informatics and literature or art history. It's a schizophrenia that's embedded into the whole field. All good media researchers have studied classical humanities, and I do not know one good media scholar who has graduated in media studies. The problem of studying media theory is that you're typically educated on a second-rate theory canon of McLuhan and everything that makes up the standard media theory reading lists."

18 Marianne van den Boomen et al. (eds), *Digital Material: Tracing New Media in Everyday Life and Technology*, Amsterdam: Amsterdam University Press, 2009. See also: <http://www2.let. uu.nl/Solis/ogc/agendaitems/10th_anniversary_new_media. htm>. The idea for this essay grew out of a short presentation that I did there, together with Florian Cramer, in which I proposed the exodus of new media out of the broadcast context of film and television studies.

19 Private email conversation, June 9, 2009.

20 Email conversation, January 1, 2010.

21 Ibid., January 1, 2010.

22 Matthew Fuller and Andrew Goffey, in Jussi Parikka and Tony Sampson, *The Spam Book: On Viruses, Porn, and Other*

Anomalies from the Dark Side of Digital Culture, Cresskill, NJ: Hampton Press, 2009; online version: <http://www.spc.org/fuller/texts/10/>.

23 Email conversation, June 9, 2009.

24 Toby Miller, "Step Away from the Croissant, Media Studies 3.0," in David Hesmondhalgh and Jason Toynbee (eds), *The Media and Social Theory*. London: Routledge, 2008, pp. 213–30; Toby Miller, "Media Studies 3.0," in *Television & New Media* 10/ 1 (2009): 5–6.

25 Email conversation, September 16, 2009.

26 Thanks to Matthew Fuller, Alexander Galloway, Josephine Berry, McKenzie Wark, Toby Miller, Florian Cramer, Mirko Tobias Schäfer, and Lev Manovich for their dialogues with the text-in-progress, and also Henry Warwick and Tim Syth for their editorial support.

CHAPTER 6: BLOGGING AFTER THE HYPE: GERMANY, FRANCE, IRAQ

1 Interview by Sabine Reul and Thomas Deichmann, November 15, 2001, in *Spiked Online*: <http://www.spiked-online.com/Articles/00000002D2C4.htm>.

2 Friedrich Nietzsche, letter toward the end of February, in F. Nietzsche, *Briefwechsel: Kritische Gesamtausgabe*, ed. G. Colli and M. Montinari, Berlin, 1975–84, pt. 3, 1: 172.

3 Dave Winer, *Scripting News*: <http://www.scripting.com/2007/01/01.html>.

4 Ibid.

5 Ibid.

6 Nick Gall: "A lot of the media are thinking about blogs as a new form of publishing but it's really a new form of conversation and a new form of community." In David Kline and Dan Burstein, *blog!*, New York: CDS Books, 2005, p. 150.

7 From Wolf-Dieter Roth, "Mein blog liest ja sowieso kein Schwein," *Telepolis*, December 27, 2005. At: <http://www.heise.de/tp/artikel/21/21643/1.html>.

8 Email interview with Pit Schultz, April 2008.

9 At: <http://www.internetworldstats.com/stats7.htm>.

10 At: <http://www.globalbydesign.com/blog/2007/12/05/marketing-opportunities-in-the-german-blogosphere/>.

11 Ibid.

12 At: <http://www.readwriteweb.com/archives/social_graph_concepts_and_issues.php>.

13 Florian Cramer, email communication.
14 Verena Kuni, email communication.
15 Florian Cramer, email communication.
16 Ibid.
17 At: <bildblog.de> and <stefan-niggemeier.de/blog>.
18 At: <http://www.vanityfair.de/extras/rainaldgoetz/>.
19 At: <http://taz.de/blogs/hitlerblog/>.
20 At: <http://www.vanityfair.de/extras/rainaldgoetz/>.
21 At: <http://www.sueddeutsche.de/computer/artikel/599/170104/3/print.html>.
22 Thomas Crampton, *France's Mysterious Embrace of Blogs*, July 28, 2006: <http://www.iht.com/articles/2006/07/27/business/blogs.php>.
23 Known as the French Joi Ito, and organizer of the LeWeb conferences (held in Paris every December), Loïc Le Meur became a controversial figure when he supported Nicolas Sarkozy during the 2007 presidential elections. Since Sarkozy arguably was the most repressive and uninformed candidate concerning digital matters, the attitude of Loïc Le Meur was perceived as a treason and a sign of the reappropriation if not colonization by politicians, journalists, and brands of the once free space called the internet. Another round of this saga is the e>G8 event that took place in Paris late May 2011, on the event of the G8 Summit, that marks "the very first time that information technology formally takes a place on the agenda of a summit of Heads of State – a recognition of how critically important these sectors are to sustaining and accelerating global economic growth." See: <http://eg8forum.com/index_EN.html>. In the lead-up to the event, it was controversially discussed as Sarkozy is known for his critical if not repressive attitude toward the internet.
24 Language Log, March 31, 2007: <http://itre.cis.upenn.edu/~myl/languagelog/archives/004352.html>.
25 See also: <http://www.customerlistening.com/>.
26 Loïc Le Meur, in conversation with German blogger Oliver Gassner, September 15, 2006: <http://netzstimmen.blogg.de/eintrag.php?id=13>.
27 Email exchange, March 2, 2008. An example of a successful newspaper website to include blogs would be: <http://www.lemonde.fr>.
28 Email exchange, March 10, 2008.
29 At:<http://www.ouinon.Net/index.php?2007/09/24/215-cartographie-blogosphere-francophone>. The map comes as a downloadable

PDF file which contains, besides an explanation, a list of URLs for the 200 selected blogs.

30 Email interview, February 12, 2008.

31 Information from Wikipedia: <http://en.wikipedia.org/wiki/Skyrock>.

32 For a review in English by Catalina Iorga, see the Masters of Media blog: <http://mastersofmedia.hum.uva.nl/2010/09/20/book-review-mythologie-du-portable-laurence-allard/>.

33 Quotes from an email interview with Laurence Allard, February 20, 2008.

34 Laurence Allard and Olivier Blondeau, "Racaille digit@le. Les émeutes de banlieues n'ont pas eu lieu," in *Contemporary French Civilization* 31/1, Université de l'Illinois, winter, 2006.

35 See: <http://parisriots.free.fr/page1/page1.html>.

36 See the Lyon conference about the work of Jack Goody: <http://barthes.enssib.fr/colloque08/programme.html>; and Paul Mathias, *Des Libertés numériques*, Paris: PUF, 2008.

37 "I was in my room, playing guitar as usual and was recording the song 'Peace Train' from Cat Stevens, and after about 30 seconds on starting the song, when reaching the first line in the song, which was 'Now I've been happy lately,' a random bullet entered my room, crashed the window and broke all the glass and a heavy shooting then took place in the street. I was like planted in my place and completely shocked because of the heavy shooting. I stopped the recording and went away from the windows to avoid getting in the cross-fire of the random bullets, and when the shooting was over, I went back to my room and checked what I recorded and here was the funny thing, that right after I said, 'I've been happy lately,' the bullet came in to my room." At: <http://nabilsblog.blogspot.com/>; April 7, 2007.

38 Riverbend. *Baghdad Burning: Girl Blog from Iraq*. New York: The Feminist Press, 2005; and *Baghdad Burning II: More Girl Blog from Iraq*. New York: The Feminist Press, 2006.

39 Niqash: <http://www.niqash.org/. Global Voices: http://globalvoicesonline.org/-/world/middle-east-north-africa/iraq/>.

40 At: <http://streamtime.org/index.php?blogId=1&op=Template&show=mission>.

41 Posted on the website of the Institute of Network Cultures, January 17, 2006, and the nettime mailing list, June 16, 2006. A slightly different version was published in *Sarai Reader* 06, Delhi, 2006.

42 More exact estimations can be found at: <http://www. iraqbodycount.org/analysis/numbers/2007/>.

43 At: <http://streamtime.org/index.php?op=Default&Date=20071 2&blogId=1>.

CHAPTER 7: RADIO AFTER RADIO: FROM PIRATE TO INTERNET EXPERIMENTS

1 See: <http://www.vrijekeyser.nl/>.

2 Dick Rijken, "Radio is dood, lang leve audio" ("Radio is Dead, Long Live Radio"). "Why do we speak of radio when it actually isn't radio?" Instead of incorporating podcasting into an (extended) understanding of radio, Dick Rijken defines podcasts as intelligent audio. "The listener can choose the program they like and can listen to it whenever and wherever suits them." See: <http://www.denieuwereporter.nl/2006/06/radio-is-dood-lang-leve-audio/> (in Dutch).

3 The crucial year of 1987, in which the Amsterdam squatters' movement of the 1980s dramatically fell apart, is described in the last chapter of Adilkno's *Cracking the Movement*, New York: Autonomedia, 1994.

4 See: <http://www.mediamatic.Net/page/5750/nl>.

5 First references to the radio practices as sovereign media can be in Bilwet, *Bewegingsleer*, Amsterdam: Uitgeverij Ravijn, 1990 (translated as Adilkno, *Cracking the Movement*). Eric Kluitenberg discusses the topic further in the chapter "Media Without an Audience," in his book *Delusive Spaces: Essays on Culture, Media and Technology*, Rotterdam: INC/NAi, 2008. For more on the shift from radio to streaming, see the chapter "Principles of Streaming Sovereignty," in Geert Lovink, *My First Recession: Critical Internet Culture in Transition*, Rotterdam: V2/ NAi, 2003.

6 The core of Chris Anderson's argument is that the numerous small companies and individual producers with very small turnovers are of greater economic significance, even in comparison to the media giants. At: <http://www.thelongtail.com/>.

7 Lynn Owens, *Cracking under Pressure*, Amsterdam: Amsterdam University Press, 2008.

8 Email interview for this essay, September 2009.

9 Ibid.

10 See: <http://www.vrijekeyser.nl/>.

11 At: <http://www.myspace.com/rietveldradio>. See also the example of the Amsterdam Oltranzista initiative, from 2007, that

presents itself as a temporary autonomous radio station: "We have designed a small media studio, we share the information on how to make your own radio with free software and cheap recycled hardware, we want to embed into interesting situations and help to create the gradient to send them to the sky." See: <http://www.radioltranzista.net/>.

12 More on the streamtime radio missions can be found here: <http://streamtime.org/index.php?blogId=1&op=Template&show=mission>.

13 Email exchange with Anja Kanngieser, January 24, 2011.

14 Stan Rijven, "DFM brengt avontuur terug in de digitale ether" ("DFM Reintroduces Adventure into the Digital Airwaves"), *Trouw*, 12 September, 2009. For further information on the 24/7 streams by DFM, see: <http://www.dfm.nu>.

15 See the pictures on their website: <http://danceradio992.cz>.

16 See: <http://www.avatarorchestra.org>.

CHAPTER 8: ONLINE VIDEO AESTHETICS OR THE ART OF WATCHING DATABASES

1 This text builds on the two introductions that I wrote for *Video Vortex Reader 1* (co-edited with Sabine Niederer), and *Video Vortex Reader* II (co-edited with Rachel Miles), Amsterdam: Institute of Network Cultures, 2008, and 2011. For a comprehensive theory of databases from a humanities perspective, see David Gugerli, "Die Welt als Datenbank," in Nach Feierabend, *Zürcher Jahrbuch für Wissensgeschichte*, Zürich: Diaphanes Verlag, 2007, pp. 11–36.

2 See: <http://www.youtube.com/watch?v=VIrjZYqJ640>.

3 See: <http://www.ctv.ca/news>.

4 Quoted from a 2007 speech at New York University; see: <http://journalism.nyu.edu/publishing/archives/bullpen/brian_williams/lecture_brian_w/>.

5 Maurizio Lazzarato, *Videophilosophie*, Berlin: b_books, 2002, p. 9.

6 John Hartley, in Jean Burgess and Joshua Green, "YouTube", in *Online Video and Participatory Culture*, Cambridge: Polity, 2009, p. 132.

7 See: <http://networkcultures.org/wpmu/videovortex/about>.

8 See: <http://mashable.com/2010/05/17/youtube-2-billion-views/>.

9 Pelle Snickars and Patrick Vonderau, *The YouTube Reader*, Stockholm: National Library of Sweden, 2009.

10 Minke Kampman, University of Amsterdam MA thesis, Media Studies/new media program, September 2009. At: <http://www.minkekampman.nl/index.php/2009/09/introduction/>.

11 See Natalie Bookchin's work, *The Trip, Mass Ornament and the Testament* (<http://bookchin.net/projects.html>); and Perry Bard's global remake of Dziga Vertov's *Man with a Movie Camera*, from 1929 (<http://dziga.perrybard.net/>).

12 Sheila Rowbotham, Lynne Segal, and Hilary Wainwright, *Beyond The Fragments: Feminism and the Making of Socialism*, London: Merlin Press, 1979.

13 See: <http://lab.softwarestudies.com/2008/09/cultural-analytics.html>.

14 Information provided by Andrew Clay during his *Video Vortex* #6 lecture, Amsterdam, March 11, 2011.

15 Nicholas Mirzoeff, *An Introduction to Visual Culture*, 2nd edn, New York: Routledge, 2009, p. 241.

CHAPTER 9: SOCIETY OF THE QUERY: THE GOOGLIZATION OF OUR LIVES

1 This chapter is an updated version of an essay published in June 2008 in the *Eurozine* magazine. It was republished in separate English and German editions of Konrad Becker and Felix Stalder (eds), *Deep Search, The Politics of Search beyond Google*, Innsbruck: StudienVerlag, 2009. Thanks to Ned Rossiter for all the useful additions and copy-editing. The article was used as a concept paper for the Society of the Query Conference, organized by the Institute of Network Cultures in Amsterdam in November 2009. In 2010, the initiative was transformed into a network of critical search-engine research, together with partners in Vienna; see: <http://networkcultures.org/wpmu/re-search/>.

2 Joseph Weizenbaum and Gunna Wendt, *Wo sind sie, die Inseln der Vernunft im Cyberstrom, Auswege aus der programmierten Gesellschaft*, Freiburg: Herder Verlag, 2006.

3 For more information on the film, see: <http://www.ilmarefilm.org/W_E_1.htm>.

4 Preface from 1983, Joseph Weizenbaum, *Computer Power and Human Reason*, London: Penguin, 1984, p. 11.

5 *Wo sind sie, die Inseln der Vernunft*, p. 29.

6 According to Wikipedia, "Powerset was working on building a natural language search engine that could find targeted answers

to user questions (as opposed to keyword based search). For example, when confronted with a question like 'Which US state has the highest income tax?', conventional search engines ignore the question phrasing and instead do a search on the keywords 'state', 'highest', 'income', and 'tax'. Powerset on the other hand, attempts to use natural language processing to understand the nature of the question and return pages containing the answer."

7   For instance, in Geert Lovink and Pit Schultz, "Academia Cybernetica," in *Jugendjahre der Netzkritik*, Amsterdam: Institute of Network Culture, 2010, pp. 68–72; and Geert Lovink, *My First Recession*, Rotterdam: V2/NAi, 2003, pp. 38–46.

8   One successful attempt to give a more or less complete overview of Google's activities was written by Dutch IT journalist Peter Olsthoorn, with his book *De Macht van Google*, Utrecht: Kosmos Uitgeverij, 2010 (in Dutch).

9   Richard MacManus, *Google App Engine: Cloud Control to Major Tom, ReadWriteWeb*, April 8, 2008. At: <http://www.readwriteweb.com/archives/google_cloud_control.php>.

10 Nathaniel Rich, "The American WikiLeaks Hacker," *Rolling Stone*, December 1, 2010. At: <http://www.rollingstone.com/culture/news/meet-the-american-hacker-behind-WikiLeaks-20101201?page=5>.

11 Jean-Noël Jeanneney, *Google and the Myth of Universal Knowledge: A View from Europe*, Chicago, IL: University of Chicago Press, 2007.

12 See the Wikipedia entry: <http://en.wikipedia.org/wiki/Quaero>. In December 2006, Germany pulled out of the Quaero project. Instead of a multimedia search engine, German engineers favored a text-based one. According to Wikipedia, "many German engineers also balked at what they thought was becoming too much of an anti-Google project, rather than a project driven by its own ideals."

13 Gerald Reischl, *Die Google Falle – Die unkontrollierte Weltmacht im Internet*, Wien: Ueberreuter, 2008. See also Dennis Deicke's review (in English), *Google Unleashed – The New Global Power?*, posted on nettime, July 2, 2009.

14 Susanne Gaschke, *Klick – Strategien gegen die digitale Verdummung*, Freiburg: Herder, 2009. See Dennis Deicke's review (in English), posted on nettime, June 26, 2009.

15 Stefan Weber, *Das Google-Copy-Paste-Syndrom*, Hanover: Heise Verlag, 2009; see Dennis Deicke's review (in English), *Brainless Text Culture and Mickey Mouse Science*, at: <http://

networkcultures.org/wpmu/query/2009/06/19/brainless-text-culture-and-mickey-mouse-science/>.

16 See: <http://www.edge.org/3rd_culture/carr08/carr08_index.html>.

17 Nicolas Carr, *The Big Switch*.

18 "The blueprints depicting Google's data center at The Dalles, Oregon are proof that the Web is no ethereal store of ideas, shimmering over our heads like the aurora borealis. It is a new heavy industry, an energy glutton that is only growing hungrier" (Ginger Strand, *Harper's Magazine*, March 2008, p. 60).

19 Lanier, quoted in Nicolas Carr, *The Big Switch*.

20 See: <http://www.googlizationofeverything.com/>.

21 Siva Vaidhyanathan, *The Googlization of Everything*, p. xii.

22 See: <http://northeastwestsouth.net/>; and the above-mentioned research blog in n.20.

CHAPTER 10: ORGANIZING NETWORKS IN CULTURE AND POLITICS

1 Malcolm Gladwell, "Small Change: Why the Revolution Will Not Be Tweeted," *The New Yorker* (October 4, 2010) at: <http://www.newyorker.com/reporting/2010/10/04/101004fa_fact_gladwell>.

2 See Evgeny Morozov, *The Net Delusion*, New York: PublicAffairs, 2011; and also his many articles related to the book release, such as "Why the World's Secret Police Want You to Join Facebook" (*The Sunday Times*, January 2, 2011).

3 Dave Winer, "Why is Technology Important?" *Scripting News*, December 2, 2009. At: <http://scripting.com/2009/12/02.html>.

4 As Cory Doctorow writes in his "Net Delusion" review in the *Guardian* (January 25, 2011): "When Morozov talks about the security risks arising form dissidents' use of Facebook he does so without ever mentioning the protracted, dire warnings of exactly this problem that have come from the 'cyber-utopian' vanguard as embodied by groups such as the Electronic Frontier Foundation, NetzPolitik, Knowledge Ecology International, Bits of Freedom, Public Knowledge and dozens of others." I could add to this list Tactical Tech, Engage Media, Hivos, Global Voices and in particular DigiActive, which created handbooks for activists on how to use Facebook and Twitter. DigiActive slowed down in 2010, precisely at the moment when the topic was hitting the mainstream.

5 Slavoj Žižek, *Living in the End Times*, London: Verso, 2010, p. 352.
6 See: <http://www.newyorker.com/reporting/2010/10/04/101004fa_fact_gladwell>.
7 John Freeman, "Not So Fast, Sending and Receiving at Breakneck Speed Can Make Life Queasy: A Manifesto for Slow Communication," in *Wall Street Journal*, August 21, 2009.
8 See: <http://www.zephoria.org/thoughts/>.
9 Mary Joyce, "What the New Facebook Privacy Rules Mean for Activists"; at: <www.digiactive.org>, December 10, 2009.
10 Chris Anderson, *The Long Tail: Why the Future of Business Is Selling Less of More*, New York: Hyperion, 2006.
11 "Sweet stranger, sweet of you to come my way, tell me you have come to stay, sweet stranger. There's danger every time I meet your glance, danger of a big romance, sweet stranger. You're a brand new brand of honey from a brand new honeycomb. You could make life sweet & sunny. Won't you step right in & make yourself at home. Sweet stranger, let me introduce you to someone who will be sweet to you, sweet stranger." Lyrics by Glenn Miller, 1937.
12 I have dealt with "upgrading" the tactical media concept in *Zero Comments* (pp. 185–206). See also Rita Raley, *Tactical Media*, Minneapolis, MN: University of Minnesota Press, 2009.
13 "Das Unbehagen an der Digitalen Macht, a sceptical dialogue," in *Frankfurter Allgemeine Zeitung* (online, only in German), April 11, 2010; at: <http://www.faz.net/s/Rub117C535CDF414415BB243B181B8B60AE/Doc~EC60D9A844BDB4FB0980E1D5030F0A9D3~ATpl~Ecommon~Scontent.html>.
14 Michael Hardt and Antonio Negri, *Commonwealth*, Cambridge, MA: Harvard University Press, 2009, p. 311.
15 See, for instance, the Rotterdam viral communications conference, organized by Florian Cramer, on April 12/13, 2010: <http://viralcommunication.nl/>.
16 More on orgnets and the collaboration with Ned Rossiter can be found in the "Introducing Organized Networks" chapter, in *Zero Comments*, pp. 239–55, and Ned Rossiter, *Organized Networks*, Rotterdam: NAi, 2006. See also Geert Lovink and Ned Rossiter, "Urgent Aphorisms, Notes on Organized Networks for the Connected Multitudes," in Mark Deuze (ed.), *Managing Media Work*, Thousand Oaks, CA: Sage, 2011, pp. 279–90.
17 Simon Critchley, *Infinitely Demanding: Ethics of Commitment, Politics of Resistance*, London: Verso, 2007, p. 103.

210

18 See: <http://www.culturemondo.org/>.
19 For a full report and links to videos and publications, see: <http://networkcultures.org/wpmu/wintercamp/>.
20 See: <http://orgnet.rixc.lv/>.
21 See the call for the event, for instance, at: <http://kyberia.sk/id/5041628>.
22 Slavoj Žižek, *In Defense of Lost Causes*, London: Verso, 2008, p. 33.
23 Ibid.
24 Ibid. p. 375.

CHAPTER 11: TECHNO-POLITICS AT WIKILEAKS

1 This is a rewritten and extended version of "Ten Theses on WikiLeaks," written with Patrice Riemens and originally published on the nettime mailing list and the INC blog on August 30, 2010, see: <http://mail.kein.org/pipermail/nettime-l/2010-August/002337.html>. The theses were updated in early December 2010 in the midst of Cablegate. The "twelve theses" received wide coverage and were translated in Dutch, German, French, Italian, and Spanish.
2 See: <http://ns1758.ca/winch/winchest.html>, for a historical overview of the cost of hard-drive storage space (reference thanks to Henry Warwick).
3 In the US, 4GB USB sticks can be purchased from around 4.50 to 11 US dollars; 16 GB sticks cost around 20 US dollars, whereas 32 gigabytes USB sticks are priced between 40 and 50 US dollars (early 2011).
4 See: <http://en.wikipedia.org/wiki/Electronic_discovery>.
5 See: <http://www.guardian.co.uk/media/2010/dec/17/julian-assange-sweden>, <http://www.nytimes.com/2010/10/24/world/24assange.html&OQ=_rQ3D1>, and *Vanity Fair*'s analysis of the troubled relationship between Assange, *The New York Times*, and the *Guardian*: <http://www.vanityfair.com/politics/features/2011/02/the-guardian-201102>.
6 Remark made in the context of the group Anonymous, their actions against the Church of Scientology, and the material that WikiLeaks published from this sect. See: Daniel Domscheit-Berg, *Inside WikiLeaks, Meine Zeit bei der gefährlichsten Webseite der Welt*, Berlin: Econ Verlag, 2011, p. 49.
7 Domscheit-Berg, p. 239.

8   Ibid., p. 253.
9   Dave Winer, *Scripting News*, September 3, 2010, at: <http://scripting.com/stories/2010/09/03/appleIsGreen.html>.
10 Quoted from the opening video at the homepage of OpenLeaks, January 2010: <http://www. OpenLeaks.org/>.
11 In WikiLeaks, *Inside Julian Assange's War on Secrecy*, written by the *Guardian* journalists David Leigh and Luke Harding (New York: PublicAffairs, 2011), we find a not necessarily correct description of how Assange (in early 2010) must have changed his mind about the collaborative "wiki" aspect of the project. "Assange had by now discovered, to his chagrin, that simply posting long lists of raw and random documents on to a website failed to change the world. He brooded about the collapse of his original 'crowd-sourcing' notion: 'Our initial idea was, "Look at all these people editing Wikipedia. Look at all the junk that they're working on … (…) surely *those* people will step forward, given fresh source material, and do something?" No, it's bullshit. In fact, people write about things because they want to display their values to their peers. Actually, they don't give a fuck about the material.'" (p. 61)
12 See: <http://en.wikipedia.org/wiki/Operations_security>.

SELECT BIBLIOGRAPHY

FREQUENTLY USED MAILINGLISTS, BLOGS, WEBSITES

Air-L, List of the Association of Internet Researchers: <www.aoir.org>.
Buzz Machine, Jeff Jarvis's blog: <http://www.buzzmachine.com/>.
Carta, overview of the German blogosphere: <http://carta.info/>.
Fibreculture, Australian list for critical Internet research and culture: <www.fibreculture.org>.
Hacker News: <http://news.ycombinator.com/>.
I Cite, blog of Jodi Dean: <http://jdeanicite.typepad.com/>.
IDC, mailinglist of the Institute for Distributed Creativity: <http://mailman.thing.net/cgi-bin/mailman/listinfo/idc>.
LINK, Australian discussion list for IT policy: <http://sunsite.anu.edu.au/link/>.
Nettime-l, International mailinglist for net criticism: <www.nettime.org>.
Nettime-nl, Dutch list for Internet culture and criticism: <www.nettime.org>.
Rohrpost, German language list for new media culture: <www.nettime.org/rohrpost>.
Rough Type, blog of ICT critic Nicholas Carr: <http://www.roughtype.com/index.php>.
Scripting News, Dave Winer's blog: <http://scripting.com/>.
Streamtime, website of the international support campaign for Iraqi bloggers: <http://www.streamtime.org/>.
Techcrunch, portal that "profiles startups, reviews new Internet products, and breaks tech news" (owned by AOL): <http://techcrunch.com>.
WL Central, WikiLeaks news, analysis, and action: <http://wlcentral.org/>.

BOOKS AND ARTICLES

Adilkno, *Cracking the Movement*, New York: Autonomedia, 1994.
Adilkno, *The Media Archive*, Brooklyn, NY: Autonomedia, 1998.

213

Adorno, T., *Jargon of Authenticity*, Evanston, IL: Northwestern University Press, 1973.

Ajouri, Philip, Klenner, Jost Philipp, and Vismann, Cornelia (eds), *Kommentieren, Zeitschrift für Ideengeschichte, Heft III/1*, Munich: C.H. Beck Verlag, Frühjahr, 2009.

Anderson, Chris, *The Long Tail: Why the Future of Business Is Selling Less of More*, New York: Hyperion, 2006.

Anderson, Chris, *Free: The Future of a Radical Price*, New York: Random House, 2009.

Assmann, J., and Gladigow, B. (eds), *Text und Kommentar, Archäologie der literarischen Kommunikation IV*, Munich: Wilhelm Fink Verlag, 1995.

Banks, Michael, *Blogging Heroes: Interviews with 30 of the World's Top Bloggers*, Indianapolis, IN: Wiley Publishing, Inc., 2008.

Barbrook, Richard, *Imaginary Futures: From Thinking Machines to the Global Village*, London: Pluto Press, 2007.

Barlow, Aaron, *The Rise of the Blogosphere*, Westport, CT: Praeger Publishers, 2007.

Baudrillard, Jean, *Fatal Strategies*, Brooklyn, NY: Semiotext(e), 1990.

Baudrillard, Jean, and Guillaume, Marc, *Radical Alterity*, Los Angeles, CA: Semiotext(e), 2008.

Becker, Konrad, and Stalder, Felix (eds), *Deep Search: The Politics of Search beyond Google*, Innsbruck: Studienverlag, 2009.

Benkler, Yochai, *The Wealth of Networks*, New Haven, CT: Yale University Press, 2006.

Berardi, "Bifo" Franco, *The Soul at Work: From Alienation to Autonomy*, Los Angeles, CA: Semiotext(e), 2009.

Berardi, "Bifo" Franco, *Precarious Rhapsody*, London: Minor Compositions, 2009.

Berger, Maurice, *The Crisis of Criticism*, New York: The New Press, 1998.

Blecher, Max, *Occurrence in the Immediate Reality*, Plymouth: University of Plymouth Press, 2009.

Blood, Rebecca (ed.), *We've Got Blog: How Weblogs Are Changing Our Culture*, Cambridge, MA: Perseus Books, 2002.

Boomen, van den, Marianne et al. (eds), *Digital Material: Tracing New Media in Everyday Life and Technology*, Amsterdam: Amsterdam University Press, 2009.

Boxer, Sarah, *Ultimate Blogs: Masterworks from the Wild Web*, New York: Vintage Books, 2008.

Braidotti, Rosi, *Op doorreis, nomadisch denken in de 21ste eeuw*, Amsterdam: Boom, 2004.

Broeckmann, Andreas, and Knowbotic Research (eds), *Opaque Presence: Manual of Latent Invisibilities*, Zurich: Diaphanes, 2010.

Bruns, Axel, *Blogs, Wikipedia, Second Life, and Beyond*, New York: Peter Lang, 2008.

Bruns, Axel, and Jacobs, Joanne (eds), *Uses of Blogs*, New York: Peter Lang Publishers, 2006.

214

Bublitz, Hannelore, *Im Beichtstuhl der Medien, Die Produktion des Selbst im öffentlichen Bekenntnis*, Bielefeld: Verlag (transcript), 2010.

Burgess, Jean, and Green, Joshua, *Online Video and Participatory Culture*, Cambridge: Polity, 2009.

Campanelli, Vito, *Web Aesthetics: How Digital Media Affect Culture and Society*, Rotterdam: NAi/Institute of Network Cultures, 2010.

Canetti, Elias, *Crowds and Power*, New York: Viking Press, 1962.

Carr, Nicholas, *The Big Switch: Rewiring the World, From Edison to Google*, New York: W.W. Norton & Company, 2008.

Carr, Nicholas, "Is Google Making Us Stupid?," *The Atlantic* (July/August), at:<http://www.theatlantic.com/magazine/archive/2008/07/is-google-making-us-stupid/6868/>.

Carr, Nicholas, *The Shallows: What the Internet is Doing to Our Brains*, New York: W.W. Norton & Company, 2010.

Carroll, Noel, *On Criticism*, New York: Routledge, 2009.

Chun, Wendy, *Control and Freedom: Power and Paranoia in the Age of Fibre Optics*, Cambridge, MA, MIT Press, 2006.

Critchley, Simon, *Infinitely Demanding: Ethics of Commitment, Politics of Resistance*, London: Verso, 2007.

Danet, Brenda, and Herring Susan C. (eds), *The Multicultural Internet: Language, Culture and Communication Online*, New York: Oxford University Press, 2007.

Dean, Jodi, *Blog Theory: Feedback and Capture in the Circuits of Drive*, Cambridge: Polity, 2010.

Dean, Jodi, Anderson, Jon W., and Lovink, Geert (eds), *Reformatting Politics: Information Society and Global Civil Society*, New York: Routledge, 2006.

Dolar, Mladen, *A Voice and Nothing More*, Cambridge, MA: MIT Press, 2006.

Domscheit-Berg, Daniel, *Inside WikiLeaks, Meine Zeit bei der gefährlichsten Website der Welt*, Berlin: Econ Verlag, 2011.

Dreyfus, Hubert, *On the Internet*, New York: Routledge, 2001.

Eagleton, Terry, *The Function of Criticism*, London: Verso, 1984.

Ehrenreich, Barbara, *Bright-sided: How the Relentless Promotion of Positive Thinking Has Undermined America*, New York: Metropolitan Books, 2009.

Elkins, James, *Visual Studies: A Skeptical Introduction*, New York: Routledge, 2003.

Elkins, James, and Newman, Michael (eds), *The State of Art Criticism*, New York: Routledge, 2008.

Farrelly, Elizabeth, *Blubberland: The Dangers of Happiness*, Sydney: University of New South Wales Press, 2007.

Figal, Günter, *Der Sinn des Verstehens*, Stuttgart: Reclam, 1996.

Fisher, Mark, *Capitalist Realism, Is There No Alternative?* Winchester: Zero Books, 2009.

Foucault, Michel, "The Order of Discourse," in Robert Young (ed.), *Untying the Text: A Poststructuralist Reader*, London: Routledge, 1981, pp. 52–64.

Foucault, Michel, *Aesthetics, Method, and Epistemology*, London: Penguin Press, 1998.

Galloway, Alexander R., *Protocol: How Control Exists After Decentralization*, Cambridge, MA: MIT Press, 2004.

Galloway, Alexander R., and Thacker, Eugene, *The Exploit: A Theory of Networks*, Minneapolis, MN: University of Minnesota Press, 2007.

Gare, Shelley, *The Triumph of the Airheads and the Retreat from Commonsense*, Sydney: Park Street Press, 2006.

Gaschke, Susanne, *Klick, Strategien gegen die digitale Verdummung*, Freiburg: Verlag Herder, 2009.

Geiselberger, Heinrich (ed.), WikiLeaks *und die Folgen, Netz-Medien-Politik*, Berlin: Suhrkamp Verlag, 2011.

Gerritzen, Mieke, and Lovink, Geert, *Everyone is a Designer in the Age of Social Media*, Amsterdam: BIS Publishers, 2010.

Goffman, Erving, *The Presentation of Self in Everyday Life*, New York: Anchor Books, 1959.

Golumbia, David, *The Cultural Logic of Computation*, Cambridge, MA: Harvard University Press, 2009.

Gugerli, David, "Die Welt als Datenbank, Zur Relation von Softwareentwicklung, Abfragetechnik und Deutungsautonomie," in *Nach Freierabend, Züricher Jahrbuch für Wissensgeschichte* 3, Zurich: Diaphanes, 2007.

Gugerli, David, *Suchmaschinen. Die Welt als Datenbank*, Frankfurt: Suhrkamp, 2009.

Gumbrecht, Hans Ulrich, *The Powers of Philology*, Chicago, IL: Illinois University Press, 2002.

Hamilton, Clive, and Denniss, Richard, *Affluenza: When Too Much is Never Enough*, Sydney: Allen & Unwin, 2005.

Hardt, Michael, and Negri, Antonio, *Multitude, War and Democracy in the Age of Empire*, New York: Penguin Press, 2004.

Hardt, Michael, and Negri, Antonio, *Commonwealth*, Cambridge, MA: Harvard University Press, 2009.

Hassan, Robert, and Purser, Ronald, *24/7, Time and Temporality in the Network Society*, Stanford, CA: Stanford University Press, 2007.

Hochschild, Arlie Russell, *The Managed Heart: Commercialization of Human Feeling*, Berkeley, CA: University of California Press, 1983.

Honneth, Axel, *Pathologies of Reason: On the Legacy of Critical Theory*, Columbia: Columbia University Press, 2009.

Horkheimer, Max, *Traditionelle und kritische Theorie*, Frankfurt: Fischer, 1992.

Illouz, Eva, *Cold Intimacies: The Making of Emotional Capitalism*, Cambridge: Polity, 2007.

Illouz, Eva, *Saving the Modern Soul: Therapy, Emotions, and the Culture of Self-Help*, Berkeley, CA: University of California Press, 2008.

Incognito, *Experiences that Defy Identification*, London: Elephant Editions, 2008.

The Invisible Committee, *The Coming Insurrection*, Los Angeles, CA, Semiotext(e), 2009.

Ippolita Collective, *The Dark Face of Google*, translation manuscript, 2009.

Jaeggi, Rahel, and Wesche, Tilo (Hrg.), *Was ist Kritik?* Frankfurt: Suhrkamp Verlag, 2009.

Janich, Peter, *Was ist Information?* Frankfurt: Suhrkamp, 2006.

Jarvis, Jeff, *What Would Google Do?* New York: Collins Business, 2009.

Jeanneney, Jean-Noël, *Google and the Myth of Universal Knowledge*, Chicago, IL: University of Chicago, 2007.

Juris, Jeffrey S., *Networking Futures: The Movements against Corporate Globalization*, Durham, NC: Duke University Press, 2008.

Karaganis, Joe (ed.), *Structures of Participation in Digital Culture*, New York; Social Science Research Council, 2007.

Keen, Andrew, *The Cult of the Amateur: How Today's Internet is Killing Our Culture and Assualting Our Economy*, London: Nicholas Brealey, 2007.

Kelty, Christopher, *Two Bits: The Cultural Significance of Free Software*, Durham, NC: Duke University Press, 2008.

Klein, Naomi, *The Shock Doctrine: The Rise of Disaster Capitalism*, London: Penguin Books, 2007.

Kleiner, Dmitri, *The Telekommunist Manifesto*, Amsterdam: Institute of Network Cultures, 2010.

Kluitenberg, Erik, *Delusive Spaces: Essays on Culture, Media and Technology*, Rotterdam: NAi/Institute of Network Cultures, 2008.

Lacy, Sarah, *Once You're Lucky, Twice You're Good: The Rebirth of Silicon Valley and the Rise of Web 2.0*, New York; Gotham Books, 2008.

Langville, Amy N., and Meyer, Carl D., *Google's PageRank and Beyond: The Science of Search Engine Rankings*, Princeton, NJ: Princeton University Press, 2006.

Lanier, Jaron, *You Are Not a Gadget: A Manifesto*, New York: Alfred A. Knopf, 2010.

Latour, Bruno, *Reassambling the Social: An Introduction to Actor-Network-Theory*, New York: Oxford University Press, 2005.

Lazzarato, Maurizio, *Videophilosophie, Zeitwahrnehmung im Postfordismus*, Berlin: b_books, 2002.

Leadbeater, Charles (and 257 other people), *We-Think: Mass Innovation, not Mass Production*, London: Profile Books, 2008.

Lessig, Lawrence, *Free Culture: How Big Media Uses Technology and the Law to Lock Down Culture and Control Creativity*, New York: Penguin Books, 2004.

Losh, Elizabeth, *Virtualpolitik*, Cambridge, MA: MIT Press, 2009.

Lovink, Geert, *Hör zu oder stirb!*, Berlin: ID-Archiv Verlag, 1992.

Lovink, Geert, *Dark Fiber: Tracking Critical Internet Culture*, Cambridge, MA: MIT Press, 2002.

Lovink, Geert. *My First Recession: Critical Internet Culture in Transition*, Rotterdam: V2/NAi Publishers, 2003.

217

Lovink, Geert, *The Principle of Networking*, Amsterdam: Amsterdam University Press, 2005.

Lovink, Geert, *Zero Comments*, New York: Routledge, 2008.

Lovink, Geert (ed.), *From Weak Ties to Organized Networks: Ideas, Reports, Critiques*, Amsterdam: Institute of Network Cultures, 2009.

Lovink, Geert, and Miles, Rachel (eds), *Video Vortex Reader II: Beyond YouTube*, Amsterdam: Institute of Network Cultures, 2011.

Lovink, Geert, and Niederer, Sabine (eds), *Video Vortex Reader: Responses to YouTube*, Amsterdam: Institute of Network Cultures, 2008.

Lovink, Geert, and Rossiter, Ned (eds), *MyCreativity Reader*, Amsterdam: Institute of Network Cultures, 2007.

Lovink, Geert, and Rossiter, Ned, "Urgent Aphorisms, Notes on Organized Networks for the Connected Multitudes," in Mark Deuze (ed.), *Managing Media Work*, Thousand Oaks, CA: Sage, 2011, pp. 279–90.

Lovink, Geert, and Scholz, Trebor (eds), *The Art of Free Cooperation*, Brooklyn, NY: Autonomedia, 2007.

McDonald, Ronan, *The Death of the Critic*, London: Continuum, 2007.

Manovich, Lev, *The Language of New Media*, Cambridge, MA: Leonardo Books, MIT Press [1999] 2002.

Meeuwsen, Frank, *Bloghelden*, Utrecht: Bruna Uitgevers, 2010.

Miller, Toby, "Step Away from the Croissant, Media Studies 3.0," in David Hesmondhalgh and Jason Toynbee (eds), *The Media and Social Theory*. London: Routledge, 2008, pp. 213–30.

Miller, Toby, "Media Studies 3.0," in *Television & New Media* 10/ 1 (2009): 5–6.

Milne, Esther, *Letters, Postcards, Email: Technologies of Presence*, New York: Routledge, 2010.

Mirzoeff, Nicholas, *An Introduction to Visual Culture*, 2nd edn, New York: Routledge, 2009.

Morozov, Evgeny, *The Net Delusion: How Not to Liberate the World*, London: Penguin Books, 2011.

Morozov, Evgeny *Net Delusion: The Dark Side of Internet Freedom*, New York: PublicAffairs, 2011.

Multitudes 36, *Google et au-delà*, Paris: Multitudes, 2009.

Nalty, Kevin, *Beyond Viral: How to Attract Customers, Promote Your Brand, and Make Money with Online Video*, Hoboken: John Wiley, 2010.

Newman, Michael, *The State of Art Criticism*, New York: Routledge, 2008.

Nietzsche, Friedrich, *Briefwechsel: Kritische Gesamtausgabe*, ed. G. Colli and M. Montinari, Berlin, 1975–84, pt. 3, 1: 172.

Olsthoorn, Peter, *De Macht van Google, Werkt Google voor jou of werk jij voor Google?* Utrecht: Kosmos Uitgevers, 2010.

Owens, Lynn, *Cracking under Pressure*, Amsterdam: Amsterdam University Press, 2008.

Parikka, Jussi, and Sampson, Tony D., *The Spam Book: On Viruses, Porn, and Other Anomalies from the Dark Side of Digital Culture*, Cresskill, NJ: Hampton Press, 2009.

Pasquinelli, Matteo, *Animal Spirits: A Bestiary of the Commons*, Rotterdam: NAi/Institute of Network Cultures, 2008.

Pax, Salam, *The Clandestine Diary of an Ordinary Iraqi*, New York: Grove Press, 2003.

Pool, Gail, *Faint Praise: The Plight of Book Reviewing in America*, Columbia, MO: University of Missouri Press, 2007.

Raley, Rita, *Tactical Media*, Minneapolis, MN: University of Minnesota Press, 2009.

Reichert, Ramon, *Amateure im Netz, Selbstmanagement und Wissenstechnik im Web 2.0*, Bielefeld: Transcript, 2008.

Reinigungsgesellschaft with Miklos Erhardt, *The Social Engine – Exploring Flexibility*, Budapest: Studio of Young Artists Association/Weimar: ACC Galerie, 2007.

Reischl, Gerald, *Die Google-Falle, Die Unkontrollierte Weltmacht im Internet*, Vienna: Verlag Carl Ueberreuter, 2008.

Reynolds, Glenn, *An Army of Davids: How Markets and Technology Empower Ordinary People to Beat Big Media, Big Government and Other Goliaths*, Nashville, TN: Nelson Current, 2006.

Rheingold, Howard, *Smart Mobs: The Next Social Revolution*, Cambridge, MA, Perseus Books, 2002.

Ricoeur, Paul, *The Conflict of Interpretations*, London/New York: Continuum, 2000.

Riverbend, *Baghdad Burning: Girl Blog from Iraq*, New York: The Feminist Press, 2005.

Riverbend, *Baghdad Burning II: More Girl Blog from Iraq*, New York: The Feminist Press, 2006.

Rogers, Richard, *The End of the Virtual*, Amsterdam: Vossius Press, 2009.

Rogoff, Irit, "What is a Theorist?," in James Elkins and Michael Newman (eds), *The State of Art Criticism*, New York: Routledge, 2008, pp. 107–9.

Rosenberg, Scott, *Say Everything: How Blogging Began, What it's Becoming and Why it Matters*, New York: Random House, 2009.

Rossiter, Ned, *Organized Networks, Media Theory, Creative Labour, New Institutions*, Rotterdam: NAi/Institute of Network Cultures, 2006.

Sheila Rowbotham, Lynne Segal, and Hilary Wainwright, *Beyond The Fragments: Feminism and the Making of Socialism*, London: Merlin Press, 1979.

Russegger, Georg, *Vom Subjekt zum Smartject, Kreative Entwurfpraktiken menschlich-medialer Selbstorganisation*, Wien: Verlag Turia Kant, 2009.

Schäfer, Mirko Tobias, "Bastard Culture! User Participation and the Extension of Cultural Industries," Utrecht: PhD dissertation, 2008.

Schirrmacher, Frank, *Payback*, Munich: Karl Blessing Verlag, 2009.

Schreyach, Michael, *The State of Art Criticism*, New York: Routledge, 2008.

Seijdel, Jorinde (ed.), *The Rise of Informal Media: How Search Engines, Weblogs and YouTube Change Public Opinion* (Open No. 13), Rotterdam: SKOR/NAi Publishers, 2007.

Sennett, Richard, *The Craftsman*, London: Penguin Books, 2008.

Shirky, Clay, *Here Comes Everybody: The Power of Organizing Without Organizations*, New York: The Penguin Press, 2008.

Sissman, L. E., "Reviewer's Dues," in Sylvia Kamerman (ed.), *Book Reviewing*, Boston, MA: The Writer, 1978, pp. 119–25.

Slater, Josephine Berry et al. (eds), *Proud To Be Flesh: A Mute Magazine Anthology of Cultural Politics after the Net*, Brooklyn: Autonomedia, 2009.

Sloterdijk, Peter, *Du mußt dein Leben ändern, Über Anthropotechnik*, Frankfurt: Suhrkamp, 2009.

Snickars, Pelle, and Vonderau, Patrick, *The YouTube Reader*, Stockholm: National Library of Sweden, 2009.

Sontag, Susan, *Against Interpretation*, New York: Dell Publishing Co., 1966.

Spink, Amanda, and Zimmer, Michael, *Web Search: Multididisciplinary Perspectives*, Berlin: Springer Verlag, 2008.

Stiegler, Bernard, *Taking Care of Youth and the Generations*, Stanford, CA: Stanford University Press, 2010.

Stiegler, Bernard, *For a New Critique of Political Economy*, Cambridge: Polity, 2010.

Strauss, Leo, *Persecution and the Art of Writing*, Chicago, IL: University of Chicago Press, 1988; 1st edn, 1952.

Sunstein, Cass R., *Republic.com 2.0*, Princeton, NJ: Princeton University Press, 2007.

Taylor, Charles, *Sources of the Self: The Making of the Modern Identity*, Cambridge: Cambridge University Press, 1989.

Terranova, Tiziana, "Another Life: The Nature of Political Economy in Foucault's Genealogy of Biopolitics," *Theory, Culture & Society* 26/6 (2009): 234–62.

Terranova, Tiziana, "New Economy, Financialization and Social Production in the Web 2.0," in Andrea Fumagalli and Sandro Mezzadra (eds), *Crisis in the Global Economy: Financial Markets, Social Struggles, and New Political Scenarios*, trans. Jason Francis McGimsey, Los Angeles, CA: Semiotext(e), 2010, pp. 153–70.

Turkle, Sherry, *Alone Together: Why We Expect More from Technology and Less from Each Other*, New York: Basic Books, 2011.

Vaidhyanathan, Siva, *The Googlization of Everything (and Why We Should Worry)*, Los Angeles, CA: University of California Press, 2011.

Vise, David A., *The Google Story*, New York: Pan Books, 2005.

Walker Rettberg, Jill, *Blogging*, Cambridge: Polity, 2008.

Wardrip-Fruin, Noah, and Montfort, Nick (eds), *The New Media Reader*, Cambridge, MA: MIT Press, 2003.

Weber, Stefan, *Das Google-Copy-Paste-Syndrom*, Hanover: Heise Verlag, 2009.

Weizenbaum, Joseph, *Computer Power and Human Reason: From Judgement to Calculation*, London: Penguin Books, 1984.

Weizenbaum, Joseph, *Computermacht und Gesellschaft,*: Suhrkamp, 2001.

Weizenbaum, Joseph, and Wendt, Gunna, *Wo sind sie, die Inseln der Vernunft im Cyberstrom? Auswege aus der programmierten Gesellschaft*, Freiburg: Herder, 2006.

Wood, James, *How Fiction Works*, New York: Picador, 2009.

Zittrain, Jonathan, *The Future of the Internet and How to Stop It*, New Haven, CT: Yale University Press, 2008.

Žižek, Slavoj, *In Defense of Lost Causes*, London: Verso, 2008.

Žižek, Slavoj, *Living in the End Times*, London: Verso, 2010.